GEORGE BLAKE
WAS MEANT TO BE A SPY

As a youth he was a loner—intelligent, mature, eccentric. When the Nazis invaded Holland, he was still in high school, but he formed resistance groups and distinguished himself as an almost fearless fighter.

GEORGE BLAKE
WAS FASCINATED WITH SPYCRAFT

In his early years he insisted that colleagues call him by a code name. He always carried a pen filled with invisible ink. He identified himself on the phone by humming a tune rather than giving his name. This colorful, flamboyant style would later become his trademark.

GEORGE BLAKE
WAS A MASTER SPY

He loyally served the British and later savagely betrayed them. Complex, shrewd, and manipulating, George Blake was a man and a spy whose story provides valuable insight into the ever-fascinating world of espionage and some of the incredible characters in the world.

D1104451

☮ ESPIONAGE/INTELLIGENCE LIBRARY ☮

GEORGE BLAKE: DOUBLE AGENT

E. H. Cookridge

BALLANTINE BOOKS • NEW YORK

ISBN 0-345-30264-8

This edition published by arrangement with Hodder Paperbacks

Manufactured in the United States of America

First Ballantine Books Edition: September 1982

CONTENTS

To FINA,
who knows

ACKNOWLEDGMENTS

Some parts of this particular account of George Blake's activities—mainly those that refer to his childhood, youth, war service, and to his imprisonment in Korea—appeared in my previous books, *Shadow of a Spy* (published by Leslie Frewin Ltd. in 1967) and *Traitor Betrayed* (Pan Books, 1962).

This volume has been completely rewritten in many of its important parts and contains much new material, which came to my knowledge during the past few years and months.

I wish to express my gratitude to E. Morland Lee, who greatly assisted me in compiling and sifting information, and to my friends Ab and Edith Visser, of Amsterdam, who afforded me warm hospitality during my research in the Netherlands some years ago. I am indebted to members of Blake's family, particularly to his uncle, Mijnheer Anton Beijderwellen; to many of Blake's acquaintances, some of whom I mention in the text, for their cooperation; to Blake's colleagues in the various organizations in which he served in Britain, Germany, the Netherlands, and the Lebanon (all of whom prefer to remain anonymous), for important information; to the brave men with whom Blake was imprisoned in Communist camps in Korea; and also to some of Blake's fellow prisoners in Wormwood Scrubs, who gave me some enlightening accounts of his activities there.

I leaned heavily on the *Report of the Inquiry into Prison Escapes and Security* by Admiral of the Fleet, the Earl Mountbatten of Burma, and I thank the Director of Publications of H.M. Stationery Office, as holder of Crown Copyright for permission to quote passages from this report. I want to thank Mr. A. D. Peters, representing Mr. Philip Deane, for permission to quote from Mr. Deane's book, *Captive in Korea*. I remember with gratitude the late Sir Vyvyan Holt, who gave me valuable information. And I owe a special debt to Philip Evans, of Hodder and Stoughton, for his revisions and advice.

Last, but not least, I want to thank Mr. Sean Bourke, who so good-humoredly recounted to me an amazing story of his adventures connected with Blake's escape from Wormwood Scrubs Prison in 1966, and of their subsequent journey to Moscow, even though I did not fully accept his interesting story.

March 1970

E. H. C.

CHAPTER ONE

THE ORDER OF LENIN

Across Moscow's Sadovaya Boulevard, a man walks briskly toward the Red Square. With his fresh, healthy complexion and brown hair with a tinge of auburn, he looks much younger than forty-eight. He has left his comfortable apartment in the skyscraper behind Vostanye Place and, like thousands of Muscovites, he is on his way to work. It is almost one and a half miles along the great thoroughfares of Gorky Street and the Street of the Twenty-fifth October to the great, gray pile of buildings in the Dzershinsky Square, the offices of the Committee of State Security—the K.G.B.—which is his place of work.

A year or two ago, George Blake, still in hiding, used his car lest he might meet one of the foreign newspaper correspondents who were so eagerly trailing him. But now he enjoys his morning walk. He has emerged from the shadow, the holder of high decorations which the Soviet government gratefully bestow on those who serve them well.

Yet he is, as he always was, a loner. His face is a mask hiding his true feelings, as it has always been. George Blake was no Agent 007, shooting his way out of danger into the silky bed of a ravishing blond. Not for him the unlikely assignments of violence and lust, the secret operator's farcical gadgets with which to fight single-handed nuclear rockets, the diamond-studded cigarette cases hiding poisoned stilettos, the sexual acrobatics with their sadistic undertones. Not even the elaborate contrived coup or the lavish disbursement of bribes.

All the spy thriller writers' armory of fantasies and in-

1

trigue and torture, of blackmail and rape, has nothing in it
to compare with the ingenuity of the real life of George
Blake, the prince of treachery.

His is a story justifying the cliché that truth is stranger
than fiction. His life has patterns incomprehensible to the
ordinary person and beyond the imagination of most of us.
No work of fiction could portray his career as credible.
No reader could be expected to identify the main character as a hero or villain in such a story—for Blake lived by
moral precepts people can neither fully despise, approve,
or understand.

Journalists and politicians, with their own ideological ax
to grind, have digested his intricate career into newspaper
headlines and solemn speeches. Legal luminaries have tried
to summarize his characters and motives in terse diatribes.

None has penetrated below the surface to give a real explanation of what made Blake the man he was, what has
prompted his actions.

He was born in 1922 in Rotterdam. His father, Albert
William Behar, was the descendant of Levantine Jews, and
became British by a quirk of political history which
brought Egypt under the British rule, and as reward for
his gallantry during the First World War. His mother
came from a titled Dutch family, and was a devout Lutheran. From infancy the boy could sense that Truth could
be two-headed. British by documentation, Dutch by upbringing, Protestant by precept, half-Jewish by blood,
George grew up an introspective, pensive boy, in a fatherless home where his mother dominated his life. When the
storm clouds were gathering over Europe in the thirties, it
was perhaps inevitable that a sensitive youth, rootless and
bewildered, should look at the world with unhappiness and
dislike. He turned to religion, yearning for the splendid
isolation of the priesthood and the vocation of creating a
kindlier world. He would have taken holy orders and sunk
into oblivion. That dream was shattered when on May 11,
1940, Nazi warplanes turned Rotterdam into a desert of
rubble. The boy grew into manhood almost overnight. He
insisted on his mother and sisters joining the refugees es-

caping to England; he himself was determined to stay and fight.

Arrested by the Gestapo, he escaped from prison, became one of the leaders of a local Resistance group and, hunted again, had to flee. In 1942 he covered, invariably alone, close to a thousand miles across Nazi-occupied Europe to reach the Spanish frontier. Caught by the Spanish police he was interned, but eventually reached Gibraltar and freedom. The fact that the youth was British carried more weight with the security officers than his pleading to be sent to England to continue to fight. He was shipped to London as a repatriate.

Here his eagerness to be trained as a secret agent and to be sent back to Holland to rejoin Dutch Resistance as an instructor or saboteur received more rebuffs. At first M.I.5 classified him as a potential suspect until otherwise proved. The best George Behar could achieve was enlistment as an Ordinary Seaman in the Royal Navy. After he legally changed his surname he was known as George Blake.

Thanks to his fluency in three languages, including German, he was recommended for a wartime commission in the R.N.V.R. and after training, attached to Naval Intelligence. Later he was transferred to the Dutch section of Special Operations, at last achieving his great ambition for secret work. After Germany's defeat he was sent to Hamburg to interrogate German prisoners of war and assist in rounding up Gestapo men, particularly those who had served in Holland and had now gone underground.

With the dedication of a fanatic and the single-mindedness of a crusader he devoted his mental energies to this task. Unable to understand his happy-go-lucky fellow officers, disgusted by the characteristic English live-and-let-live policy and the bumbling failure to mete out punishment where punishment was due, Blake realized that a sense of belonging still eluded him. Perhaps he compared his superiors and colleagues with the ruthless and disciplined Soviet Intelligence officers who now swarmed the Western zones of Germany with some equivocal missions.

That first chink in his mental armor did not, of course,

appear on his record, which showed his devoted and reliable work, when he was recruited for the British secret service. At last he had a job where his isolation was an asset. An agent should have no friends, no emotional ties, none of the virtues and vices which make up a gregarious human being. Now at least he could feel that he was right to be a loner.

It is small wonder that he rose rapidly in his self-chosen profession. He became a senior agent in the Secret Intelligence Service, the legendary M.I.6. Sent to Korea in 1950 as a key agent with the rank of a vice-consul, he was captured by the North Koreans and for nearly three years suffered severe hardships.

While American and a few British prisoners succumbed to brainwashing by Russian and Chinese indoctrinators, Blake emerged from the prison camps without any tangible evidence that his strong anti-Communist views had changed. Little blame can be attached to the security officers who "vetted" him. Blake had had already, then, a lifetime of learning that his opinions were best kept to himself. Moreover, if he began to believe that communism was the better hope for mankind's future, he was still a long way from crossing the line. His slow conversion came about by his own thought processes, and not by brainwashing. The future double agent was not a robot manipulated by Soviet indoctrinators, but the master of his own thoughts and actions.

An eighteenth-century proverb says that "a solitary man is either a brute or an angel." George Blake made his choice. His career was brutish to the men who trusted him, the two scores of his agents he betrayed without pity. It was only in his warped mind that he saw it as that of an avenging angel, bent on destroying a society which spurned him.

For long and terrible years he zealously worked for the downfall of his country, proving his genius in the practice of perfidy. From his station of the Secret Intelligence Service in West Berlin, he turned over to the Russians every secret document, every tidbit of information he could lay his hands on. He kept Moscow informed on vital political decisions made in London and Washington. He betrayed the Berlin telecommunication tunnel which promised to give the West's Intelligence services an edge on their Soviet opponents.

He named every important Western agent operating from West Germany, consigning them to the firing squad or a Siberian prison camp.

In 1961 the master traitor was himself betrayed. Tried and sentenced to forty-two years' imprisonment—the heaviest sentence in Britain's modern legal history—his faith in his masters did not waver. Within five years the model prisoner was free again. His escape from Wormwood Scrubs in October 1966 was arranged by the K.G.B. octopus, whose tentacles could safely probe into the heart of a London jail, using Blake's guileless former fellow prisoner, Sean Bourke, as a willing dupe.

The police and security forces of the West failed to waylay the two fugitives as they leisurely proceeded across Europe to Moscow and safety. Nothing was heard of Blake for several years. It seemed that this phenomenon of the Anonymous Man had disappeared into oblivion.

In February 1970, *Izvestya*, the official newspaper of the Presidium of the Supreme Soviet of the U.S.S.R. announced the award of the Order of Lenin, an honor ranking second only to the Gold Star of a Hero of the Soviet Union, to "Comrade George Blake, the merited Soviet secret agent, who has rendered eminent services which, over a long period of years, foiled the operations of the British secret service directed against the Soviet Union and other Socialist countries."

Thus did George Blake, in the forty-eighth year of his adventurous life, emerge once more from the shadow to enjoy—if this is the word—the official stamp of traitor from those who knew best. The citation served the twofold purpose of extolling the resourcefulness of the Soviet Intelligence and showing its active agents how well they are being looked after, as well as of trying to drive a wedge between the British and American services by stressing that it was a British agent who had betrayed C.I.A. operations. The previous award of the Military Order of the Red Banner to Blake was not publicized and did not carry so specific a citation of the manner in which honor paid for dishonor.

The summary of Blake's activities as published in *Izvestya* almost coincides in its terms with the pronouncement of Lord Chief Justice Parker, when passing sentence on Blake at the Old Bailey in 1961: "Your confession reveals that for some years you have been working continuously as an agent and spy for a foreign power. The information communicated was clearly of the utmost importance . . . and has rendered much of this country's efforts completely useless . . . Your conduct in many other countries would undoubtedly carry the death penalty."

With the deviousness which typifies so many actions and statements by the Soviet government, Moscow for years denied that Blake worked for them and that after his escape he had reached Russia. Two and a half years passed between an event which finally dispersed any doubts about Blake's whereabouts and the official publication in Moscow describing him as "a merited Soviet agent" and announcing his high decoration. This event took place in September 1967, but the Soviet government decided to turn a blind eye.

On September 21, 1967, the Foreign Office in London issued this statement:

> A man calling himself Bourke called at the British embassy in Moscow on September 4, and saying that he was staying with George Blake in Moscow, whose escape he had arranged, asked about returning to Britain.
>
> The man had no proof of identity. The Embassy officials explained that they would have to establish his identity and he would have to obtain a Soviet exit visa. Authority also had to be sought from the Irish Republic, as Bourke said he was an Irish citizen.
>
> Accordingly, he was asked to call again. He has not, so far, done so.

It has been confirmed through photographs that the man was indeed Bourke, for whose arrest there is a warrant in the United Kingdom.

The Embassy was given the necessary instructions to enable them to act if Bourke should call again.

A Foreign Office spokesman added, a trifle unnecessarily, that the British authorities were now satisfied that George Blake was in Russia, and he said, somewhat naïvely, that it would be impossible to get him out of Russia without Soviet consent as Britain had no extradition treaty with the Soviet Union. The Soviet government, probably satisfied with the reaction to this blatantly contrived leak, remained silent. They did, in fact, encourage Bourke to go home and in the meantime—after he had quarreled with Blake—provided him with a comfortable apartment on his own and a generous allowance of seventy-five roubles (about thirty pounds) per week. This was part of the reward to the man who, however colorful and diverse the accounts he later gave, had been the key operator in the scheme to spring Blake from Wormwood Scrubs. It was by no means certain that Bourke, once outside Russia, would not be handed over to the British authorities, tried and severely punished. This did not trouble the Soviet masters. He had done his stint and was, of course, entirely expendable. In the event, the Irish courts refused Bourke's extradition after his return to Dublin.

Eventually, in February 1970, the announcement of the high award bestowed on Blake was accompanied by a five-thousand-word "interview" serialized in two consecutive issues of the *Izvestya*, an almost unique feature in the official newspaper not given to sensational stories. The publication was intended no doubt mainly for overseas consumption.

The narrative can be faulted on many of the incidents described. The familiar Communist jargon indicates that, whatever Blake did or did not say to his interviewers (who signed themselves V. Lyadov and V. Rozin), they injected the official line to produce a plethora of banal propaganda.

After the stereotyped dirge about "the perfidy of capitalist imperialist aggression against the peace-loving Socialist countries," Blake talked for the first time about his work for the British secret service, greatly magnifying his position—important though indeed it was—by claiming to have been deputy head of a "Technical Operations Section" of the Secret Intelligence Service in London in 1953 (after his return from Korea) and to have held similar rank in "Section Y," concerned with telephone tapping and diplomatic-mail interception. It is, of course, perfectly safe for him to make these specific claims. The Secret Intelligence Service, he and his K.G.B. masters know, will never rise to the bait and confirm or deny them.

Likewise, he could safely spin his yarn about his role in various odious operations of the S.I.S., designed to plant microphones in the offices of Soviet embassy and trade-mission officials not only in London, but also in Brussels, Copenhagen, and other European capitals.

His account of his work in West Berlin, where he began his prolonged treacherous activities, of his regular attendances at top secret conferences of British S.I.S. and American C.I.A. chiefs in London and elsewhere, is possibly correct if taken with several grains of salt. He enlarged on the "Operation Gold," the scheme to construct a tunnel in Berlin in order to tap the telephone cables linking the Soviet *Kommandatura* and the East German government offices with Moscow, and proudly stressed that he had betrayed this operation "just in time."

But he omitted many of the salient contributions he made, for instance his betrayal of some forty British and West German agents, although he had boasted to Sean Bourke that, in fact, he betrayed more than one hundred of them to the Soviet espionage chiefs.

The book of memoirs he says he is writing "will make more disclosures of the dangerous and contemptible machinations of the British and American intelligence services."

In the sporting terms which Blake so admired despite his ambivalent regard for British customs and conventions, he is "on a good wicket" in saying or writing whatever he wishes about the British Intelligence Service. Virtually nothing about his work has ever been officially revealed by Whitehall. The 1961 trial was conducted almost entirely in secret session. Questions in Parliament were expertly parried, and debates petered out in vagaries. The published version of the report of the Committee of Inquiry into Security Procedures, presided over by Lord Radcliffe after Blake's trial, shed no light on his prolonged betrayals. Lord Mountbatten's report on prison security after Blake's escape in 1966, while describing in great detail the events before and after the escape, was concerned with prison security and with measures to prevent similar jailbreaks in the future.

It was understandable that in 1961 the British authorities decided to brush the Blake affair neatly under the carpet. The biggest pile of dust needing concealment lay in one place where public curiosity might have seized on it and blown it into an international storm. This place was Berlin.

Blake's trial coincided with secret negotiations between London, Washington, and Moscow on the city's future. Two years before, Khrushchev had demanded "the demilitarization of West Berlin, and its reunification with East Berlin into a 'Free City,'" the implication being the withdrawal of the Allied troops from its western sectors, but leaving it ringed by the many Soviet divisions stationed in East Germany and by the quarter of a million strong "People's army" and militia of the East German regime. Khrushchev threatened to sign a treaty with the East German government and return to it the control of all access routes to West Berlin if his demand was not accepted. Britain and the United States flatly rejected this demand, which acceptance would have meant the end of freedom for West Berlin, leaving its two million inhabitants at the mercy of the Communists. Washington denounced Moscow's statement as a "war threat"* and President Eisenhower proposed a Four Power summit meeting—to take place in Paris on May 15, 1960—to reach some solution of the grave crisis. When the leaders of the United States, Britain, and France arrived, Khrushchev exploited the shooting down of the American U-2 "spy aircraft" over Russia to break up the meeting.

When Kennedy followed Eisenhower as president, he again attempted to call a conference with Khruschchev. Berlin was to be the first item on the agenda. The conference took place in Vienna on June 3–4, 1961, a few weeks after Blake's trial at the Old Bailey, and ended inconclusively. Kennedy described the situation as "somber," Khrushchev darkened the situation still further by sending the American president a savage note accusing the Western powers of "saber-rattling militarism" and claiming that West Germany "had established a powerful military base for aggressive plans, to kindle a dangerous hotbed of conflict on German soil." In East Germany Soviet troops and armor were reported on the move, and on the city borders the Berlin Wall was being erected.

In Washington President Kennedy delivered on radio and television a speech to the nation, speaking of "an immediate threat to free men" and announcing that "to deter and destroy any aggressor" fifty percent of the United States B-52 and B-47 aircraft, carrying nuclear bombs, were put on a fifteen-minutes warning alert.

A minor incident, a shot across the Berlin border, could have started World War III. The British government had no desire to aggravate relations with the Soviets, particularly as Mr. Macmillan was trying to act as a mediator between Washington and Moscow. Moreover, any further disclosures about Blake's successful, and for many years undetected, treachery would have been extremely painful to secret service chiefs, who had been made to look foolish by the scant information already revealed.

* *Berlin,* a document issued by the U.S. Department of State, Washington, D.C., August 1961.

So what was one of the major cases of postwar espionage was allowed to lapse into oblivion once the prison gates closed behind its main character. The Berlin crisis abated, and for nearly ten years the Soviet government made no attempt to extract any propaganda value out of their notorious agent.

But no one who had studied Moscow's methods could have any doubts that one day Blake would be presented to the world as a hero.

CHAPTER TWO

BARTERING SPIES

The blueprint for the processing of Western traitors welcomed back into the fold was the case of the "Missing Diplomats," Donald Maclean and Guy Burgess. For five years after their disappearance in 1951, the Soviet government denied any knowledge of their whereabouts or even of their existence. Soviet newspapers* even alleged that it was the British secret service who, for some unexplained reasons, had engineered their disappearance, or even "had them put away."

Then Maclean and Burgess were produced with a fanfare of publicity shortly before Khrushchev and Bulganin visited London in 1956. Several reasons for the timing of their sudden reappearance were suggested, for instance that Moscow assumed it would create a better climate for the state visit in Britain, where there was strong resentment about Moscow's persistent and devious denials and allegations. But the main reason for the decision to produce Maclean and Burgess was, no doubt, that Khrush-

* For instance, in *Novy Mir*, October 4, 1951.

chev saw an opportunity to drive a wedge between London and Washington just as his state visit began. The two British ex-diplomats were made to say at their first public appearance on February 11, 1956, at a Moscow press conference for foreign correspondents that the United States was the chief fomentor of the cold war policy, dragging a rather unwilling Britain along with her.

The rigmarole of denial, contrived leak, and finally full publicity was also adopted in the case of Colonel Rudolph Abel, the master spy of the K.G.B., who was arrested in New York in 1957. Abel had lived under many aliases in the United States since 1948, heading a spy network which extended all over the country and into Central and South America. When he was sentenced to thirty years' imprisonment, Soviet officials and Moscow newspapers indignantly denied any knowledge of him, stated that he was not a Soviet citizen, and described him as "one more innocent victim of the Fascist witch-hunt by the bouncing Pinkertons from the F.B.I. and C.I.A., framed by *agents provocateurs* and denounced by a professional swindle." This mouthful was published by *Pravda,* while the highbrow journal *Literatournaya Gazeta* dismissed Abel's trial as "a hoax whose authors concocted a fantastic crime fiction story and made a poor New York photographer into the brains of a spy ring which never existed."

Like Blake, Abel was consigned to oblivion for five years in prison. Like Blake, his employers had not forgotten him. The five years, which seems to be the standard period Soviet spies must be prepared to serve, was up. Thereupon the release machinery was put in motion. Semi-official feelers were put out from Moscow about the possibility of exchanging Gary Powers, pilot of the American U-2 spy plane, serving a ten-year sentence in Russia, for the hitherto disavowed Abel. The exchange, a splendid bargain for the K.G.B., took place in Berlin in February 1962. Moscow insisted that it was agreed upon solely for humanitarian reasons, because of the pleading by Abel's suddenly produced wife and daughter in East Germany.

Colonel Abel was not heard of for three years after his

release and exchange. Then, in May 1965, the full propaganda treatment put him on display in Moscow as "the great hero of Soviet state security." Moscow produced him on television and it was announced that he was decorated with the Order of Lenin and other medals. To top it all, no lesser personage than Vladimir Semichastny, then chairman of the U.S.S.R. Council of Ministers' Committee for State Security (K.G.B.), wrote his eulogy:* "On the eve of the great victory holiday [the twentieth anniversary of Germany's surrender] one cannot fail to express special appreciation and profound gratitude to valiant Soviet Intelligence agents who . . . like the agent known by the name of Rudolph Abel, performed difficult but honorable tasks in the struggle against the enemy. This was truly labor demanding great mental effort, audacity, determination, boundless love, and loyalty to the homeland. The time has not yet come when all the names of all these intrepid people can be mentioned, but history will be generous to them as they rightfully deserve. It is to their selflessness, their extremely difficult service in complex conditions, far from homeland, family, and friends, that we are indebted for the disclosures of insidious plans . . . against the Soviet Union."

Comrade Semichastny was now in position to decide the time had come for admitting the existence of yet another of these "intrepid people." This was the pseudo-Canadian Gordon Lonsdale—in reality the K.G.B. Colonel Conon Trofimovich Molody—sentenced to twenty-five years' imprisonment in 1962 in London for his leading part in the naval spy ring, in which were involved Peter and Helen Kroger and the two British civil servants, Harry Houghton and Ethel Gee.

This time Soviet admission of Lonsdale's spying activities was made discreetly, with overtures for an exchange of this man for a British agent, Greville Wynne, imprisoned in Russia. Wynne, an exhibition salesman, was somewhat inadvisedly enlisted by the British secret service

* In *Pravda*, May 7, 1965, p. 4.

as a courier to Colonel Oleg Penkovsky in Moscow, who had supplied Western intelligence with valuable information."* Arrested in Hungary, Wynne pleaded "guilty with certain qualifications" at his trial in Moscow, stating that he had been commanded and threatened by the British secret service when he tried to terminate his assignment. "They started to squeeze the vise tighter and threatened me," he explained, "and in the last stage it was quite clear to me that I was in such a fix that I had no choice whatsoever in the matter."†

Wynne was given a comparatively mild sentence of eight years. He was out and home within eleven months in exchange for Lonsdale who had served three years and one month of his twenty-five years' sentence. Lonsdale, emerging from nonexistence to fame and glory in the familiar way, received a hero's welcome in Moscow, plus the inevitable decorations. By this time the Soviet propaganda machine had devised fresh publicity novelties. Lonsdale was assisted in writing his memoirs for the edification of the Soviet public and the mortification of the Western secret services. For the edition of his book‡ in Britain he received the agreeable fee of ten thousand pounds tax free. He also starred in a film as the brilliant Soviet agent "Lonsfield," outwitting the secret services of imperialism. With the adroit interpolation of scenes from travel films the unnamed country of the film plot was clearly Britain, and a seaside town named "Dorgate" was intended to portray the Portland naval base, where Lonsdale and his accomplices had stolen the secrets. Colonel Abel lent his prestige to the film by giving the introductory commentary.

* Compare *The Penkovskiy Papers*, Collins, London, 1965.

† Mr. Wynne, after his return to Britain, retracted these statements and explained they were made under duress. In his book *The Man From Moscow* (Hutchinson, London, 1967) he stated that his depositions at his trial had been prepared and approved by his superiors in London for the eventuality of his arrest.

‡ *Spy* (published by Spearman, London, 1965 and serialized in *The People* newspaper).

The spy barter system worked admirably for the K.G.B. Big Russian fish were retrieved for little ones. The master spies Peter and Helen Kroger sipped champagne on their homeward flight and, one hopes, gave a silent toast to Gerald Brooke, the idealistic young lecturer who had indulged in some abortive efforts of anti-Communist propaganda in Moscow and had been held as a hostage until the British government was blackmailed into releasing the Krogers.*

But in spite of the many successes in retrieving their star agents from prisons in the West by barter, Moscow came to realize that George Blake could not be bought in return for a courier, or a pilot, or a few captured tourists unfortunately straying into Communist territory. He was a British subject when caught and tried, and the British government could not and would not exchange him.

Blake's welfare was, therefore, a challenge to the K.G.B.'s ingenuity. One can be sure that all over the world Soviet agents at work were watching closely, and with anxious foreboding, Blake's fate. They knew that the K.G.B. had an almost maternal regard for their safety. None of them could be under any illusion that this was a humane or sentimental feeling, but a dividend payable on their "labor with audacity, determination, and boundless loyalty," as one of their chiefs put it. Their knowledge that a Soviet agent, when caught, would eventually be rescued by the K.G.B. was a priceless asset to the K.G.B. in recruitment as well as in the agents' subsequent devotion to the job. Indeed, every Soviet agent goes about his business today with an invisible insurance policy in his pocket: whatever happens to him and however heavy a sentence he might get, he knows that his employers will not let him down and that, in the end, he will be free and honored.

Blake knew all this, too. In his *Izvestya* interview he said that he never despaired after his trial. He knew he would not serve more than a few years; indeed he quite

* In *A Spy for A Spy* I give a full account of the many spy exchanges, disclosing hitherto unpublished documentary details.

exactly estimated his term: five years, which he accepted as a reasonable price for his exploits. He told his interviewers: "After the trial my mother put my clothes into mothballs. I told her, when she visited me, I shall need them again in about five years." In the event he was "sprung" from Wormwood Scrubs—after Moscow's offers for his exchange misfired—five years and four months after he began his forty-two-year sentence.

It is reasonably certain that the complete and unvarnished story of the criminal organization needed to get Blake out of prison and then out of the country and across Europe to Moscow will never be known. Blake might give a fictitious account when he publishes his book. Sean Bourke, who claims to have carried out this major coup single-handed, does not know the real and complete story, and he has good reasons not to give a detailed account of what he does know.

I have had a lively correspondence with this flamboyant and likable Irishman both during his stay in Moscow and since his return to Ireland. In January 1970, when I was invited to address the Philosophical Society of Trinity College, Dublin, on the subject of espionage, I met Sean Bourke face-to-face for the first time. At my suggestion he came to the lecture hall and gave a colorful and amusing account of his role in Blake's escape in October 1966. His story did not, however, bear too close an analysis. When I pointed out various contradictions, he tried to laugh it off. This very Irish character has, in the role of a true raconteur, more regard for the manner of telling a story than for the matter of it.

My own careful and prolonged researches into the Blake escape, yielding valuable information from British officials insofar as it did not infringe the Official Secrets Act, coupled with my own experience in the spy game, have prompted me to conclusions which I have every reason to believe to be reasonably accurate and comprehensive. These are given in more detail in Chapter 20 of this book.

The Blake case was the curtain raiser to a series of sen-

sational spy dramas. They ranged from the Portland Naval
Spy Ring of Lonsdale, the Krogers, Houghton, and Miss
Gee, to the homosexual Admiralty clerk William Vassall;
from the role Captain Evgeny Ivanov, Soviet agent and
naval attaché at the London embassy, played in the Pro-
fumo-Keeler affair, to Frank Bossard, the Ministry of
Aviation guided weapons scientist, and R.A.F. Chief Tech-
nician Ronald Britten.*

The motives of these traitors were all too typical of the
corruptive weaknesses of human beings. Houghton, Bossard, and Britten sold their country's secrets for a cash return to satisfy their craving for drink and high life. Vassall
was a sexual degenerate and a victim of blackmail as a
result. Miss Gee was a weak, infatuated woman sup-
pressing her conscience to please her lover.

None of them was clever enough or important enough
to do irreparable harm to national security.

George Blake and Kim Philby were traitors of a very
different kind and their treachery caused prolonged and
extreme harm to the defense of the Western democracies.
Both were ideological and dedicated double agents. Both
held vital positions within the British secret service. Both
were clever enough to carry on their nefarious work undetected for years on end.

The Philby case has been widely covered both by the
main character in it and by expert observers.† It warrants
no further mention here except to stress some remarkable parallels of Philby's career with that of Blake. The
similarities apply to the mentality and the official position

* Peter and Helen Kroger were both sentenced to twenty years'
imprisonment, Harry Houghton and Ethel Gee to fifteen years; William Vassall in 1962 to eighteen years; Frank Bossard in 1965 to
twenty-one years, and Ronald Britten in 1968 also to twenty-one
years.

† My own book *The Third Man—The true story of Kim Philby*
(Barker, London, 1968); Professor Hugh Trevor-Roper's *The Philby
Affair* (Kimber, 1968), Kim Philby's *My Silent War* (MacGibbon
and Kee, 1968), Eleanor Philby's *The Spy I Loved* (Hamish Hamil-
ton, 1968) and the account by a team of *Sunday Times* reporters.

of both men after they had taken the decision to work for
Moscow. They do not apply to their background or the
motives which prompted them.

Philby was by birth, family background, environment,
and education a typical product of British Establishment.
To his superiors, acquaintances, and intimate friends he
remained so even after doubts arose about his Communist
leanings. He says in his book that his conversion to communism began when he was an undergraduate at Cambridge. As a member of the University Socialist Society,
he "became gradually aware that the Labour party stood
well apart from the mainstream of the Left as a worldwide
force." The real turning point in his thinking, he says,
"came with the demoralization and rout of the Labour
party in 1931 . . . which should be so helpless against the
strength which reaction could mobilize in time of crisis."
He confesses that his conversion was a slow and brain-
racking process, but he left Cambridge "with the conviction that my life must be devoted to communism."

Like many of his generation, Philby watched fascism
spread like a disease from Italy to Germany, Austria,
Spain. He detested the appeasement policy of the Bald-
win-Chamberlain era. Many thousands of ordinary and decent people felt the same. Some became avowed and overt
Communists. Not so Philby. For thirty years he lived a
double life, choosing the crooked path of a traitor. He enjoyed, and took advantage of, the confidence of friends,
colleagues and superiors. The British government paid him
a comfortable living. He climbed the ladder of promotion
in the British secret service until at one time he was
mooted to become head of its main organization. And day
by day, for many years, he betrayed the trust of his employers and the vital interests of his country. He enjoyed
the power over his subordinates who trusted him and he
delivered them to a cruel enemy. An honest rebel against
society and its institutions, fighting them openly, can claim
and deserves respect by his opponents. Philby can make
no such claim; even in the tawdry annals of treason he
reaches the nadir of dishonor.

Like Philby, George Blake, too, became a brilliant craftsman in his self-chosen strange profession, a high-powered, trusted secret agent in important positions. But, in contrast to Philby, he had no cause for disillusion with the policies of Britain when he entered it. He moved toward treason through a very different motivation. He came to Britain when the country—of which he was a citizen by legal right though not by birth—was the very symbol of the fight for freedom against Nazi tyranny. Whatever bewilderment he felt in the difficult task for a foreigner to understand British mentality, only after many years did bewilderment change to disenchantment, and disenchantment to hostility and treachery. The usual reprehensible, but rational, motives for treason, intrigue, and perfidy seemed to be missing.

In order to find out how and why George Blake became a traitor, I have made as rigorous a series of investigations as, I believe, is humanly possible. In the Netherlands, the country of his birth, childhood, and youth, I talked to members of his family, his school fellows and teachers, the men who fought beside him in the Dutch Resistance. In Britain, Berlin, and Beirut I met men and women who had been his close colleagues, and though he spurned intimate friendship, believed they knew him well. I interviewed the men who shared with him the horrors of Korean prison camps. I have drawn on my own brief acquaintance with Blake, and on the more extensive memoirs of several of his superiors in the organizations of which he was once an important member, and which he tried to destroy.

What my researches have elicited is deeply perturbing. It points to a psychological malaise, which—undetected or minimized by a secret agent's superiors—must lead to a situation of grave danger for the organization which employs him. Blake was mentally and emotionally insecure, with an inability to adjust himself to the complicated life into which ancestry, environment, and the tasks assigned to him had thrust him.

His foreign descent led to a contrariety of his emotions, one yearning to be accepted as "British," to belong to his adopted country. The other growing into hatred because of the real or imagined rebuffs he experienced. Consciously or subconsciously he must have decided that his superior intelligence, his devotion to duty, his coveted ambitions were never rewarded in the manner he believed he was entitled to expect, certainly not in the manner they are rewarded for men who "belong" to England. He was driven by an extraordinary ambition to excel, he wanted power over events and people—and suffered wounding frustration. This must have created a feeling of inferiority. To compensate for this, Blake was driven to turn to actions by which he could prove to himself, if not to others, his superiority. The results of such an emotional conflict cannot be shaped by reason.

Blake's motives to become a traitor were as irrational as Philby's were frighteningly rational. It is, therefore, unlikely that anyone—and that includes Blake himself—can ever give a fully satisfactory explanation for his actions. His Soviet mentors may order him to publish an acceptable and reasoned theme. Observers such as myself may probe his actions, may illuminate some facets of his character and explain factual events. But there will always remain the mysteries buried in the dark recesses of his mind.

Blake's downfall really began when his British superiors in West Berlin acquiesced to his suggestion that he should become a double agent. They agreed that he should contact the chiefs of the East Berlin headquarters of the K.G.B. under the pretext of readiness to work for them. The purpose of this exercise was to plant fabricated material—mystifying but, in fact, worthless—thus gaining their trust and ferreting out valuable information from them.

The dividing line between outwitting the adversary and traducing one's own side is almost invisible. Even the most resourceful and coolheaded double agent can slip up. He must dispense with all the normal feelings of honor, decency, and trust. By all civilized standards he is a conscienceless scoundrel. If he brings back more than he gives away, his employers will praise him as a hero; if he gives away more than he brings back, they will brand him as a traitor.

George Blake clearly dreamed of being a hero. In the end, goaded by his desire to excel, he got himself into an impasse from which there was no escape. Obdurate, ruthless men, far more clever than he, molded him with guile and flattery. If he saw through them, he tried to escape from his mental torment by consoling himself that by joining the Communist side he was helping—as he later put it—"in establishing what I came to believe to be a balanced and more just society."

The price he paid was loss of all integrity. He became one more victim of the omnipotent and omnipresent Communist conspiracy.

CHAPTER THREE

THE BOY APART

Spy, traitor, double agent. The labels tell us nothing about the nature of the man whom they are designed to throw into the ugly notoriety of newspaper headlines. When George Blake stood his trial, there were in effect only the headlines to read and no supporting text. No facts were given in court during the public session, which lasted for fifty-three minutes. No clue was given to the actual nature of his crimes or the motives behind them.

"The prisoner had made a complete confession," said Sir Reginald Manningham-Buller, the attorney general. And he added that the contents of the confession, except for short passages to which he proposed to refer, "must remain secret." It was as if the finger of accusation had been pointed at an inanimate object: "The Traitor Blake," a figure from Madame Tussaud's wax cabinet.

What manner of man was he? What was he like as a person before the prison gates closed on him?

To meet him socially he was good-looking, intelligent, and cultured. He was a good conversationalist, well informed on many subjects and able to compel attention. Yet one found it easier to remember the way he held one's attention than to recall what he had said. By reputation he was brave and energetic and these qualities were easily credible after a few minutes in his company. He enjoyed comfort, good food and wine, but did not drink heavily.

He seemed entirely English and yet one soon assumed that he came from a foreign, cosmopolitan background. He could be brash and a little boastful in his twenties, when I first knew him. In later years his attitude seemed more relaxed, he appeared to be more confident even though he sometimes affected somewhat eccentric habits.

One wondered how much he had in common with his colleagues at the Foreign Office and in "the Service," born into the Establishment, who behind his back might have at times referred to him as "that funny foreigner." After his return from the prisons of Korea, described by his fellow prisoners—professional diplomats and English missionaries—as the most reliable, unselfish, and steadfast of men, I assume that he had reached with his colleagues a new relationship of mutual respect and even of affection.

The political views he expressed were cautious and acceptable, as befitted a member of the Foreign Office. To some people he gave the impression not so much of wanting to avoid political discussion, as of mental vacuity where politics were concerned.

He was shy in the company of women but not more than many young Englishmen of that period. Later he seemed to be happily married and was a devoted father of his two pretty children. He spoke rarely about his family, but sometimes remarked on his great attachment to his mother.

When in the spring of 1961 the news broke of the arrest of George Blake on a serious charge under the Official Secrets Act, I realized that I knew very little of the real

man. None of his much closer acquaintances seem to
know anything about his origin, his background, and his
early life. The picture which began to shape of the "government official" who had been arrested after his recall
from a diplomatic post in the Middle East, was out of fo-
cus. Even Scotland Yard was mystified; records at the Foreign Office and the security service contained only bare
and incomplete facts. Inquiries in Holland were difficult
because registry records in his birthplace Rotterdam had
been destroyed during the German bombing raid in May
1940. It took some time to establish the identify of his father when reporters were searching after a "Mr. William
Blake," a shadowy Englishman believed to have abandoned his family many years before. It was the name
"Blake" that first misled the searchers. There was never a
"Mr. Blake" senior. George was born George Behar, and
he had adopted the name "Blake" only after his arrival in
England in 1943, a prudent anglicization. Soon after the
trial I went to Rotterdam and, after many wrong turns, I
managed to build up a complete dossier of Blake's family,
background, and childhood.

George's father, Albert William Behar, born on August
10, 1889, in Cairo, was the son of a wealthy Sephardic
banker, whose family tree was more than six hundred
years old. The Sephardim are regarded as the aristocrats
of the Jewish race. They originate from Portugal and
Spain, where they occupied a privileged position, enjoyed
power and acquired wealth as merchants and financiers
during the Middle Ages.

Albert Behar's family descended from Isaak Abravanel,
who was treasurer and minister to King Ferdinand V of
Aragon in the fifteenth century. In 1492 the Sephardic
Jews were expelled from Spain and six years later the
same fate overtook their community in Portugal. Most of
them emigrated to countries of the Mediterranean, Greece,
Turkey, Egypt, and North Africa.

The Behars (the accent is on the "a") settled in Turkey
and Egypt nearly five centuries ago and prospered.
George's grandfather was financial adviser to the Khedive

of Egypt, but by the time his father, Albert, was born the country was ruled by Lord Cromer on behalf of Queen Victoria. The Behar family became "British protected persons."

Albert Behar served in the British army in the First World War, fought in Flanders, was wounded twice and badly gassed. He later served on Field Marshal Haig's Intelligence Staff, received several awards for gallantry, and also the Order of the British Empire and the French Legion of Honor.

In 1919, in London, Captain Behar met a young Dutch girl, Catherine Gertrud Beijderwellen. She came from a no less respectable, but a very different background; the family of Beijderwellen and Van Asperen had been supplying the Kingdom and the General States of the Netherlands with church dignitaries, public servants, and naval commanders since the middle of the seventeenth century.

Albert and Catherine fell deeply in love but, at first, their families did not approve of the match. However, after much heart-searching and firmness of purpose by the young couple, the consent of both families was obtained. Albert Behar and Catherine Beijderwellen were married in London, on January 11, 1922.

Albert had relatives in Holland and the young couple decided to settle in Rotterdam, where many of the Beijderwellens had resided for generations. He became a partner in a sporting-goods business and he also represented several British firms in Holland. The newly married couple rented a house, No. 104, Gedempte Botorsloot in a pleasant district of Rotterdam.

Their first child was born there on November 11, 1922, and named George, in honor of King George V.

A year later the family moved to a larger house which had become vacant next door, at No. 102, and when their second child, Adele Gertrud, was born, Mr. Behar bought a large house at 40C, Spengensekade; there in 1925 the second daughter, Elizabeth, was born.

Albert Behar retained his loyalty to Britain and regularly visited London and Cairo on business and family af-

fairs. He also retained his British nationality, and friends
and acquaintances always thought of him as British. His
wife's family were staunch and conservative Protestants
and the three children were brought up with strict Lutheran instruction. But Mr. Behar never made any attempt
at concealing that he was of Jewish origin.

Plain for all to see was the sacrifice he had made for
the country of his adoption during the war. He suffered
badly from the aftereffects of the phosgene or mustard gas
used by the Germans on the battlefield during his service
with the British army. In 1935 he fell seriously ill with
lung trouble, contracted peritonitis and died in April of
the following year at the age of forty-six.

His widow and her three young children lived in a villa
in Maasstraat No. 4 in the famous seaside resort of
Scheveningen. Behar had made full provision for his
family and his widow was able to maintain a comfortable
home, employing two maids. Frequent visitors were Grand-
mama Beijderwellen and her unmarried daughter Truus.
George, who had become the only male in a household
full of women, went to a select school at The Hague.

One of the maids, who served the family loyally for
several years, was Dina Regoort, now Mrs. Emans, whom
I visited at her spotless home at Overschie. She spoke to
me with sincere affection for the "rather lonely little boy,"
as she remembered George during and after the illness of
his father. During the family ordeal, she says, he was inevitably left to himself more than would otherwise have been
the case.

"Although he was a sweet, polite boy I always felt he
was apart and he was often sad," Dina told me.

"George had no friends of his own age," she continued.
"He did not play with his schoolmates or other boys. And
he missed his father very much. . . ."

George played elaborate games of imagination on his
own. All children like pretending.

But one of George's favorite games of make-believe, as
recounted by Dina, had about it a macabre quality in the
light of subsequent events.

He would dress up in his mother's black silk gown, place an old black hat on his head and order Dina to spread a green cloth over the dining-room table, at which he would seat himself with magisterial dignity.

Then, rapping the table hard with a little hammer from the toolbox, he would call the court to order and announce the beginning of a "trial." George was always the judge. Dina was his favorite prisoner, because she so readily confessed to all the crimes the "judge" read out. But if she was busy in the kitchen, little Adele and Elizabeth had to stand in. They were usually accused of serious crimes, which the small girls hardly understood, and they were invariably found guilty. Sentences were always severe and pronounced with great dignity.

His father seems to have been aware on his sickbed of the danger of a fatherless home for his only son. He made his wife promise that, in the event of his death, she would send the boy to relatives in Cairo, for a year or two. Mr. Behar had a sister there, married to a wealthy banker, and there were several boys in that family. Mrs. Behar agreed, albeit with a heavy heart, and in the autumn of 1936, George—by then thirteen and a half years old—traveled to Egypt. While staying there he attended the English school in Cairo. He continued to do very well in his studies and acquired fluent French, which was the second language after English in his uncle and aunt's household.

Every year he came home to Rotterdam for a holiday with his mother, sisters, and grandmother and also stayed with his uncle, Mijnheer Anthony Beijderwellen, who had no children of his own.

When George had been in Cairo for two and a half years his mother, acting on the advice of her brother, decided that the boy should continue his education at a Dutch high school, and so he came home "for good" just before Christmas 1938.

At the age of sixteen he became a pupil at the *M.U.L.O.*, the abbreviated name for the Rotterdam High School *Meer Uitgebreid Lager Onderwijs*. As his mother and sisters stayed on at the villa at Scheveningen, George lived with his grandmother in a pleasant, three-storied house at No. 35A, Burgemeester Meinesz Plein in Rotterdam. With the grandmother lived his maiden aunt Truus and Dina presided in the kitchen.

George was physically mature for his age and had grown into a dark, handsome young lad, nearly six feet tall. He had, of course, learned to speak and write English from early childhood and the English College in Cairo had given him mastery of the language. In later life, few people detected any trace of an accent when he spoke English. He had also acquired a very good knowledge of German. Rotterdam claims with justification to be Europe's greatest port, but when George returned it was to a provincial bourgeois atmosphere, compared with the luxury of his uncle's house and the sophistication of life in Cairo, where his uncle entertained a succession of guests from many different countries. When in the squalor of the Korean prison camp, Commissioner Lord found that George Blake "had exquisite manners and was a man of the world," he did not know that his fellow prisoner had acquired these qualities in his early youth.

Yet, despite his newly won social ease, George remained "a boy apart" when he returned to Rotterdam. He had a lively intelligence and unusual poise for a young man of his age. They enabled him to become almost unnaturally self-sufficient.

Trusted Dina had left the Beijderwellens to marry a respectable artisan and she sent her sister Jo Regoort to take her place. This was the description she gave me of George, as she remembered him in 1939: "He was a very nice, pleasant boy, always polite and helpful, never causing any trouble. But he was so serious . . . never up to any pranks like other boys. He kept himself to himself."

Her impression was confirmed by all his contemporaries. Their descriptions are in all essentials almost identical: pleasant, conscientious, ambitious, but somehow withdrawn.

I spent several hours discussing George's school days with Heer Roélof Cornelis Kistemaker, having collected him from the hubbub on the floor of the Rotterdam Stock Exchange where he holds an important position. A cheerful, burly family man, Heer Kistemaker clapped his hand to his head in a gesture of bewilderment and distress when he described his reactions to the newspaper reports of Blake's trial.

"I read that George was convicted for treason. The one thing I shall never believe is that he did anything dishonest or wicked . . . As you know, schoolboys are not always paragons of virtue. They tell lies to escape punishment, they crib, they deceive their teachers and parents from time to time. I reckon we were no better and no worse than other boys at sixteen or seventeen . . . But George Behar really was an exception. He was the most decent boy in our class. I do not remember him ever telling a lie. He never involved himself in one of our petty intrigues or took advantage of another schoolfellow. He was always ready to help others. He knew English, French, and German much better than any of us at *M.U.L.O.*, and he was always willing to help us with homework.

"Yes, it's true he kept himself to himself. Although we passed his house every day, he never asked me in and I don't think he invited any of the other classmates. You know, in those days, Rotterdam was a more homely town, perhaps rather provincial, if you wish. We boys used to pop in at each other's place, uninvited. But none of us would have gone to George's. Perhaps we felt that we were not wanted.

"I think George Behar spent most of his spare time reading. He did not join in with 'the gang' which went to the cinema, football matches, cycle racing. But he wasn't a softie either. He did well in physical training—we call it gymnastics—and he was quite a good athlete and swimmer. . . .

"He wasn't interested in girls when we were having our first childish crushes," continued Heer Kistemaker, "but again I must qualify that by saying that he seemed more, not less, mature than boys of his own age."

Heer Kistemaker rubbed his chin. "You know, I simply

do not understand how the George that I knew could have betrayed not only his country but also his wife and children. It just does not make sense to me. . . ."

Heer Kistemaker, like other people in Holland who knew George as a youngster, was baffled and upset.

The boy who shared the same desk with George at the *M.U.L.O.* is today the director of a leading company in the international hides and skin trade. Heer Henrik Dentro broke away from a series of urgent telephone calls in his office to tell me about George.

"I think he was a very introspective boy. To us lads, brought up in the strict tradition of Dutch middle-class respectability, he was a somewhat exotic figure. He had traveled widely and mixed with important people. He told us sometimes about his visits to the Pyramids and the Sphinx, the marvels of Luxor, sailing on the Nile, but he never boasted about it or bragged about his rich uncle in Cairo, or anything like that.

"He mentioned that his father served in the British army . . . I believe he had something to do with the Intelligence Service.

"We admired George and also envied him a little, because he was so good at schoolwork. He knew several languages and he often helped the other boys when they got stuck with a précis or a composition. . . .

"No, he never had a very close friend. I sat next to him for a long time, but we never became very close. It wasn't in George's nature to open up."

George's form-master, Dr. Levy, who was Jewish, had been deported by the Nazis during the war and died in a concentration camp. I found two of George's schoolmasters at *M.U.L.O.* but they could contribute little beyond what I had already heard: "a pleasant, conscientious boy, the brightest in the class, a little reticent and dreamy, perhaps . . ."

Thus a consistent picture of George as a boy emerged from the memories of those who knew him before the war. All found much to praise and none had a harsh word to say about his character or behavior. All refused to be-

lieve that he could have become a Communist or a traitor.
Indeed, some made the point that his indifference to politics was exceptional in 1939, when the schoolboys in Holland took sides on the issues which were tearing Europe
apart.

Hitler's Third Reich was only a few miles away. Austria
and Czechoslovakia had been seized. Many people in Holland feared a Nazi invasion and many of the *M.U.L.O.*
boys joined patriotic organizations and cadet units. George
did none of these things. If he was asked why not, he
would reply that he was British and never discussed Dutch
politics.

His lack of interest in politics was genuine, if only because his interests lay in a different direction. One of his
schoolmasters told me that George had remarked several
times that he would like to study for the priesthood, after
passing his examinations. With his mother and sisters he
was a regular worshiper at the Lutheran church.

Later he began to train for Holy Orders, but he never
completed his studies because he had to fly from the
Gestapo.

The discovery that he had taken such serious interest in
religion came as a surprise to me, but it was not out of
character. Years later he would make passing references to
religious matters and philosophy which betokened a
greater knowledge than one might have expected from a
man who had been unable to go to a university.

Another attribute which his masters and schoolfellows
emphasized was that George was very ambitious and was
driven by the desire to excel at whatever he was doing.
This did not surprise me. It fitted with what I knew of him
myself and with the opinions of others who knew him in
later years.

CHAPTER FOUR

THE TEENAGE HERO

During 1939, when he was a pupil at the *M.U.L.O.* high school, George Blake lived with his grandmother at her house at 35A, Burgemeester Meinesz Plein, in Rotterdam. Since then the house has been converted into flats but Heer Verhoeff, the jovial butcher on the corner, remembers George well. "He was a tall, polite lad. He often called to collect meat for his dog.

"George Behar was here one day when the 'phony war' was on," said Heer Verhoeff. "We talked about it occasionally. He told me that he could not believe the war would come to the Netherlands and even if it did he would stay on to complete his examinations. He said he hoped to win a scholarship for the priesthood."

The war could come to Holland and, when it did, it arrived in the most terrifying manner. Wave after wave of German paratroopers descended upon carefully selected targets, of which Walcheren airfield near Rotterdam and the roads between Rotterdam and The Hague were two of the most important. The German panzers came from the south. There was only a small Dutch garrison in Rotterdam but when the German commanders sent an emissary to demand its surrender, this was promptly refused by the garrison commandant, Colonel Scharoo.

Within hours the Germans began a merciless bombardment of the great port and city. At 1:30 P.M. the first Luftwaffe bombers flew low over the virtually undefended city. By 3:30 P.M. more than 150,000 of its inhabitants had lost their homes. No fewer than 26,000 houses were destroyed; the center of the city, including the Coolsingel,

31

Rotterdam's Piccadilly, was flattened. The bombers departed but the fires raged on. By 6:00 P.M. Rotterdam was one huge conflagration.

Death came indiscriminately, by high explosives, incendiaries, drowning in the underground shelters when water mains burst, by collapsing buildings, by fire, and by exploding gas and lack of medical attention.

Like most of the surviving people of Rotterdam, George never forgot nor forgave the Germans. He walked through the ruins of the city and watched the German troops goose-step past in the victory parade. He was there when the S.S. men and Gestapo arrived. One of his grandmother's neighbors was a member of the Dutch Nazi party and a few days later he denounced George as a *Britischer* to the Gestapo men, who were busy rounding up aliens and suspects. George was arrested and taken to the internment camp at Schoorl north of Amsterdam. This former military camp of the Dutch army was crowded with Britons, Frenchmen, Indian and Lascar seamen, Senegalese, Poles, and Jews.

Mrs. Behar and her two daughters were still in Scheveningen on the day of the invasion. A British friend of the family, Commander D. W. Child, a British Intelligence officer, advised her to go immediately with the two girls to the Hook of Holland, where three British destroyers had arrived to take the Dutch Royal Family, the Dutch government and a few British families aboard and carry them to England. Mrs. Behar had to leave all her belongings behind and hurry to the port.

The German panzers and mechanized columns were racing north and west from Hilversum, Amsterdam, and Rotterdam toward the North Sea. At the Hook, Queen Wilhelmina and the Dutch government members boarded H.M.S. *Hereward*. Mrs. Behar and her daughters were among a handful of British families to join a group of other Dutch officials aboard another British destroyer. German Stukas were dive-bombing the ships and a third British destroyer was hit and sunk. The two other warships reached Harwich safely, although they were machine-gunned and bombed during the journey.

George had seen his mother and sisters for the last time on April 28 when there was a family reunion at his grandmother's home to celebrate the old lady's birthday. There was some talk of Mrs. Behar and her children going to England. The family realized that, in the case of a German invasion, they would be in danger becuse of their British nationality. George told his mother he was determined to stay in Holland to finish his examinations. "And when the Nazis come, I shall fight them. . . ." he added. Mijnheer Beijderwellen promised his sister that he would look after the boy.

After George's arrest by the Gestapo at his grandmother's house, his uncle searched desperately "through the width and breadth of Holland" for the boy. "At last I found him at school," he told me, "and I went to see the Gestapo commandant. I asked him: 'Since when do the Germans make war on children? I have come to collect my nephew.' But the S.S. man just laughed. They would not let George go."

The camp was heavily guarded by S.S. troops, but this did not prevent George making the first of many daring escapes of his life.

He made his way eastward, almost across Holland, to his uncle's home at Warnveld near Zutfen, in the province of Gelderland. He reached it on October 16, 1940. Mijnheer Beijderwellen, a director of a grain company, hid him for a time, but the situation was dangerous because the Gestapo was looking for the boy. He managed to arrange a safer hiding place for George with a farmer, Boer Weenink, who had a farm called *De Koesterd* ("The Cow's Tail") at a village near Hummelo.

There George met the parish priest, Pastor Goedhaart, and began to study theology seriously. He was still determined to become a clergyman.

Mijnheer Anthony Beijderwellen, who lives at the seaside resort of Zaandvoort near Amsterdam, told me of this period of his nephew's life. Dutch Resistance organizations were being formed in the cities and towns of the Netherlands, but in the rural peace of the Gelderland progress was slow. George made a few friends among the young farmers of Hummelo. Suddenly he put away his theological volumes and treatises and gathered a few determined men around him. The eighteen-year-old boy became one of the leaders of the first local Resistance group.

His uncle, though a staunch patriot, was worried about his nephew's dangerous enterprise. After all, George was a British subject, wanted by the Gestapo, and if he were to be caught as an *onderduiker,* an underground fighter, he would almost certainly be put to death by the Nazis.

George, usually so obedient and polite to his elders, was adamant. He said he had joined the fight for freedom and he could not give up. He assumed the name of "Max de Vries" in his Resistance group and during the days he worked as a farmhand for Boer Weenink, in the cowsheds and the dairy. At night George and his men met to plan Resistance and sabotage actions against the Nazi invaders.

They possessed neither arms nor explosives and all they could do was cut telephone lines, slash the tires of German military vehicles, and strew nails in the path of army convoys.

Dissatisfied with this state of affairs George was constantly on the watch for more powerful Resistance groups with properly organized supplies. He heard that just such a unit was at Limburg, a town some eighty miles south of the "Cow's Tail Farm." He was on the point of going there when the German *Sicherheitsdienst,* the Gestapo's security police, became aware of his rather paltry activities as a saboteur and put a price on his head.

George had to leave the farm hastily and hide with a miller at Emper near Voorst, but the fact that the Germans were searching for him did not stop him from going to Limburg a few days later.

He discovered that the patriots in the town were, indeed, well organized and ready for action. They had established one of the first units of the *Orde Dienst.* This was a country-wide Resistance organization composed mainly of officers and men from the disbanded Dutch army, navy, and gendarmerie. *Orde Dienst* means "Order Service" and from it grew the Dutch Secret Army of the Interior, which defied the Germans for more than four years and made an important contribution to their disarray at the time of the liberation. In the meantime the O.D. helped the Allied cause by supplying information to Britain.

It was the Resistance organization which worked closely with the Dutch government in exile in London and the British secret service.

One of the first measures taken by Winston Churchill when he became prime minister in May 1940 was to order the formation of an organization to send agents over to the Continent. The instrument forged to this end was the Special Operations Executive, headed at first by Sir Frank Nelson, and subsequently by Sir Charles Hambro, the international banker, and Major General (later Sir) Colin McVean Gubbins of the Military Intelligence.

The S.O.E.'s mandate from Churchill "to set Europe ablaze" embraced a wide range of subversive and sabotage activities against the Germans. During the war the S.O.E. dispatched more than three thousand secret agents into occupied Europe, by boat and parachute. These men and women were all volunteers and came from many countries, including Britain, Canada, France, Norway, Denmark, Poland, Czechoslovakia, Italy, Greece, and, of course, Holland.*

The S.O.E. officers acted as liaison men with existing Resistance movements, helped to establish new organizations, worked as instructors, training the freedom fighters for the day of a *levée en masse* when the Allies invaded Europe, planned and commanded sabotage actions, and set

* In my books *Inside S.O.E.* (Barker, London, 1966) and *Set Europe Ablaze* (Pan Books, London, 1969), I described the Special Operations in Holland and Western Europe.

up a number of secret radio posts in the occupied countries, supplying information to the S.O.E. headquarters and
through it to the Allied military leaders.

George Behar, not yet nineteen, became one of the
Resistance members who helped to receive S.O.E. officers
sent from Britain to Nazi-occupied Holland.

The first S.O.E. agent parachuted into Holland was
Lieutenant L.A.H. van Hammel, a Dutch army officer
who had escaped to England after the German invasion.
The sending of any single agent from Britain to Nazi-occupied Europe always involved painstaking and dangerous
preparation for his reception by the Resistance fighters in
the field.

George Behar was involved in this process which would
begin with the exchange of coded messages on secret radio
transmitters, the fixing of the expected time of the arrival,
the selection of a safe dropping zone, and rise to a climax
with a reception committee of Resistance men and women
waiting at night to guide the aircraft by torch signals and
take care of the body. George was in the Limburg area
when several S.O.E. officers were dispatched from England
in the wake of Lieutenant van Hammel.

Initially, German treatment of the Dutch people was
korrekt. Hitler's gauleiter, Seyss-Inquart, announced that
there was "no intention on the part of the German of op-
pressing the kindred Dutch people." He said he considered
the Dutch "to be his first cousins" and he would "respect
their national character."

The Dutch, remembering the mass slaughter of Rotterdam, did not respond to the blandishments of their self-appointed "cousin." For the first few months the Resistance
movement was weak and preoccupied with the task of
bringing itself into existence. The first signs of discontent
only became apparent during the winter of 1940–41. The
Germans began to requisition thousands of tons of food-
stuffs and other goods for transport to the fatherland.
Stringent rationing was enforced in Holland. Attacks began on the trains carrying the plunder away, some S.S.
men were beaten up, and strikes broke out.

The honeyed words of Seyss-Inquart were soon followed by threats by his chief of security, S.S. Obergruppen-fuehrer Rauter. When the only reaction was an increase in the amount of sabotage, Rauter decided that the honeymoon was over. By February 1941, the first hostages were arrested and subsequently executed.

Rauter asked Berlin for some "energetic experts," capable of dealing with the British agents and Dutch "terrorists." Two counterespionage experts arrived in The Hague. One was Major H. J. Giskes, who had already proved himself a specialist in catching British agents in France, where he had been a senior officer of the *Abwehr* (German Military Intelligence). The other was S.S. Sturmbannfuehrer Joseph Schreieder, of the *Sicherheitsdienst* of Himmler's Gestapo.

These two men quickly scored their first successes in Holland. A Dutch Nazi was instrumental in betraying several S.O.E. officers soon after their arrival and in this way Giskes and Schreieder acquired three S.O.E. radio posts intact. From two of the captured men they managed to extract the secret signal codes of the S.O.E. Dutch Section in London. The chiefs of the S.O.E. Dutch Section did not realize that the agents and their transmitters had fallen into the hands of the Germans. Giskes and Schreieder began sending fake messages to England and received messages in return which allowed them to build up a store of knowledge about the whole S.O.E. network in Holland.

Thus began the fatal *England Spiel*, the radio game, which London failed to detect for nearly three years. It led to the capture of eighteen radio links by the Nazis and of fifty-four S.O.E. agents dropped by parachute or landed in Holland. Of these S.O.E. volunteers forty-seven were subsequently put to death in the extermination camp of Mauthausen.

The lack of mountain and forests in the Low Countries made it almost impossible to assemble secret camps to train the *onderduikers* (literally "divers", i.e., underground

fighters) in the handling of arms and the reception of
agents and materials dropped from the R.A.F. "Moon-
squadrons." A few wooded areas in the Limburg and Gelderland provinces provided some cover. There a number
of camps were set up and George Behar became one of
the active workers. People who knew him then recall his
tremendous drive. He could keep going at top pitch for
days and would often cycle through the night for thirty
or forty miles. One of his Resistance comrades described
him to me as follows:

> "He never seemed to be tired. He was a youngster, but
> men twice his age accepted his authority without a mur-
> mur. He seemed to be shy, but he had a strong person-
> ality and could make quick decisions which were right,
> when older fellows would bite their nails and scratch
> their heads . . ."

In this way George became an enthusiastic if very junior
participant in the link between S.O.E. and the Dutch Resistance movement. It was hardly surprising that he later
overestimated his own importance and believed himself to
have played a prominent part in the fight against the Nazis
in Holland. On the other hand it would be wrong to dis-
miss the effectiveness of his work. He was dedicated,
clever, and courageous. He volunteered for several dangerous missions and by the summer of 1942 the Gestapo was
looking for that young "terrorist" Van Vries, which was
the alias George Behar had assumed.

In June 1942 the Dutch exile-government in London, in
cooperation with the British Chiefs of Staff and S.O.E., decided to dispatch to the Netherlands an important emissary. He was Professor George Louis Jambroes, a member
of the Resistance Council. Jambroes had reached England
a year earlier and was now being sent back as the representative of Dutch Prime Minister Gerbrandy in London.

Jambroes was to bring from London the "Plan Holland," a document devised by British and Dutch planners
of the Allied Chiefs of Staff. It envisaged a reorganization

of the *Orde Dienst*, the unification of the various Resistance groups, then divided on political and religious lines, the division of the Netherlands into seventeen military districts, and ultimately the creation of a Secret Army of the Interior. Jambroes himself was assigned a high post in the new organization.

Carrying a suitcase stuffed with coded documents and instructions, and accompanied by a radio operator, Jan Joseph Bukkens, Professor Jambroes left England during the night of June 27, 1942, aboard an R.A.F. aircraft. Preceding Jambroes's and Bukkens's dispatch, the S.O.E. Dutch Section sent a series of signals to radio posts in Holland which had already been captured by the Germans and the two managers of the *England Spiel* succeeded in bamboozling London into a cunningly laid trap.

Giskes and Schreieder had radioed to London four alternative areas; near Ermelo; at Woudenberg, some twenty kilometers from Utrecht; at Doorn; and near Woltrum. After an exchange of signals London settled on the dropping zone at Doorn and was assured that "a safe reception will be prepared." The Germans were as good as their word. The instant Jambroes and Bukkens landed they were surrounded by a "reception committee" of Dutch traitors on the Gestapo's payroll, who played the parts of genuine Resistance men. The two secret agents were led to a road where an S.S. squad was waiting.

After long interrogations at the German counterespionage headquarters they were taken to the Gestapo prison at Haaren. Both were ultimately executed at the extermination camp of Mauthausen in Austria.

The Germans found on Jambroes the "Plan Holland" documents and had not much difficulty in decoding them. The dossier was sent to the *Reichs-Sicherheits-Hauptamt* in Berlin and was soon on Hitler's desk.

London expected, of course, a stream of signals from Jambroes, providing information about his work and the expected success of his mission. Giskes manufactured a number of messages and, using Jambroes's code and transmitter, could deceive London for some time.

London patiently waited for new developments. But disturbed by Jambroes's apparent inability to fulfill his task, the Dutch secret service chiefs in London and the S.O.E. Dutch Section ultimately ordered him to return to England by the French escape route. This order was sent to one of the captured radio posts and received by Giskes and Schreieder. They replied that such a journey would be both inopportune and too dangerous at the moment.

In the meantime *Orde Dienst* leaders were anxiously waiting for the arrival of the emissary from London. George Behar, the redoubtable young courier "Van Vries," was one of the Resistance members assigned to look out for the two expected arrivals. As they were safely behind lock and bars at the Gestapo prison, he and his friends had hardly a chance of finding them. At the other end, the Germans had gained knowledge that *Orde Dienst* and Resistance members were trying to establish the whereabouts of the two agents from England.

Although George had been only a small and unimportant pawn in this great game played around "Plan Holland," the Germans somehow got on his trail. Once again the British Intelligence agent, Commander D. W. Child, proved helpful. When George got in touch with him, Child warned him that the Gestapo was searching for him and he urgently advised him to leave Holland. He explained to George the working of the S.O.E. escape routes from Belgium, across France, to Spain and hence to Gibraltar, and he gave him the addresses of "safe houses" and British agents in Brussels and at several places in France.

George was enthusiastic about the prospects of reaching England. After all, he was a British subject; he wanted to join one of the secret organizations in London, of which he had vaguely heard, receive training as an agent and, if possible, return to Holland to take charge of a network. Surely, he must have seen himself as a future fully fledged secret agent and organizer.

Commander Child, himself hunted by the Gestapo, had to leave, too. He used the escape route a few weeks after George's departure and, after a dangerous journey across

France and Spain, reached London from Gibraltar late in 1942. Although he warned British secret service chiefs that the Germans had infiltrated at least a number of radio posts in Holland, his warnings were at first disregarded and the *England Spiel* continued for several months with disastrous results.

During the third week of July, George journeyed to Breda, from where he intended to cross the frontier to Belgium. With some money his uncle Anthony Beijderwellen had sent him, he bought a bicycle. Characteristically, he decided to embellish his escape with a really good disguise. From a Catholic priest, whom he had met in the Resistance, he obtained the clothes of a Trappist monk.

In the brown habit and black capula of a frater of the St. Servatius monastery, George, now transformed into "Brother Peter," made his way toward Belgium. A monk on a bicycle was a common sight in the Roman Catholic south of the Low Countries. German field policemen would shout a rude word or laugh about the monk on the bike, but would not molest him. He reached Brussels and the "safe house" of which Commander Child had told him. It was one of the relay points of the "Pat" escape organization, run by the Belgian doctor Albert Guérisse, better known in London as the legendary Pat O'Leary. This organization had conducted many hundreds of escaped prisoners of war, shot-down Allied airmen, and secret agents on the run through France to the Pyrenees and safety.

After crossing the French frontier, George was stopped by a field police patrol near Lille and told that he would be taken to the police station for an identity check. But just as he was being bundled into a car there was an air raid and the young "monk" used the confusion to make a quick getaway. In Lille he found a hiding place with a French family, just by knocking at a door and asking for refuge. The householder was a local Resistance leader and he arranged George's journey to Paris by providing him with a forged travel document, and sending him off with his two young daughters who had genuine German passes, being employed by a business company engaged on work for the Germans.

With a recommendation from his newly won friends in Lille, he found refuge in a monastery near Sacré Cœur, and the next day reported at the house of Jean de la Olla, "Pat's" chief assistant. He was told to travel to Lyons, where he was to get in touch with a one-legged woman called Renée, who worked for the American consul, George Whittinghill.

The fugitive did not know that "Renée" was one of the great heroines of S.O.E., Virginia Hall, a former correspondent of the *New York Post* in Paris, who led a fantastic double life. She was quite legitimately accredited to Marshal Pétain's Vichy government and also worked part-time at the U.S. consulate. But she also ran a successful S.O.E. circuit in Lyons and was one of the chief organizers of the "Spanish escape route."

At first Renée thought that it would be best to provide the young escapee with American documents, describing him as a citizen of the United States, aged under sixteen, who wanted to leave France for Spain. The Vichy authorities usually made no difficulties for American children and issued them exit visas. Thus George, who looked very young for his age—he was then nineteen and a half years old—might have reached Spain quite legitimately and in comparative comfort. But before the application, submitted by the American consul, was granted, the Allied landing in North Africa took place and the Germans entered the hitherto unoccupied Vichy zone. Within days the Gestapo took over in Lyons, and Americans, whatever their age, were rounded up as enemy aliens and treated no better than British subjects, which meant immediate internment.

So George decided to leave Lyons and make his way to the Spanish frontier in the same perilous manner as the thousands of escapees, refugees, and fugitives from the Gestapo. A small group of them, accompanied by "The Woman in Red," Denise Mitrani, one of the most courageous and efficient members of the Lyons escape organization, eventually reached the Pyrenees. Denise handed her wards to a couple of Spanish smugglers who, for a good price, guided escapees across the passes.

Freedom, or so it seemed, lay just across the mountains. But as was the case with so many escapees, George and his companions were spotted by Spanish frontier guards and taken to the internment camp of Mirando de Ebro.

Not all Spanish officials were pro-German. Indeed, in 1943, after El Alamein and Stalingrad, the Allied invasion of Italy and Mussolini's downfall, most people in Spain had lost confidence in a German victory and the attitude of the authorities, from General Franco down, had become much more sympathetic toward the Allies. While escapees continued to be arrested and interned, the Spanish government did not put great obstacles in the way of their release and deportation to Portugal and Gibraltar, so long as some face-saving was observed to preserve its neutrality. At the camp former military barracks had been converted into fairly comfortable if badly crowded lodgings. At times there were as many as four thousand internees there, people of all nationalities, many of them stateless. In the case of British and American escapees, treatment was usually good and the British or U.S. embassies in Madrid were regularly notified of their arrival.

George was allowed to write to the British embassy and one day an official arrived and took him and a few other British nationals by car to Madrid. From there they were sent on to Gibraltar, where Major Donald Darling of M.I.9 interrogated them and, having confirmed their *bona fides,* arranged their journey to England.

Arrivals from the Continent in Britain during the war were greeted with caution and George was no exception. He was held in custody for several days while M.I.5 and Special Branch interrogators examined him with the pensive attention of art experts looking at a painting of doubtful origin.

Among the "escapees" from Nazi-occupied Europe there were a few fakes. This made it essential to check and recheck all new arrivals with utmost care. The danger of allowing the entry of people often unable to prove their identity—during their escapes they perforce used false papers—and thus admitting to Britain German spies was, however, small. The enemy's efforts in this diretcion were inept and unsuccessful. The more real threat was posed by refugees who had taken the more direct route, across the Channel. A high proportion of the German attempts to infiltrate agents into Britain by the North Sea and Channel routes originated in Blake's home country, Holland, where the *Abwehr* and the *Sicherheitsdienst* were playing the *England Spiel* so actively.

Near Wandsworth Prison, where several German spies were hanged in 1942, stood the institution designed to catch them before they were let loose in war-time Britain. It was the Royal Victoria Patriotic School on Wandsworth Heath, which belonged to the Patriotic Fund for the education of orphaned daughters of servicemen. The building had been taken over by the Ministry of Home Security, and for most of the war it served as the main interrogation center for escapees and refugees arriving in Britain from Nazi-occupied and neutral countries.

It was known as the "Patriotic School," which was a good name for a place where examinations of a very special kind were held.

It was there that George Behar, as he was then, got his first experience of Britain.

Although he had been thoroughly vetted by M.I.9 officers in Gibraltar after his release from the Spanish internment camp at Miranda de Ebro, George was nevertheless detained for several days before his *bona fides* were established beyond doubt. This was not too difficult. He could name Commander Child as a referee, and Special Branch officers found that his mother and two sisters were living in Buckinghamshire.

I worked for a spell at the "Patriotic School" and a wearing and depressing business it was for interrogators and interrogated alike. It was rather unpleasant to have to maintain suspicion and even animosity toward people who were decent and brave souls and whose dearest wish was to enjoy the dignity of personal freedom in Britain, after all the humiliating and dangerous experiences in Nazi-occupied Europe. Most of them had just emerged from such harrowing experiences and had landed in England with a sense of great relief and justifiable pride in getting here at all. All of them—that is with the exception of the few who had come as German agents—were eager to do whatever they were asked to help the Allied war effort. To be received with suspicion and kept under police guard came as a severe shock which caused a variety of unhappy reactions. Only few of these people were prepared to accept the necessity of the precautions taken by the British counterespionage and police.

George Behar certainly took it as an affront to his pride. Surely, he asked his interrogators, word of his achievements as a member of the Dutch Resistance had reached London? As so often later in his life, he displayed a sense of self-importance and self-assertion, which was in contrast with his otherwise retiring disposition.

He had expected to be enrolled immediately in one of the secret service organizations. As soon as he was released from the detention at the "Patriotic School," he visited the office of the Dutch secret service. But he was told there that, being a British subject, he must apply to the War Office, which might direct him into one of the Intelligence organizations, or perhaps recommend him to be trained with Special Operations Executive. He spent a few weeks with his mother and sisters who were guests of an English family on a farm near High Wycombe. He felt bitter and disappointed, and he could not understand that none of the organizations he had approached wanted him.

In London he met Commander D. W. Child again, and on his advice he volunteered for the Royal Navy. A few days before his twenty-first birthday, in November 1943, he became an Ordinary Seaman, a position in which he certainly had not expected to find himself in Britain. He was sent to Portsmouth and after a brief shore training he was posted to a mine-sweeper. A few months later—it seems that his superiors had somewhat belatedly discovered that he was fluent in three languages, English, Dutch, and French, and had a good knowledge of German—he was recommended for a commission and sent to an officers' training course in H.M.S. *King Alfred* at Hove. In the spring of 1944 he passed out with excellent marks as a sub-lieutenant, with a wartime commission in the Royal Naval Volunteer Reserve.

He applied once again for Intelligence work, but was sent to a submarine training course instead. He spent a few weeks at Fort Blockhouse at Portsmouth. It may well be that he had been promised to be sent in a submarine to German-occupied Europe, but he did not like the posting. At the earliest opportunity he complained to an R.N. surgeon that his hearing was affected by deep-water tests, and applied for a posting away from the submarine depot. At last he achieved what he had desired for more than a year: he was posted to Naval Intelligence.

George Behar had changed his name to "Blake"* and completed courses at three Special Training Schools with glowing reports from instructors who noted his toughness, enthusiasm, intelligence, and initiative. Through no reluctance on his part he was unable to use his qualifications behind enemy lines. His requests for sending him as a secret agent to Holland were turned down and he was once again given a desk job.

In May 1944 his ambition was, however, satisfied up to a degree. He was posted as an interpreter to the staff of the newly created Supreme Headquarters Allied Expeditionary Force (S.H.A.E.F.) and subsequently to A.N.C.X.F., which was the code name of the Allied Naval Expeditionary Force H.Q.s of Admiral Sir Bertram Ramsey, at Southwick House, north of Portsmouth. During the final preparations for the Allied invasion of France Blake also worked at Norfolk House, the headquarters of General Eisenhower and General Sir Bernard Montgomery. It was in Room 126 of Norfolk House that the Allied invasion chiefs—Eisenhower, Montgomery, Air Chief Marshal

---

* His mother and sisters also adopted this name by deed poll.

Tedder, General Bradley, Admiral Ramsey, Air Chief Marshal Leigh-Mallory, and General Bedell Smith met for their momentous conferences.

This is not the place to describe, however briefly, the preparations for *Overlord* and, in any case, Sub-Lieutenant George Blake, R.N.V.R., played an infinitesimal part in them, being one of the youngest subalterns among the many hundreds of British and American officers on the S.H.A.E.F. staff.

One of his duties was to assist in translation and interpretation of German documents captured by agents of S.O.E., S.I.S. (Secret Intelligence Service), and O.S.S. and transmitted from German-occupied Europe.

Blake had acquitted himself well of the minor tasks he had been assigned. He had also gained some experience in interrogations of German prisoners captured in *coup de main* landings on the French coast. His reports and translations were lucid and to the point and he was commended for his work.

Some weeks after D day Blake crossed the Channel and set foot again on the continent from which he had had to fly two years before.

In April 1945 George Blake was at the headquarters of Field Marshal Montgomery and on May 4 he was present at the surrender of the German army corps in Northwest Germany, Netherlands, and Denmark. Three days previously a German radio announcement from Hamburg declared that Hitler had "died defending the Reich Chancellery in Berlin" and that Grand Admiral Doenitz had succeeded him as "führer."

Field Marshal Montgomery established his mobile headquarters in his famous caravan at the Lüneberg Heath and it was there that Blake watched one of the final episodes in the collapse of the "Thousand-Year-Reich" that had lasted only twelve years.

A photograph of that historic occasion shows Sub-Lieutenant Blake, in blue naval battle-dress standing not far from his commander in chief, as a grim-faced Admiral von Friedeburg hands over the document of unconditional surrender on behalf of Doenitz to "Monty."

It was five years, almost to the day, since he had stood as a teenager in the blazing ruins of his birthplace Rotterdam. What a banquet it was to a man with his appetite for drama.

A short while after the surrender at Lüneburg, Blake was sent to Hamburg, officially posted to H.M.S. *Royal Albert*. He was now a British Intelligence officer. For his wartime service with the Dutch Resistance and the Dutch S.O.E. section in London, Queen Wilhelmina of the Netherlands had awarded him the Cross of the Order of Nassau, fourth class (corresponding to a British M.B.E.).

While the world was still cheering Churchill's proclamation of the end of the war, the intense young officer plunged feverishly into his new assignment that was to lead him into the perilous game of espionage.

CHAPTER FIVE

YOUNG MAN AT THE HELM

In Hamburg George Blake, now a full Lieutenant R.N.V.R. at the age of twenty-three, was put in charge of his own Naval Intelligence unit.

He installed himself in an office in the huge building in the Flottbeker Chaussee in Hamburg's dockland of Othmarschen which had been the headquarters of Grand Admiral Doenitz, the C.-in-C. of the German navy. It was from this building that Raeder and Doenitz directed the U-boat warfare against Allied shipping, a campaign which at one time nearly succeeded in defeating Britain.

Opposite this headquarters spread out the enormous shipyards of the *Deutsche Werft* where many of the U-boats for the Battle of the Atlantic were built.

Blake was ordered to lay his hands on as many U-boat commanders and technical experts as he could and interrogate them as quickly as possible. His Intelligence unit had various other duties but investigation of the German submarine service was the first priority. The Royal Navy wanted to compile a complete record of Germany's conduct of the war at sea, required by the Allied governments for the Nuremberg trial of Nazi war criminals. Furthermore, their Lordships of the Admiralty wanted all the available facts on subjects ranging from the strategy of German pocket-battleships to the psychology of U-boat crews. The German invention of the revolutionary "Schnorkel" breathing system for submarines, the magnetic and pressure mines, ingeniously constructed torpedoes that had given the Allies so much trouble, war crimes committed against drowning men, women and children: all these came within the purview of Naval Intelligence and Blake's special unit.

Within a week of arriving in Hamburg Blake and his small staff were hard at work. He had been promoted, but he was still only a boyish-looking twenty-three-year-old. Hardly enough, one might have thought, to outgun the *Kapitän-Leutnants and Korvetten-Kapitäns* who rapidly formed a queue outside his door. These officers and U-boat commanders were disinherited but uncowed members of the Third Reich's élite; many were unrepentant members of the Nazi party. Their huts in the P.O.W. camps were still decorated with swastikas and pictures of Hitler, Raeder, and Doenitz.

George Blake, however, was a fair match for them, largely I think because he enjoyed conducting the interrogations. The sheer exuberance of his interviewing technique came as a nasty surprise to his charges, whose previous dealings with the British may have given them the impression that they were in for a fairly gentle ride.

I have no reason to believe that Blake ever overstepped the bounds of legality. He certainly never used physical violence. But I know that he rejoiced in applying every trick of verbal interrogation. His German was perfect. Vitriolic tirades about Hitler would alternate with affable service anecdotes and glasses of whiskey, though Blake rarely emptied them himself. Tea and cigarettes would be followed by moody but not seriously meant threats of "instant execution."

I am not a great believer in historic justice but I think the letting loose of George Blake among the U-boat commanders was one of the better things to happen after the war. These German officers were not in the same category as the repulsive Gestapo and S.S. criminals whom Allied investigators were beginning to question, with mounting horror. The U-boat captains were hard, but honorable according to their flawed code. If Germany was to have any sort of civilized future, they and officers like them of the German army and Luftwaffe were worth saving from their own political beliefs. A tall order, indeed, for any interrogator, however brilliant. I do not suggest that Blake wrought a miraculous conversion to democratic ideals in a single one of the officers he interviewed; in any case the object of the exercise was to acquire information, not to save souls. I am, however, sure that George's combination of zealous moral certitude and naval expertise stimulated some of the U-boat aces to reappraise their ideas where a more languid interview would have left them quite unmoved and enhanced their arrogance.

George Blake's performance during this period not only revealed the strength of his character, but also disclosed another trait distinct already in his childhood: his great zeal and ambition to improve himself.

For many weeks he spent all his spare time studying marine technology and naval tactics with the result that, before long, he could talk with a fair degree of authority with Royal Naval officers and engineers who had spent a lifetime at sea. This addiction to homework was one aspect of that serious-minded self-importance of his which was to set him apart from his brother officers, as it set him apart from his schoolfellows at the Rotterdam *M.U.L.O.* college.

Only those of us who saw service in Germany in 1945 and 1946 have some memories of the chaos which followed the sudden disintegration of Hitler's Third Reich and its inundation by millions of homeless, half-starved people, German refugees from the east and "displaced persons" of all nationalities from the forced labor camps, as well as British, American, French, Russian, Belgian, Dutch, Czech, and Polish armies.

In order to place George Blake's life at that period in perspective and also to outline some of the factors that must have influenced his character, it is worth mentioning some of the events taking place at that time.

Following Germany's unconditional surrender, and while German forces were being disarmed, Allied orders were transmitted through the self-appointed German government headed by Admiral Doenitz, whom Hitler had named his successor before committing suicide in his Berlin bunker. On May 23, 1945, this government was suppressed and Doenitz, members of the German High Command, and an assortment of Nazi leaders were taken into custody. On June 3 the Allied commanders in chief met in Berlin and announced the formation of the Allied Control Committee consisting, in the first instance, of themselves: General Dwight D. Eisenhower, Field Marshal Sir Bernard Montgomery, General de Lattre de Tassigny, and Marshal Gregory Konstantionovich Zhukov. The committee divided Germany into four zones. Berlin, inside the Soviet zone, was divided into four Allied sectors.

The British zone of Germany in the north and west corresponded roughly to the area which had been taken by the Twenty-first Army Group under Montgomery's command. It extended from the Dutch and Belgian borders in the west to the river Elbe and Brunswick in the east, where the demarcation line between it and the Russian zone ran down through the center of Europe for more than three hundred miles. From the Danish border and the North Sea it extended into the Rhineland in the south, where it met the French and American zones.

The British were thus called upon to administer the

most densely populated and highly industrialized area of
Germany. Their zone included the Ruhr, the industrial
centers of Essen, Düsseldorf, Dortmund, Hanover, the
great seaports of Hamburg, Bremen, Lübeck, Kiel, and
Wilhelmshaven, all having suffered the heaviest bombardment during the war.

On August 2, 1945, the final communiqué of the
Potsdam Conference was published. President Harry S
Truman, Generalissimo Joseph Stalin, and Prime Minister
Clement Attlee had signed an agreement. It laid down the
Allied plan for Germany, Central and Southeast Europe in
fourteen paragraphs.

The purpose of the occupation of Germany was given
in a long separate schedule. It stipulated "the complete
disarmament and demilitarization of Germany and the
elimination or control of all German industry that could
be used for military production."

All German land, sea, and air forces, the S.S., the S.A.,
the S.D., and Gestapo, the General Staff, the Officers'
Corps, the Reserve Corps, military schools, all other military or quasi-military organizations, clubs and associations
were to be completely and finally abolished. All arms, ammunition, and implements of war were to be destroyed or
kept at the disposal of the Allies.

The agreement declared that "in order to convince the
German people that they have suffered total military defeat and that they cannot escape responsibility for what
they have brought upon themselves, since their own
ruthless warfare and the fanatical Nazi resistance have
destroyed the German economy and made chaos and suffering inevitable," the Allies had decided "to destroy the
National-Socialist party and its affiliated organizations and
to ensure that they are not revived in any form. All Nazi
laws which provided the basis of the Hitler regime, established discrimination on grounds of race, creed, or political opinion were abolished; war criminals and those
who participated in atrocities were to be brought to justice. . . ."

When George Blake first read this document he was elated.

For the next few days he talked of little else. But it did not take him long to realize that either the Allies would not, or could not, cleanse Germany of all traces of Nazism.

He read the solemn words of the Potsdam Agreement: "It is not the intention of the Allies to enslave the German people. It is the intention of the Allies that the German people be given the opportunity to prepare for the reconstruction of their life on a democratic and peaceful basis. If their own efforts are steadily directed to this end, it will be possible for them in due course to take their place among the free and peaceful peoples of the world."

Looking round him he was disillusioned by the contrast between the decisions taken at a conference hall and their implementation in real life.

Before the signatures on the document had dried, the Allies had began to quarrel. The Russians had sealed the frontiers of their zone, refusing to admit British and American missions. There were signs of disagreement between the French and the British, the British and the Americans, the Americans and the French.

The immediate difficulty with which the Allies had to contend was the desperate shortage of German officials qualified to carry out any administration. Most of those who could be put to restore public services, schools and hospitals, local government, cultural institutions and newspapers, trains and drains, had been members or officials of the Nazi party.

From the window of his office in Hamburg Blake watched crowds marching to the headquarters of the British military government. Housewives demonstrated noisily against food rationing and their cries were: "Britishers, end the hunger blockade!"

Admittedly, life in Hamburg was difficult. More than two-thirds of the houses in which one and a half million people had lived before the bombing now lay in ruins.

However, the people of Hamburg were eating whole-

some bread, made from shiploads of Canadian wheat
hurriedly diverted from British ports to the "starving Germans," while Britons were still having to content themselves with strictly rationed loaves of an indeterminate
color, tasting of sawdust.

In fact, the take-home food rations of the "starving
Germans" was very soon approaching British levels and in
some regards—sugar and potatoes, for instance—exceed-
ing them. Shopping queues in Hamburg were no longer
than those in London. Hamburg restaurants provided, at a
price, truly Teutonic meals of soup, fried fish, leg of pork
or roast veal, with liberal helpings of vegetables and a big
lump of pudding, all without coupons, while in London
restaurants people were rationed to one main course.

Through hard work and with Allied help the Germans
were able to restore surprisingly quickly prosperity and a
high standard of living, even though by 1945 the economic
structure of the country had been shattered. Already during the war black-marketing was rampant throughout Hitler Germany, partly based on the loot German officers and
soldiers carried home from subjugated France, Holland, or
Denmark. Now, coinciding with a decline in the discipline
of the Allied occupation forces, the black market achieved
fantastic proportions.

Massive thefts from British and American stores were a
routine business and almost respectable. I remember the
case of a British captain who made a profit of ten thousand pounds in about three days by "organizing" the sale
of a Regimental Mess's consignment of whiskey and gin
on the German black market.

George Blake rarely visited the haunts of his brother officers. If he did, he could watch at Hamburg's Atlantic
Hotel, one of several officers' clubs, or at the *Ratskeller*
which had been turned into a club for British N.C.O.s,
scenes of historic drinking bouts. At any time of the day
or night one could see groups in British uniforms absorb-
ing awe-inspiring quantities of liquor, wine, and beer. A
nip of whiskey or brandy cost four shillings. But the price
of drinks, three times that in Britain at that time, did not

matter because a pound of coffee, "organized" from the
N.A.A.F.I. would fetch one thousand marks or twenty-five
pounds. The pockets of British servicemen, if not their
physiques, could easily withstand the strain.

An atmosphere of drunkenness and sexual abandon per-
vaded the city. Hamburg was never exactly a center of pi-
ety and its waterfront district of St. Pauli was reputed to
possess more brothels and gaming dens than any other
place on earth. The Nazi rulers had been inclined to discourage the tradition until the latter part of the war when
they found it useful for keeping up the morale of German
sailors and soldiers on leave. In 1945 vice and crime returned to Hamburg with a vengeance.

Reports sent back caused alarm in London and were
followed by many questions and debates in the House of
Commons.

The handful of British Intelligence officers and men of
the Special Investigation Branch of the British army of the
Rhine could not begin to cope with the spreading demoralization of the troops. Even cautious ministerial statements
in the House of Commons admitted that one in five British
officers in Germany was involved in black-market deals.
There was widespread "fraternization with undesirable
women" and cases of venereal diseases among British soldiers, particularly young National Servicemen, mounted
alarmingly.

How did George Blake react to these feverish conditions? So far as the black market, drinking, or lechery
were concerned he was one of the few members of the Occupation forces who remained entirely immune.

He did not stoop even to the most minor infringement
of the theoretically strict rules. I am sure he never sold a
single packet of cigarettes to one of the black marketeers
who ran after every British officer with a bundle of paper
money in their outstretched hands. In any case, George
was a nonsmoker.

He drank occasionally, a glass of beer or a whiskey and
soda. He did not womanize. In contrast to the remarkably
unprincipled behavior of nearly all the younger officers,

who are now doubtless pillars of respectable society, George's life was modest and restrained, perhaps unnaturally so. He had remained the same nice boy, of whom his schoolfellow, Mijnheer Kistemaker of Rotterdam, said: "George would never do a wicked thing. . . ."

There is no record of an affair with a girl. He might have had one or two fleeting adventures. But when his leg was pulled by his fellow officers, who changed their girl friends as often as their shirts, he had a standard reply: "Don't be silly, we have a job to do. I have no time for women here, anyway not for women of that kind. . . ."

Although he was sexually a completely normal person, his shyness with women persisted throughout his life. In Hamburg in 1945 it resulted in the unkind sobriquet "Mummy's boy," given to him by some of his boisterous brother officers; in Berlin in the 1950s it earned him the repute of being a model husband; in Moscow in 1967 Sean Bourke, himself a "gay lad," who soon acquired a pretty Russian girl friend, Nerissa, told me that he never discovered that Blake had a romantic affair when they shared the same home for more than six months.

Blake had a touching respect for women which might be explained by his strong attachment to his mother. In his *Izvestya* interview in 1970 he made a special point of this deep affection: "After my mother's departure from Rotterdam to London in 1940, I missed her terribly. When I stayed behind I always dreamed of a reunion with her, and although I wanted to continue my work in the Dutch Resistance, one of the reasons for my escape to England in 1942 was to see my mother again."

The main reason, however, for his almost monkish behavior in Hamburg was that he devoted all his energy and time to his work. Combined with his vaulting ambition this was to estrange him from his more carefree colleagues. From his desk at the Flottbeker Chausee came an interminable flow of reports, minutes, and memoranda. He liked to remind his colleagues that he was a "professional Intelligence officer" while they were mere amateurs. His equals and subordinates found him irritating and bumptious. Like he they were in the R.N.V.R., the "Wavy Navy," and most of them much older. One was a former Liverpool dock manager, another an Oxford don, two were Jews, naval engineers of German origin who had found refuge in Britain before the war. All of them had better qualifications for the work they were doing than George Blake. They resented his often arrogant "know better" attitude; they were infuriated by his almost unreasonable dedication and by the security pantomimes in which he would indulge.

The officers had been warned that Soviet spies were busy in the Western zones of Germany. They were told to provide normal facilities for Soviet liaison officers and accredited Soviet missions, but to be cautious with unauthorized Russians who showed great curiosity for everything in the British and American military offices. Blake, who expressed strong opinions about "those Red spies," constantly impressed upon his colleagues the need for utmost watchfulness lest a Soviet agent might penetrate their secret work. He devised special security precautions.

On entering a room, one of his favorite tricks was to close the door, wait a few moments, and then to whip it open again—to see whether any Red spy was posted at the keyhole outside. He went around the office trying the locks of steel cabinets and telling the typists and messengers to burn the contents of wastepaper baskets every evening. With hindsight, one could wrongly assume that all this was clever pretense and that Blake already used at that time the cover of a particularly security-minded Intelligence man for some clandestine relations with the Russians. Many years later in Moscow he made vague remarks of having gained pro-Communist convictions soon after the end of the war, but even he put the beginning of his conversion not earlier than after Churchill's Fulton speech in the spring of 1946. I completely reject this claim of Blake's, which in his present situation is one of convenience. The Russians dislike and distrust defectors of more recent origin. It is quite natural that George Blake now tries to pose as a sort of "Old Bolshevik." There is no

shred of evidence that he changed sides before his return
from Korea in 1953, even though his political opinions
might have undergone certain changes at an earlier time.
Even though he had contacts with Soviet agents in London, there is no evidence that he became seriously involved in outright treachery before he went to Berlin in
1954.

Some of the regular Royal Navy officers, his superiors
in the Naval Intelligence in Hamburg, strongly disliked
him. They say he was throwing his weight about and that
his behavior would be unacceptable in an admiral and was
intolerable in a R.N.V.R. two-striper. Some thought they
could detect in his attitude an "un-English" streak of ruth-
lessness and even cruelty. Sean Bourke who for several
years lived more closely to Blake, in prison and in Moscow, than any other man, strongly shares this opinion.
Looking back, I recall an incident which might confirm it.

I was visiting Kiel, the great German naval base, where
after the German surrender the British found the pocket-
battleship *Admiral Scheer,* the cruiser *Admiral Hipper,* the
famous *Emden,* and a number of light warships wrecked
by the bombs of British and American air raids. The *Admiral Scheer,* once the pride of Hitler's navy, was completely capsized, but salvageable. The naval yards and
docks were an incredible shambles. Just before the surrender, some forty U-boats and other vessels had been
scuttled by their own crews. Royal Navy officers assembled gangs of German prisoners of war and gave them the
order: "You put them down, you put them up."

I stood on a pier with other British officers, watching
the salvage operations. It was grim work for the divers,
going down to patch up the hulls before giant cranes were
brought into action to lift them. The harbor was full of
corpses of air-raid victims. Sometimes a diver came up
and was violently sick. He told us that some corpses of
drowned German sailors and dockers were standing upright in the mud of the riverbed. When he walked through
the water, his wash made some of the bloated bodies move
and follow him. One or two corpses, crawling with worms

and marine life, had fallen on him in a horrifying embrace.

The sunken U-boats had to be pumped full of air before they could be lifted. The submarines which had been fished out lay in a heap on the dockside like giant stranded sharks. A great lot of wrecks of every kind would have to be cleared before the harbor could be used again. The entrance was blocked; a particularly difficult problem had been set by the wreck of *Admiral Hipper* which, in her dying spasm, had rolled over into the same creek as the *Emden*. A crane could lift 350 tons, two lifted a thousand deadweight tons, though in the words of a British engineer, "they bent at the knees." But some of the huge wrecks had firmly settled in the mud, the *Hipper* sprang a big leak, and half went down in the shallow water.

A young lieutenant-commander suggested blowing the hulls to pieces by high explosives. A gray-haired Royal Navy captain shook his head: "No, the blast would be terrific . . . many houses would be ruined near the dockside and there could be serious casualties," he protested. "We can't do it to the townspeople."

Lieutenant Blake then made his contribution to the discussion. "That wouldn't matter," he said calmly, "only ten percent of the town is habitable, and it's only jerries, anyway."

It was a frivolous remark any man might have made in the circumstances without arousing comment. But now there was a slight, embarrassed pause, when it came from Blake. The captain cleared his throat. We all realized that in his precise manner George Blake meant exactly what he said.

CHAPTER SIX

THE RUSSIAN EXPERT

Blake's superiors at the Naval Intelligence headquarters in Hamburg found him difficult. But a few high-ranking officers in the Intelligence division of the British military government's "Whitehall" in the pleasant little Westphalian town of Luebbecke, the headquarters of Major-General (now Field Marshal Sir Gerald) Templer, had noted that he had drive and got results.

Unlike the Naval Intelligence, with which they were traditionally at loggerheads, the chiefs of Military Intelligence and the Secret Intelligence Service (the so-called M.I.6) felt that this young naval lieutenant might be useful in a situation which was causing more and more anxiety: the infiltration of the Western zones in Germany by Soviet agents.

The most immediate worry was the underhand methods adopted by the Soviet allies in matters of technical and industrial intelligence. The Potsdam Agreement provided for an inter-Allied control of all German industrial and scientific institutions. Allied intelligence officers were to collect and collate the enormous output of German scientific and technological research during the war, and to sift the blueprints and reports of secret inventions and improvements produced by German scientists and technicians and their colleagues from many European countries, whom the Nazis had forcibly employed.

When General Templer became the director of military government, he established a Combined Intelligence Objectives Committee under Sir Patrick Linstead, the distinguished professor at the Imperial College of Science and director of scientific research of the Ministry of Supply during the war. The collection of the German material proved difficult because Hitler had ordered in March 1945 the destruction of all such documents, reports, statistics, and blueprints to prevent their falling into Allied hands.

Leaders of German industry, who had readily acquiesced in the use of slave labor and the pursuit of Nazi policy during the war, became greatly disturbed about this order. They foresaw the need of keeping the results of years of scientific and technical research and planning for their businesses, once their Führer's regime had become a regrettable but fading memory. During the last months of the war they were secretly supported by some of Hitler's more enlightened henchmen, such as Albert Speer, the minister of war production, Neumann, in charge of Hitler's Four-Year-Plan, Albert Pitsch, the president of the Reichbank, Albert Krupp, the armament king, and decided that Hitler's order must be ignored. They ordered industrial managers and heads of scientific institutions and laboratories to hide all important papers, plans, prototypes, and models.

When the search parties of the Allied Intelligence Committee went out to find information about German technological wartime secrets, they had literally to unearth them from steel safes and strong rooms, often buried beneath ruined factories, laboratories, and office buildings. In many instances units of Royal engineers had to be called in to dig for caches lying under tons of rubble or concealed in walls and cellars in the bombed cities of the Ruhr and the Rhineland.

George Blake assisted several of these teams. The great game of hunt the thimble, which combined the fascination of archaeology with the excitement of criminal detection, was very much to his taste. Thus, besides his newly acquired knowledge of naval matters, he became versatile in scientific and industrial Intelligence.

Meanwhile a similar hunt was proceeding in the American and French zones, and all the experts in the West cooperated closely. Their findings and the results of their

examinations were freely and fully available to the teams
of Russian scientists and technicians scouring the Soviet
zone and paying frequent visits to the Western zones of
Germany.

But the Russians did not reciprocate. While the Western
Allies made slow but methodical progress, the Russians
went about the same business much more ruthlessly. They
did not hand over the fruits of their labors to the Allies.
They sent all papers they could find to Moscow. They
rounded up more than two thousand German scientists
and technicians and bundled them off to Russia. Many
never returned.

The important research centers which had fallen into
Russian hands, such as the Kaiser Wilhelm Institute in
Berlin (where the Germans had conducted atomic research),
the rocket station at Peenemünde, rocket manufacturing
plants in Brandenburg, optical and precision instrument
factories in Thuringia, and many others, were stripped
bare and the contents loaded onto trains and sent off to
Russia. Large quantities of ordinary German machinery,
from plants such as the Opel motorcar works, textile mills
in Leipzig and Saxony, engineering works at Brunswick,
were also sent back, piece by piece.

The Soviet Union was entitled to do so under the Potsdam Agreement which provided for German reparations
to compensate "for the damage, destruction, loss and
suffering the Soviet people had endured during the war."
In addition to reparation extracted from its own zone of
occupation, the Soviet Union was to receive twenty-five
percent of the capital equipment of metallurgical, chemi-
cal, and machine industries in the three Western zones.

Many Soviet missions came to the British, American,
and French zones to organize and supervise the removal
of the machinery and goods. Other missions led by Soviet
Intelligence officers and security men of the N.K.V.D.
(the predecessor of the K.G.B.) arrived on the pretext of
flushing out German war criminals. With the missions
came hundreds of secret agents and they embarked on es-

pionage against the Allies and political subversion of the Germans in the Western zones.

They made a dead set at any German employed by the British, U.S., and French military governments and U.N.R.R.A (United Nations Relief and Rehabilitation Administration) which looked after the millions of displaced persons in Germany. The aim was to subvert these Germans for Stalin's plan to conquer Europe from within. In a disrupted continent, with powerful Communist parties in France and Italy, this plan seemed to have a very real chance of success. The borders of the Soviet zone extended to a line 110 miles west of Berlin. The western boundaries of the Soviet empire had moved to a line four-fifths of the way from the Soviet Union's prewar frontiers toward the Netherlands, Belgium, France, and Italy.

The Russians did not have to start from scratch in building their underground networks in West Germany. Throughout the war, against long odds, they had preserved an espionage system in Hitler's Reich. Losses to the Gestapo had been very heavy: in 1942 and 1943 eighty-two Communist agents were executed by the Nazis alone from among operators of the network in Berlin, known as the "Red Orchestra." But when victory came there were many Soviet agents still in position and they were reinforced by many hundreds of new ones including highly trained graduates of Beria's spy schools. Immediately after the German defeat and surrender, Beria had set up headquarters of the N.K.V.D. and the new State Security Commissariat at Karlshorst in East Berlin and in Baden near Vienna. Hundreds of his emissaries went to the United States, Canada, Britain, France, Italy, Greece to strengthen existing spy rings and to establish new outposts of espionage and subversion.

In Berlin, General Ivan Serov—who eventually succeeded Beria as supreme spy master—was in command for a time. When he returned to Moscow for higher duties, he left Major General Nicolai Ivanovich Melinkov and Colonel Igor Tulpanov in charge of the "apparatus" for the infiltration of the Western zones. One of their early operations was to recruit informers, to set up clandestine cells in British, American, and French establishments, and to organize shortwave radio transmitting posts in the Western zones, tuned to the Karlshorst H.Q.s.

Their efforts were soon rewarded, particularly in the American zone. One of their spies, Ernst Bosenhard, managed to obtain an appointment as a clerk in the U.S. Intelligence H.Q. at Oberammergau. Before he was caught, Bosenhard sent back copies of hundreds of top secret documents, including Intelligence reports from General Lucius D. Clay, the director of the U.S. military government to President Truman. At Bosenhard's trial the president of the court stated that he "had secured documents from the very nerve center of our defense." Another German, Erwin Andres, managed to obtain employment at the U.S. Air Force base in West Berlin. He had served in Hitler's army, was taken prisoner by the Russians in 1944, and after brainwashing was trained as a spy. Back in Germany, his "controller," Major Nikofor Stolarov, sent him first to West Berlin. Later he worked with another Soviet agent, Alfred Krieg, at the United States military government in Frankfurt and Oberursel. These were two of many serious cases.

British Intelligence was aware of the spy jamboree taking place from the Elbe to the English Channel, but was prevented from hitting back, at least for many months. Attlee and his Foreign Secretary, Ernest Bevin, had their eyes wide open, but they were trying to come to terms with Stalin. Bevin's instructions to the chiefs of the Secret Intelligence Service and Military Intelligence were to tread cautiously and take no drastic action which might have caused a diplomatic incident and a worsening of relations with Moscow. All the efforts to keep Stalin sweet were, of course, doomed to failure. He became more and more intractable. The precarious wartime alliance between East and West was rapidly disintegrating. A few months after the victory, Stalin was resorting to threats and abuse against his British and American Allies. Addressing a parade of two million Red Army men, back from the fronts, he said: "We are carefully watching the intrigues and plots of the reactionaries in Washington and London who are hatching plans for a new war against our Socialist motherland. Constant vigilance is needed to protect the strength of our armed forces who may be called upon to smash a new capitalist aggression. . . ."

The Iron Curtain was coming down and the Cold War was about to begin.

One of the early, if most junior, fighters recruited for it by the Secret Intelligence Service was the energetic and dedicated young Naval Intelligence officer in Hamburg, Lieutenant George Blake.

For many months he had been seeking a transfer from Naval Intelligence to the "real" secret service. While many of his "amateur" colleagues had been impatiently waiting for their demobilization, or had gladly returned to their civilian occupations in offices, universities, or legal chambers, Blake's experience in Hamburg had only sharpened his appetite for the game of espionage.

He was thrilled when he was summoned to an interview with a senior official of the British military government. Although this man ostensibly occupied an inconspicuous post, Blake knew that he was, in fact, one of the station chiefs of M.I.6 in Germany. When Blake was asked whether he was prepared to serve in a department concerned with countering Soviet espionage, he eagerly agreed. He felt that this appointment both rewarded his hard work and vindicated the verbal and written reports in which he warned of the activities of Soviet agents in his area. He was jubilant and raring to have a go at his first assignment. But it was explained to him that he would have to undergo further training and learn Russian. Meanwhile he was to return to his post in Hamburg.

What Blake had not been told, and what he could not possibly have known in his lowly position, was that the Secret Intelligence Service was undergoing thorough reorganization. Great changes had taken place at the London headquarters when its transition from wartime to no less difficult peacetime tasks was carried out. Major General

Sir Stewart Menzies, who had occupied the time-honored position of "C"—that of chief of the legendary M.I.6—throughout the war since he had succeeded Admiral Sir Hugh Sinclair ("Quex") after his death in November 1939, remained in charge. But several of his deputies, such as Colonel Sir Claude Dansey ("Uncle Claude") and Colonel Valentine Vivian ("Ve-Ve") were replaced. The new vice-chief was General Sir John Sinclair ('Sindbad"), a former director of Military Intelligence; Air Commodore (later Sir James) Easton became deputy chief, and several new deputy directors were appointed.

By an ironical twist of fate, the section concerned with counterespionage against the Soviet Union and Communist countries in Eastern Europe, for which George Blake had been earmarked as an agent, was put in charge of Kim Philby, who during the war headed the Iberian section. The reorganization dragged on until the summer of 1946, and Philby was eventually appointed head of the S.I.S. station in Istanbul, which he later described as "the main base for Intelligence work directed against the Soviet Union and the Communist countries in the Balkans."

Meanwhile, George Blake was biding his time, but he set about to justify his claim that he was already "a professional secret agent" with a missionary zeal that verged on the ludicrous. The Intelligence officers whom he began to bombard with unasked-for reports examined them with a mixture of irritation and amusement.

His reports grew longer and more frequent. He always carried two fountain pens filled with invisible ink in his breast pocket. He insisted on exchanging passwords with his own superiors and, as for his equals or juniors in rank, he told them never to expect him to answer the telephone by name or extension number. Instead he would hum a prearranged tune.

He disappeared from the office, for days at a time, dressed in rags, disguised as a "displaced person." His destination was the border of the Soviet zone. The port of Lübeck, only a few miles from the Soviet barbed-wire fences and watchtowers, became one of his favorite haunts, in which to look busily for Soviet spies. Every visit there was good for a voluminous report.

When he traveled by car, even in Hamburg, he would often order the driver to stop and change the number plates from the large stock Blake had collected for this purpose.

He became increasingly isolated from his fellow officers, emitting a truly fantastic aura of mystery wherever he went. His dreamworld had taken possession of his better sense.

His new chiefs were remarkably indulgent. Sometimes "that mad Dutchman" exasperated them but his antics never caused serious trouble and he seemed to be making some headway.

The first case in which he was involved, and which he considered to be of the utmost importance, was the apprehension of two Soviet officers, Sedov and Shulkin. They arrived with one of the many "technical missions" in the spring of 1946 and began questioning some German clerks and messengers at the British headquarters.

George Blake discovered what they were doing and produced an epic report, attributing most of the current world problems to the activities of the two Russian subalterns. By then the pair had left the British zone and were asking the same kind of rather silly questions from the same kind of people in the American zone. Blake insisted that signals be flashed to the U.S. headquarters at Frankfurt and the Americans warned of the coming disaster.

The two Russians were detained, held in custody for a while and, when their unimportance was recognized, pushed back quietly into the Soviet zone. Sedov and Shulkin were not regarded as worth a major quarrel with Moscow. But George Blake could carve two notches in his swordstick. He was convinced that he had run to earth two dangerous Soviet spies. . . .

Another little acorn of a case did grow, much later, into something like a tree: George Blake gathered evidence in the affair of Fräulein Edith Seefeld, a German telephonist employed by the British military government, who had given a classified British telephone directory to another German, Robert Koch. He sold it to a Soviet agent, Karlheinz Tejkl, for four hundred marks.

The British military tribunal convicted Koch, but dismissed Fräulein Seefeld from the case. She had tearfully told the judge that she had not realized that the directory contained the addresses of British military establishment and that it might have been useful to the Russians. Neither the British secret service chiefs, nor those of the N.Q.V.D., considered this case a historic coup of espionage.

And so it went on. Minor cases, usually involving German employees, and commonplace investigations, which George Blake rarely saw through to the end. Soviet agents were happily blackmailing black-market dealers and arrests were frequent but it was hard for Blake to distinguish himself.

He caught a few German informers, produced sheaves of lengthy reports. Among his quarry were some of the members of the newborn German officialdom whose ranks were riddled with ex-Nazis.

By January 1947 the British and American governments decided to introduce "home rule" in their zones. The Americans had already sponsored local elections in part of the Rhineland, Hesse, and Bavaria. Hamburg elected its own city senate for the first time in fourteen years, and in April 1947 elections were held in three of the counties within the British zone.

A new Germany was rising after twelve years of tyranny and two years of occupation, although another two years were to elapse before a West German parliament was elected and a federal government formed by Dr. Konrad Adenauer.

The liberalization of British and American rule in Western Germany resulted in even greater malevolence on the part of Stalin toward his former allies. The Cold War was soon to enter a dangerous phase, with the Russian blockade of West Berlin and the Western countermove in staging the great "Airlift" of 1948.

On the other hand, the discovery of the Canadian spy

ring, with its evidence that the Soviets had been spying on their Allies since 1942, put the West on the alert. The Canadian spy case did, in a roundabout way, enhance George Blake's modest reputation. He had, if somewhat naïvely, foreseen the threat posed by Communist espionage long before it was fashionable to do so. He had drawn attention to it again and again when some of his superiors were whooping it up with the Russians at caviar and vodka parties.

At last, in the spring of 1947, came the call to London. Blake's wish to go on to the higher things he undoubtedly deserved was a heaven-sent relief to his superiors in Germany. To get rid of "that intense Dutchman" was an eminently desirable objective. A laudatory report about Lieutenant Blake was quickly dispatched to the London office. The chummy "old boy" circle in Hamburg was able to ship home its zealous but wearisome junior secret agent without fuss.

On his arrival in London, Blake expected an important assignment to be waiting for him. But he got a damping reception at Broadway Buildings, the hush-hush headquarters of the Secret Intelligence Service. He was told his file had been passed to the Foreign Office and he was to remain in ignorance for several weeks before discovering the reason for this desultory interlude. With growing tension he waited for news. He spent part of his leave with his mother at Chalfont St. Peter in Buckinghamshire and went to the local photographer to have a last picture taken in his naval uniform, of which he had been so proud before; soon it was packed away in mothballs.

When the summons eventually came to attend an interview at the Foreign Office he was greatly relieved. All his life George Blake was confident that, given a chance, he could carve his way to the career he had set his heart upon.

At the Foreign Office he discussed the plan to learn Russian and was told he would be given a serviceman's scholarship to Cambridge. There was, however, to be no question of going for a degree. He was to take a "sand-

wich course," learn Russian and study Russian history
with particular emphasis on the political development and
organization of the Soviet Union. He was to go up to
Cambridge in the autumn; meanwhile he would be working in a department of the Foreign Office to get an initial
training for his future work. In peacetime, the British do
not go for training spies in secret colleges. They rely on
intelligent "amateurs" and improvisation and by 1947 the
Special Operations Executive had been disbanded and its
Special Training Schools closed.

He arrived in Cambridge in October 1947, was admitted
to Downing College, and became an assiduous student. He
did not take lodgings in Cambridge, but rented a room
with a kindly old lady at Madingley and cycled every
morning to the college. Within weeks he was completely
engrossed in the study of the difficult declension, conjuga-
tion, and syntax of the Russian language. He had already
been taking Russian lessons in Hamburg and within three
months he could read Maxim Gorky's *Childhood* in the
original, and soon advanced to Lenin's *Tshto delat?*
("What is to be done?").

At Cambridge George did not take part in undergraduate activities, neither did he join any of the students' clubs
or societies. In 1947 many Cambridge undergraduates
were ex-servicemen and quite a few were married. They
were seriously preparing themselves for civilian jobs. He
found a few friends among them and, like them, he had
neither taste nor the time for pranks and womanizing.
Throughout his stay at Cambridge he visited London at
least twice a month to pop in and out of the various secret
service offices which occupied a lot of floor space in
Whitehall, St. James's, and Northumberland Avenue.

As things turned out he need not have worried. Although his presence in Naval Intelligence had been somewhat abrasive, the secret service had more room for mild
eccentrics. They were even prepared to close an eye on the
strict regulations governing the entry into the Foreign
Service.

The first rule was that only candidates "born in the

United Kingdom and Northern Ireland or one of the self-governing dominions overseas" could be considered. Furthermore, the candidates had to prove that "their parents were similarly born."

None of this, of course, applied to George Blake and should have made him ineligible. His birthplace was Rotterdam and so was his mother's. His father, Albert Behar, was born in Cairo, and though he had a British passport, neither of his parents were born British. But, after making inquiries into George's family background and taking into consideration his father's gallant service in the British army during the First World War as well as George's own naval service, this rule was waived.

There was another hurdle to jump. Entry into the Foreign Service was conditional upon the candidate having obtained a Matriculation Certificate and a good university degree. Most Foreign Office men were honors graduates. George Blake had, of course, neither. So, the second rule regarding the candidate's educational record was waived too. It appears that the secret service chiefs who decided to offer him employment reasoned that, if not quite the usual kind of chap, he would be most useful to have around the place. By the time he came down from Cambridge he would have five languages and that was four more than most of their recruits had.

When he came down at the end of Easter term of 1948, George was told by Mr. D. V. Staines, the establishment officer at the Foreign Office, that he would be joining the Foreign Service, Branch A grade IX, with the rank of vice-consul (temporary) at a salary of 640 pounds a year plus the usual emoluments and annual increments.

Then came the surprise: he would be attached to the Far Eastern Department, under Counselor R. H. Scott (who later became a deputy under secretary of state), and would be given a posting overseas in due course.

The routine official announcement of his appointment was dated September 1, 1948, and subsequently his name and rank were published in the Annual Foreign Service List. He bought a few copies at the Stationery Office and proudly sent one to his mother and another to his uncle, Mijnheer Anthony Beijderwellen. It was also the occasion for a visit to the printer. The delicately embossed visiting cards were inscribed: "George Blake, His Britannic Majesty's Vice-Consul."

CHAPTER SEVEN

SECRET ASSIGNMENT IN THE FAR EAST

The appointment to the Far Eastern Department was, however, a bitter disappointment to George. He had been looking forward to returning to Germany in triumph; scoring a few points with his former Naval Intelligence colleagues who had sniggered behind his back. But he was more than reconciled to it by the time his foreign post came through. He was told he was going to Seoul, the capital of the Republic of Korea. His pleasure at this may seem surprising. It would be difficult to think of a more obscure position than that of a vice-consul at a legation in the capital of a country which few people could have pointed out on a map in 1948.

But the officials at the Foreign Office who did know the whereabouts of this newly created state of Korea were gloomily sure that the world would soon become aware of its existence. George Blake was one of them. He had learned enough during the few months at his desk in the Far Eastern Department not to doubt the importance of his superior's interest in Seoul, despite the fact that the British legation there did not even rate a minister.

Blake also knew that "Our Man in Seoul," the British *chargé d'affaires*, Captain Vyvyan Holt, was an old hand at the game he himself was so keen to play. Holt (later knighted) was a highly competent and gallant veteran of "the Service." He had come from the Military Intelligence, had been Oriental Secretary—that is an exponent of the secret service—in Iraq, and Counselor at the British embassy in Teheran, before he was given the Seoul post.

George Blake was looking forward to becoming his assistant. He knew that important and delicate work was waiting for him. With his zeal for self-improvement he also hoped to pick up a few tricks of the trade from such an experienced man as his new chief.

For centuries Korea had been a subject kingdom of the Chinese emperors and, until the nineteenth century, it was a "sacred land," closed to foreigners. After the Russo-Japanese war in 1905, it became a Japanese "protectorate" and was formally annexed by Japan in 1910. Westernization of the colony, renamed "General Government Chosen," proceeded slowly compared with the rapid modernization and industrialization of Imperial Japan.

Only during the last twenty years had Seoul, or at least its center, become a modern city, and when George Blake arrived there he found it a bustling place of almost two million inhabitants.

In 1945 the Russians entered Korea from the north. Russia had always been anxious to extend her "area of influence" in the Far East southward from Vladivostock. The last-minute entry of the Soviet Union into the West's war with Japan, on August 8, 1945, two days after the Americans had dropped the first atom bomb on Hiroshima, was partly due to Moscow's desire to stake a claim in Korea.

On September 8, 1945, the Americans landed in South Korea. The American and Soviet commanders reached a temporary agreement in which Korea was partitioned along the 38th parallel. All the Allied Powers pledged themselves to restore Korea to full independence after five years of tutelage.

By May 1946, however, negotiations to this end between the United States and the Soviet Union had broken down. The Russians were busily setting up a Communist régime in the north, while the Americans found in Dr.

Syngman Rhee, an aged political émigré who spent the
war in the United States, a willing president for a nomi-
nally democratic Republic of Korea in the south.

Meanwhile, the civil war on the Chinese mainland, between the Communist armies of Mao Tse-tung and the
Nationalists of Generalissimo Chaing Kai-shek was nearing its end. Eventually, Chiang Kai-shek fled with 200,000
of his men to Formosa and American protection.

The Communists had come to power in China and
had proclaimed the "People's Republic." They began to
arrest and expel British and American residents who had
been in control of many business undertakings, particularly in Shanghai, for generations. It was of little avail that
the British government recognized the new Communist
régime, causing bitter resentment in America. Most of the
Britons had to go.

To the Foreign Office and the secret service this meant
that all their outposts were lost almost overnight. Such information as they were able to extract had to come by
way of Hong Kong, Formosa, by courtesy of the Americans, and the Portuguese colony of Macao, which became
one of the main espionage centers in the Far East.

Communist China, a gigantic new power, was thrusting
herself slowly but menacingly into the arena of world politics and as she did so, rebellion and terrorism erupted in
Malaya and Indochina. The Chinese were quick to supply
arms and "volunteers" to the rebels. Every scrap of a clue
as to Chinese intentions in Malaya, Hong Kong, Singapore, was of vital concern to the British government.

Unexpectedly, Seoul, capital of the new Republic of
Korea, became a good place to gather at least some useful
information.

Since his appointment as *chargé d'affaires* in Seoul early
in 1948, Captain Holt left London in no doubt about the
mounting Communist pressure in North Korea.

Strong missions of Soviet military instructors and "technicians" were busily at work and there was a steady flow
of consignments of arms, tanks, vehicles, and ammunition
on the trans-Siberian-Manchurian Railway. There was also

increasing infiltration of Soviet and Chinese emissaries into South Korea.

With his experience of the Russians in Europe and newly acquired command of the Russian language, Blake was a sensible choice to assist Captain Holt and his consul, Norman Owen, who comprised the whole of the diplomatic staff of the British legation.

Apart from his stay in Cairo as a schoolboy, George Blake had never traveled in the Orient. He enjoyed his first eighteen months in Seoul tremendously. He took an immediate liking to the Korean people who are of ancient Ural-Altac origin and only remotely related to the Chinese and Japanese. He soon discovered that if they had any preference it was for the Chinese, whose ancient culture and philosophy the educated Koreans admired and imitated. The friendly feelings of the ordinary Koreans for the Chinese was easily explained as the result of the oppressive domination of their country by the Japanese.

Blake realized that among educated Koreans there were many who were in sympathy with the new Chinese Communist régime, if for no other reason than that it was a new régime which offered all Eastern peoples a message of national dignity and vigor. To his dismay Blake also recognized that the Americans, who were now in control of many South Korean institutions, were overlooking this fact.

Within a few weeks of his arrival Blake made friends with the intellectual set in Seoul. Although the Koreans are reticent people, his friendly curiosity went down very well with them. With his leaning to religious discussions and his interest in theology, Blake also sought and found the friendship of several English missionaries. One, with whom he later shared the hardships in Communist prison camps, was the Right Reverend Alfred Cecil Cooper, the Anglican bishop of Korea, who had arrived there in 1908 and spent forty years as a missionary and bishop in that remote country.

Bishop Cooper, who after his return from prison became chaplain to the Convent of the Society of the Love of God at Burwash in Sussex, told me: "I saw a lot of George Blake. My house and the English Church Mission in Seoul was just over the wall from the British legation and George used often to pop in. He was a fine chap, a good Christian and a regular churchgoer. . . ."

He also became friendly with the head of the Mission of the Salvation Army, Commissioner Herbert Lord, who had served in Korea since 1909 and carried out a phenomenal amount of charitable work, building hostels, schools, hospitals, and orphanages.

Describing Blake as he knew him during the Seoul days, Mr. Lord said: "George Blake appeared to be a very typical Foreign Office type, a man of the world, but serious-minded and rather reserved until you got to know him well. I always thought of him as a man of great self-respect and an ambitious and energetic fellow. . . ."

Through these English missionaries Blake not only met Koreans in important positions, but he also gained much knowledge of the people and the country. It is characteristic of Blake's attitude to life that he sought the company of mature and wise men, like Bishop Cooper and Commissioner Lord, rather than that of American diplomats and officers, whose behavior in Seoul was as rumbustious and promiscuous as that of those of his fellow British officers in Hamburg whom he had avoided.

His Korean acquaintances, among whom were professors and teachers at the National University and the Prince Li Art Institute, were prepared to talk freely to him. These conversations fully corroborated the view of Captain Holt that opposition to the régime of Syngman Rhee was disorganized but strong.

The Americans supported Rhee's government for lack of an alternative but the fact remains that it was an autocratic, corrupt régime which relied heavily on politicians and officials who had been collaborators with the Japanese during the war. When the Communist invasion came, the mass of the people did not support Rhee and the Communists were able to overrun the country and capture the capital within four days.

George Blake also confirmed, and reported to London, that there were strong anti-American feelings at all levels of Korean society. The Koreans did not take kindly to the boisterousness of the American G.I.s who represented the might and the way of life of the Western world. This, more than any conscious resentment at American support of the unpopular Syngman Rhee régime, lay at the root of the distrust and dislike which existed.

Thoughtful South Koreans were not blind to the reality that the U.S. Army units stationed in their country were the only protection against invasion from the north and, whatever respect they may have nurtured for progressive ideas, they certainly did not want to be invaded and unified with the backward and impoverished Communist north.

The anti-American prejudice of the Korean intelligentsia was not violent and it did not extend to other Western nations. Britain under a Labour government was more to their liking and they spoke highly of the work of the English missionaries. The number of Blake's acquaintances among liberal and Socialist politicians, lawyers, and teachers grew rapidly. This was very useful because they in turn maintained contacts with the leaders of the Democratic and Chendogno parties which had formed a coalition with the Communists at Yyongyang, the capital of the northern "People's Republic."

By this route Blake gathered valuable information about political and military events beyond the 38th parallel, as well as about developments in China, reports which the Communist censorship would not have passed.

Sir Vyvyan Holt told me, after his return to London in 1953, that as early as 1949 he was convinced that a clash between the opposing régimes of North and South Korea was inevitable. He did not, of course, divulge to me the contents of diplomatic dispatches but he did indicate that, according to his information at the time, some of which was supplied by George Blake, Syngman Rhee had been preparing plans for the unification of Korea. Such plans were, of course, doomed to failure because the Soviet

Union and China would have never agreed to them. However, Rhee was not discouraged from his dangerous line of thought by the chiefs of the U.S. Military and Political Missions.

There were frequent armed clashes on the frontier, and many of them were precipitated by Syngman Rhee's troops, violating the 38th parallel agreement. The Communists also claimed that Rhee had been sending "assassins" who tried to poison the president of the "People's Republic," Kin Du-bong, and its prime minister, Kim-Il-sung. Moscow sent a series of protest notes to Washington on the subject, but the State Department replied that these were matters of Korean internal politics.

While some of the accusations against Syngman Rhee were justified, it is also a fact that the Russians bore a full share of responsibility for the destruction of the truce and that they and the Chinese were sending hundreds of Moscow-trained agitators and secret agents to spread subversion in South Korea.

In February 1950 Captain Holt had warned the Foreign Office that armed conflict between North and South Korea was now only a matter of time. He advised the British government to refrain from military intervention should the Americans embark on any adventure, because of the repercussions such action would have throughout Southeast Asia, including Hong Kong, Malaya, and Singapore. All these territories were vulnerable to a possible retaliatory attack by the Chinese Communists. Captain Holt also told me that he had then formed the opinion that China certainly, and the Soviet Union probably, would give armed support to the Korean Communists. This could have caused world war.

Captain Holt was proved to be right. Humanity came perilously close to the brink, and 600,000 Chinese "volunteers" poured across the 38th parallel and swept south forcing American and United Nations troops into a humiliating retreat.

Although the United States maintained large diplomatic and military missions in South Korea, and well-staffed Intelligence headquarters in Seoul, the State Department, the C.I.A., and the Pentagon were taken by surprise when the Communist attack came.

The British Foreign Office was not quite so startled. Britain and some of the Commonwealth governments, notably Australia and Canada, had been treating the Korean problem with caution and counseled caution, too, in Washington. It was not for lack of warnings from the British legation in Seoul that the Korean war cost the United States heavy initial defeats, 53,000 dead and 103,000 wounded, and many billions of dollars.

In his cautious and by far not truthful "confession" after his arrest in 1961, and more clearly in his interview in the *Izvestya* in 1970, George Blake stated that he had already then realized the superiority of the Communist cause. But in 1950 he had still a long way to go from toying with ideological problems to becoming a traitor. Indeed, as we shall see, he was to suffer untold hardships from the hands of his future comrades.

CHAPTER EIGHT

PRISONER OF THE COMMUNISTS

North Korea invaded the southern republic on June 25, 1950. The Communist troops encountered only weak resistance, Seoul was occupied four days later. President Syngman Rhee, his cabinet, and the American military and political missions comprising two hundred and thirty members fled from the capital and took refuge in the town of Taejon.

Communications with Hong Kong were broken and, having no instructions from London, Captain Holt decided it was his duty to stay in Seoul and provide protection for his fellow countrymen. So did the French minister, M. Georges Perruche. While the Communist invaders might have turned on the Americans, the two diplomats had every reason to believe that they, their staff, and British and French citizens would be treated as neutrals.

The British legation compound was situated in Chong-dong, north of the modern Japanese district of Seoul.

As soon as the Communist troops entered the city, rioting and looting began. Armed mobs attacked houses and shops belonging to Europeans, Japanese, and Indians, and many were set afire.

George Blake hurried across to the English Church Mission, but Bishop Cooper was out, visiting some of his parishes in the country. He collected Commissioner Lord from the Salvation Army Mission Hall and returned to the legation, where refugees were beginning to arrive. Among them was the Catholic missionary, Father Charles Hunt, whose house had been burned down.

Seoul was in a turmoil. Communist tanks were patrolling the streets but instead of calming the populace, the soldiers encouraged them to ransack the houses of the "capitalists" and burn down churches. A drunken throng celebrated the liberation all through the night.

On the morning of the thirtieth a group of civilians, wearing red armbands to indicate that they were members of the new People's Militia, entered the legation compound. Brandishing automatic pistols the militiamen demanded that the legation's cars be handed over to them. Blake went out to parley with them, accompanied by Commissioner Lord who spoke Korean and acted as an interpreter. In spite of their protests the cars were driven away.

The next twenty-four hours were uneventful, except for the noise of sporadic firing, the blaze of burning buildings, and the smoke which now enveloped part of the capital.

The following day a short, stout man in the uniform of a major of the North Korean army arrived with several soldiers. He introduced himself as Major Choe and demanded to see Captain Holt. He said the Union Jack should be lowered because "the sight of it might provoke the anger of the liberated people."

Captain Holt told Blake to reject this demand. The major then ordered some of his soldiers to climb on to the legation's roof and take the flag down. When this was done the major folded up the Union Jack neatly, bowed politely, and gave it to Blake.

Major Choe said no one would harm the British diplomats because he was leaving two sentries behind for their protection. An hour later a band of ragged men, all armed and some firing into the air, surrounded the compound. Their leader demanded whiskey and cigarettes.

Blake had been helping Captain Holt and Consul Owen to burn the legation's files and code books in the garden. Fortunately, he had taken another precaution on his own initiative: he took most of the bottles from the legation's cellar and poured their contents down the drain. When the Korean visitors persisted in their demand for liquor, Blake took them out to the gutter.

"Look here and smell," he told them with a grin. "Whiskey gone, all gone!" The men gazed in astonishment at the sad puddle of scotch by the drain. Some of them promptly went on their knees to lap up a few mouthfuls of the precious but by now rather dirty liquid.

Blake and Mr. Lord assured them there was not a drop left inside the building. Then Blake started to push the heavily armed men gently toward the gate. He shooed them off like a gang of naughty boys who had tried to steal apples from an orchard. Defeated by the forces of temperance, the invaders departed, sadly but quietly.

Two more days passed in anxious waiting. Blake ventured out into the street to try and discover what was happening. When no one molested him in Chongdong, he walked on, through the center of the town, the only European who dared to show his face. Soldiers pushed him off the pavement, but he returned unharmed.

From the little he could understand, it seemed that the Communist armies were advancing rapidly southward. He saw columns of Communist tanks clattering through the streets and he picked up a rumor that Syngman Rhee and his ministers had been captured and killed.

A tradesman he knew told him from behind the shutters of his shop: "All Americans dead . . . all *meisho* [generals] dead . . ."

Other reports, brought to the legation later in the day, said the Communists were distributing newssheets with the announcement that "Britain and France had joined the American capitalists in a criminal attack on the people of Korea." They also said they had heard that British troops were already on the way to Korea and that the French legation had been raided and the diplomats taken away.

The isolated group at the British legation treated all these rumors with caution. The electricity supply had failed, like all the other public services, and they were unable to pick up radio stations outside Korea with the battery receiver. Their contact with the outside world had ceased.

Early in the morning of July 2, several police vans drove up to the front gate of the compound. Blake went to the door. He opened it to find the genial Major Choe with two police officers and a posse of soldiers. Blake took him into the drawing room where Captain Holt, Consul Owen, Commissioner Lord, and Father Hunt were waiting.

With a bow, Major Choe told the British minister that he and his honorable friends must come to the police headquarters.

"We only desire to check your credentials," he said. "Once your diplomatic status is established you will be allowed to return. We do not want to molest you, but I have my orders."

The three British diplomats and their guests were driven to the police headquarters near the Nan-zan Palace. Major Choe assured them they would be brought back "within twenty minutes."

They were left waiting in a small room, guarded by several armed men, without a meal or drink, for eight hours. Then Captain Holt was asked to produce his diplomatic credentials. He explained that the King's Commission and all other documents were in his safe at the legation. He was driven to the legation to collect the papers. When the car arrived at the gates of the compound, parts of the building were on fire. The remaining rooms swarmed with looters who were throwing furniture, bed linen, and kitchen utensils out of the window, every article being picked up by eager hands outside.

The police officer who accompanied the minister ordered the driver to return to the police office. Back there the interrogations began in earnest. George Blake was questioned for several hours. The examination was punctuated by the noise of sporadic bursts of rifle and machine-gun fire in the city. Blake's session with the commissar was enlivened by a stray bullet which came in through the open window and embedded itself in the table between the two men. Apologetically the commissar remarked: "Those boys are having some fun there. . . ."

George Blake banged his fist on the table and roared: "Why can't we have some fun, too?"

The inkwell leaped into the air and splattered its contents on the commissar's face and tunic. The Communist took it stoically. There was a pause for polite apologies and some tidying up during which Commissioner Lord advised Blake to refrain from having any more fun.

Then a colonel of the North Korean Security Police came to ask the commissar about some South Korean officials who had been arrested the day before.

The commissar sprang to attention. "Oh, we have shot them already, comrade Colonel," he said.

"But that was wrong," retorted the colonel angrily, "I wanted to question them. I did not give you any orders to shoot them."

The commissar bowed deeply. "I am very sorry, comrade, but I thought you were very busy, so I ordered the executions myself."

Captain Holt did not understand much Korean and was, therefore, unable to know precisely what attitude the Comminists were adopting toward himself and the group from the legation. He maintained his composure throughout the ordeal and protested solemnly against the abuse of diplomatic privileges to which he and his colleagues were being subjected.

The Communists, however, were in no mood for further discussions. After further detention of several hours in a locked room, the British minister, Consul Owen, Vice-Consul Blake, Commissioner Lord, Father Hunt, a White Russian employed as a driver at the legation, and two American businessmen were ordered to board a truck.

They were told they would be driven a hundred and forty miles to Pyongyand, the Communist capital, for more questioning.

In Pyongyang the renewed interrogations were conducted by officials of the North Korean Security Police, but this time a Russian—apparently an agent of the M.V.D.—was present. He did not say a word, but he made copious notes.

Then the five Britons were taken to a dilapidated school building. The sixth prisoner, the White Russian, was taken away and they never saw or heard of him again.

The school was surrounded with barbed wire and sentries were posted inside and out. Captain Holt was told that it was "an internment camp for important civilians." The internees were treated fairly; there was no manhandling although some of their guards were sulky and rough. They got three meals a day, consisting in the main of soup, pork stew, cabbage, rice, and bread.

On July 20 another transport arrived from Seoul. It brought M. Georges Perruche, the French minister, M. Jean Meadmore, his consul general, the legation's chancellor, M. Charles Martell and his seventy-six-year-old mother, Madame Amelie Martell, M. Matti, a Swiss citizen, who had been general manager of the Chosum Hotel, and surprisingly enough, a citizen of Communist East Germany, Frau Lotte Gliese.

With them came a large party of missionaries, headed by the apostolic delegate (papal ambassador), Bishop Patrick Burns, the Prefect Apostolic Monsignor Thomas

Quinlan, the eighty-two-year-old Father Paul Villemot, and Father Francis Canavan, an Irishman. This group included priests of every Christian denomination and many nuns and Protestant deaconesses.

Notable among them were the mother superior of the Order of Barefoot Carmelites, who with her nuns had spent a lifetime in Korea looking after orphans and old people, Miss Nellie Dwyer, a well-known American Methodist missionary, and Father Jules Gombert, a French Catholic priest.

All these people had already spent several weeks in prison at Seoul under indescribable conditions. Later they were joined by Mr. Philip Deane, the special correspondent of *The Observer*, who had been badly wounded and taken prisoner with the Seventy-first U.S. Tank Company near Taejon.

George Blake proved invaluable to his fellow prisoners. Being the youngest and fittest, he volunteered to do many chores. He carried the food containers, served meals, washed up, swept up, and looked after the primitive washing and sanitary arrangements.

Commissioner Lord told me: "George was a good man to be interned with. He turned his hand willingly to any kind of job, cooking, cleaning, and all the other chores we had to do. . . . He did it all with good humor, always ready to help others."

The French minister also kept his good humor. He had traveled to Pyongyang in a sealed cattle truck with his party, but had somehow managed to keep his hands on a suitcase. Under the clothes he had hidden several bottles of vintage Château Burgundy. On the long journey in the dark cattle truck he had opened two of them to celebrate the *Quatorze Juillet*, the French national holiday, with his compatriots. With acclaim, they drank that pre-Communist revolutionary toast, *"Liberté, Egalité, Fraternité!"*

When the prisoners heard on the radio, to which they were allowed to listen occasionally, that Princess Anne had been born on August 15, M. Perruche sacrificed the last of his precious Burgundy at a party at which he proposed the toast *à Sa Majesté, le roi d'Angleterre, à la princesse Elizabeth, et à la jeune princesse!*

That was late in August and the comparatively gentle days in the schoolrooms were coming to an end. On several occasions the prisoners were nearly killed during American B-29 bomber raids which caused widespread destruction in the capital. Eventually the Communists decided to move the "V.I.P. internees" to a safer place. They obviously considered them valuable hostages.

On September 5 they were taken from the school first to the Central Prison and then with a number of American P.O.W.s to the railway station. The journey lasted six days and nights. Often the long train was stationary for many hours. There were several heavy air attacks by American bombers. Food and water were distributed very infrequently. An old Catholic priest and a number of G.I.s died on the way.

At last, on September 11, 1950, the prisoners reached the town of Man-po on the river Yalu, near the Manchurian frontier. The civilians were put into an old building, formerly used as customs quarantine quarters by the Japanese. Their "quarantine" was to be a long one.

CHAPTER NINE

ESCAPE ON THE DEATH MARCH

The few weeks George Blake and his companions spent at Man-po were a summer idyll compared with the ordeals which lay ahead. Their guards were amenable and the prisoners could barter their watches, fountain pens, and other personal possessions in exchange for small favors. Blake, Deane, and some of the other younger men went swimming in the Yalu while the good weather lasted. The rations were reasonable: meat three times a week, rice, sugar, oil, an egg a day for each prisoner.

Things changed, however, when the Communists began to sustain reverses at the front. On October 20 the North Korean capital of Pyongyang was captured by American troops and the Communist forces began to retreat northward in a state of disorder.

By then the prisoners had some idea of what was going on in the outside world. George Blake and Philip Deane had organized an information service in which the key figure was a fifteen-year-old boy, educated at a Presbyterian mission. He was allowed to run errands for the internees and every morning he brought them a summary of radio bulletins.

Just when the reports of the successful American offensive were beginning to raise the prisoners' hopes, the mood of their guards became ugly. The prisoners were no longer allowed to leave the camp and rations were cut.

Confined as they were, they could see signs of collapse of the North Korean forces. Stragglers, separated from their units passed by the camp in large numbers. Many seemed to have discarded their uniforms and thrown away their rifles. But in the opposite direction, across the bridges of the Yalu, came the first Chinese "volunteers." They included long convoys of artillery and antiaircraft batteries.

The idyll was over. On October 9 the prisoners were marched fifteen miles down the river to the village of Ko-Sang Djin. The weather was getting very cold and they shivered in the threadbare summer clothes which they had been wearing since their arrest. Blake gave his tunic to an elderly nun and continued to face the biting winds in his light flannels and sports coat.

After a few days the prisoners were moved again, to the mining village of Chuiam Nee. They were put into the primitive huts which had served the miners as homes, bare of any furniture and verminous.

The scarecrow caravan of civilian prisoners had already been swollen by intakes of South Korean officials, policemen, and politicians, including Syngman Rhee's minister of the interior, Kim Hyu Suk. It was further augmented by several hundred American officers and men. They were in a pitiful state. They had been captured in their summer fatigue uniforms which were now in shreds. Most of them were barefoot, the North Koreans having seized their boots, a coveted prize.

The hostility of the guards toward the prisoners grew in direct proportion to the worsening news from the front. By October 20 the guards' excitement rose to fever pitch as the mutter of American artillery gradually grew into a steady rumble and American bombers roared overhead.

Blake heard from one of the guards that units of the U.S. Seventh Division had been reported near the Yalu River, only a few miles away. On October 26 came the order to bring the prisoners back to Man-po. The prisoners were formed into a column and as it marched toward Man-po, which it reached on October 30, it was passed by never-ending convoys of Chinese troops. The arrival of these massive reinforcements marked the beginning of a new Communist offensive.

Man-po looked very different from its appearance a few weeks earlier. It had been bombed heavily and some of the ruins were still burning as the prisoners struggled toward the center of the town.

The cold was intense and the only food distributed to the captives were some half-boiled corncobs. Starving Korean children picked up the chewed remains from the ground.

The commander decided he must "thin out" the convoy of prisoners. The meager stock of food had to be kept for those whom he now regarded as hostages against the arrival of United Nations troops. A batch of South Korean officials and policemen was taken outside the town and shot.

Blake had already planned an escape at the mining village. He was in a better physical condition than most of his companions and he felt the proximity of American forces was a challenge to action. During the night, when the guards had kicked out the fires as a precaution against air raids, Blake crawled out of the camp and up a steep hill near Man-po. Then he walked south through a forest to tackle another hill. At dawn he reached a valley where he thought he would find American tank patrols.

While he was looking for the advanced units of the Americans, he ran straight into a Communist patrol, doing the same thing. The soldiers took him to a farmhouse and marched him before their captain.

"You are a spy," said the officer without further ado. "You have been caught red-handed and you will be shot immediately."

He ordered his men to tie Blake's hands behind his back and they pushed him out of the house toward a wall. They cocked their rifles ready for the execution.

Not for the first time in his life Blake faced the likelihood of violent death, but this was his first experience of firing-squad procedure. He found he could not remember any of the Korean words he had learned but with a flash of inspiration, which saved his life, he shouted to the officer in Russian:

"I am not a spy. I am a civilian internee, a British diplomat. I went out of the camp of Man-po and I lost my way."

His last-minute words had a dramatic effect on the captain who, like many North Korean officers, had received military training in the Soviet Union. He dismissed the firing squad and congratulated Blake on his command of Russian. He then escorted him back to the farmhouse, invited him to share a meal of pork soup and sweet rice, and gave him cigarettes.

Blake was brought back just in time to join the long column of prisoners as it was about to move off on another march.

In front marched the American prisoners of war, followed by the civilian internees. All were in an equally dreadful condition.

Disease, wounds, exhaustion, hunger, and cold were taking their toll. Prisoners who could not walk had to be carried. Blake and Deane were among those still fit enough to carry some of their fellow marchers, often for hours at a time.

But then, standards of fitness were not high. Philip Deane recalls how Monsignor Quinlan, himself weak and in his late fifties, carried the eighty-two-year-old French missionary, Father Villemot, for many miles.

Father Charles Hunt tore his chasuble, the garment which is the emblem of charity at the Holy Mass and which "makes the yoke of Christ light and agreeable," and wrapped the two pieces around the frostbitten, shoeless feet of Consul Owen, who was suffering from dysentery and was near collapse. Father Hunt's condition soon became nearly as bad. Commissioner Lord carried him for a stretch and then helped Madame Funderat, a seventy-year-old woman. He tied a rope around her waist with which to drag her forward every time she wanted to lie down and die.

Commissioner Lord was also the interpreter for the prisoners. He had the task of relaying the Communist commander's orders. The first of these was that no one must drop out. If anyone did, he or she would be shot. If anyone died the corpse would have to be carried.

On November 1 some of the G.I.s dropped out, collapsing on the ground. The commander stopped the column and called one of the American officers, Lieutenant Cordus Thornton, a twenty-three-year-old Texan, to him.

He said: "Some of your men have dropped out. You have disobeyed my orders. I will now shoot you all." He ordered Commissioner Lord to translate this. Mr. Lord began to plead for the lives of the Americans. The commander put his revolver to Lord's head and said: "All right, I shall shoot you, too." This did not stop the Salvation Army man's entreaties on behalf of his fellow prisoners.

The Communist grew impatient, He turned to the American officer and said: "I shall now hold a court-martial." Then he asked his soldiers a question: "Did this prisoner disobey my orders?" The soldiers replied: "Yes, he did." The commander asked: "What is the punishment for disobedience?" and the soldiers shouted: "Death. Kill him!" The commander calmly told Lieutenant Thornton, "Now you have had your court-martial and you were sentenced to death."

Thornton stood rigidly to attention throughout. When the Communist pulled the trigger and the bullet went through the American's neck, he fell slowly where he had been standing. Blake was a close witness of this murder.

That night many American soldiers died from exhaustion and cold. The commander ordered that they should be buried, like Lieutenant Thornton, in a field by the road. He added: "The tops of the graves must be left without mounds."

The next morning Mother Superior Beatrice of the Order of St. Paul, who had kept an orphanage for Korean children for thirty-five years, collapsed. As she lay unconscious, the commander shot her through the head. Then he held his revolver to Commissioner Lord's head and ordered him to write another "death certificate," stating that the nun had died of heart failure.

The death march went on for many days. Occasionally there were overnight stops in villages. Usually the civilian internees were packed into one room which had no windows and was covered with vermin and excrement.

On November 4 the column stumbled across a mountain pass in a terrible blizzard. More and more G.I.s were falling by the way. A group of children of the civilian internees strove desperately to keep up with the adults. Philip Deane recalls: "A young redheaded kid who could still walk, was trying, weeping, to carry his dying pal. A guard kicked him on. He stumbled off, sobbing."

Those who fell lay by the side of the road, watching mutely as the column passed them by. Deane says: "We heard many shots . . . the dying were pushed into the ditch."

When the marchers arrived at their destination, the village of Chung-Kang-Djin, on November 8, 1950, Commissioner Lord, helped by George Blake and Philip Deane, made a rough estimate of the casualties. They found that at least a hundred people had died or had been shot during the march.

A school was transformed into a prison for the more important civilian prisoners. The morning after the arrival the commander, whom the prisoners named "The Tiger," ordered "physical exercises," as a punishment for "bad behavior during the march." The prisoners were made to run, although many only succeeded in crawling on all fours. Sister Mary Clare, an Anglican deaconess, collapsed and died during this purposeless torment. Further deaths among the civilians were Father Paul Villemot and Father Jules Gombert, aged seventy-two. Monsignor Quinlan stood at their graves in his torn soutane and said the Mass for the Dead. There were very many deaths among the American soldiers.

After a few days in Chung-Kang-Djin and several air raids, the prisoners were moved on to a neighboring village, Hadjang.

There a large camp had been established, mainly for American prisoners of war. The diplomats and missionaries were billeted in the house of a tobacconist. It had only three rooms and all of them were crammed with the old chests in which the owner had once kept his stock.

Seventeen people, including Captain Holt, Consul Owen, George Blake, Bishop Burns, Commissioner Lord, several priests, and seven South Korean ex-ministers and politicians shared the little house. In January 1951 there were twelve degrees of frost. Food consisted mainly of rice and vegetables. Small portions of sugar and oil were given to the sick.

George Blake withstood the hardships fairly well. He had his share of illness, suffering from prolonged bouts of dysentery and influenza and, like all the other prisoners, severe frostbite, but he remained active and imperturbable, comforting the less fortunate prisoners and nursing the sick. For many days and nights he sat at the side of Captain Holt and Consul Owen who had fallen very ill and believed that their last hour had come.

Philip Deane, who shared this vigil with Blake, recalls: "There is a story that vermin leave a dying man before he dies. While nursing Captain Vyvyan Holt and Norman Owen, I slept between them. One morning I noticed a stream of lice crawling away from their bodies and towards me. I felt very frightened. A few more lice did not matter. I already had thousands; but I remembered that story of the vermin and the dead. . . ."

Buddhist communities have a custom whereby elderly people who fall sick are taken to special "death houses," in which they squat, waiting for the end. "The Tiger" introduced this practice at the Hadjang camp, except that the "death houses" were called "hospital huts." When he decreed that a prisoner was beyond his help, the patient was taken to the "hospital" and left there to die.

Only the combined efforts of Blake, Deane, and the French consul Martell prevented the removal of Captain Holt and Norman Owen to the "hospital." Several others in their group could not be saved. Bishop Burns, the apostolic delegate, Father Francis Canavan, and M. Matti, the Swiss hotel manager, were dragged to the hut and died there.

George Blake succeeded in persuading "The Tiger" that the deaths of the two British diplomats might get him into trouble with his superiors. "The Tiger," realizing the value of the two important "hostages," sent the medical sergeant off on a search for drugs. He returned after five days, not a moment too soon, with some phials of penicillin and a bottle of sulfa-pyridine tablets from a North Korean army hospital.

Captain Holt and Consul Owen were so near death they hardly knew what was happening. Not long after their return to Britain both these men died, their health broken during the terrible hardships of their imprisonment.

When I saw Sir Vyvyan Holt in London, in 1953, he told me: "If it were not for George Blake and Philip Deane I would not have survived even the last lap of the death march. They nursed me and Consul Owen and gave us their rations, although they were themselves sick and hungry."

Temperatures during the Korean winter of 1950–1951 sometimes fell to seventy degrees below freezing. Hadjang had become a camp for dying.

In addition to all the other hardships there was a shortage of water. Prisoners had to bring water from the river, after hacking up the thick ice that covered it.

George Blake and Philip Deane were usually detailed for this duty. As a rule, they each had to carry twenty-five gallons. On December 5 a guard ordered Blake to bring a hundred gallons from the river. It was a long walk and Blake, feverish and exhausted, refused.

The guard dragged him out and ordered him to kneel in the snow. Blake remained in this position until he had nearly frozen to death. Then the guard told him he would receive punishment for disobeying an order and so, too, would Philip Deane who had tried to remonstrate.

Deane described what happened in these restrained words: "The guard accused us of insulting the Koreans, and of not carrying the amount of water laid down in regulations. We replied that this was not so. The guard said he would teach us not to lie, and he beat us with the butt of his rifle, kicked us and slapped us.

"George Blake, who got the worst of it, smiled throughout the ordeal, his left eyebrow cocked ironically at the guard, his Elizabethan beard aggressively thrust forward. . . ."

One can scarcely imagine a less propitious moment to try and convince European prisoners that the Communist cause in Korea was just, or that it was likely to succeed. Yet, the Communists began their essays at indoctrination at Hadjang.

These were so inept that any suspicion they might have influenced George Blake must be, at least, doubtful. The indoctrination was administered in the form of "lectures" by simpleminded, barely literate North Korean police officers. The instruction was welcomed by the captive, sick, but mentally alert audience as a blessedly entertaining diversion.

The "lecturers" distributed a few books in English and Russian and ordered the prisoners to read them. This they did with pleasure, having an interest in any subject capable of yielding some intellectual stimulation. They soon discovered that the "lecturers'" knowledge of Communist theory and history was minimal; the table was often turned as one of the prisoners gave his mentors a simplified explanation of a point of Marxist teaching.

More often than not the "examinations" conducted by the Koreans, with the aid of the missionaries acting as interpreters, were transformed into a discussion on any subject which happened to arouse the interest of the prisoners taking part.

Captain Holt was particularly adroit at changing the subject to one of his taste. For instance, when the Koreans were warming up to their theme of capitalist imperialism and colonial oppression in general and the crimes of Britain and France in particular, they might have been unwise enough to mention the Middle East. Holt, an Arabic scholar, would drop a promising tidbit on archaeology, camel riding, or Arabic calligraphy, and the Koreans would listen fascinated, forgetting the questions they were supposed to be asking about the prisoners' proficiency in Lenin's works.

Blake was also an able classroom performer. On one occasion the indoctrinators discovered that he was of Dutch origin and they began to ask him about the exploitation of Dutch workers by the rich capitalists. In return they received an interesting description of the works of Rembrandt and Franz Hals.

Sometimes, of course, the indoctrinators stuck doggedly to the point but they were still easy victims to waylaying techniques perfected years before by their pupils under schoolmasters made of much sterner stuff.

The "lecturer" might begin ponderously enough: "At the Seventeenth Congress of the Communist party of the Soviet Union, the great Stalin said . . ." but after a few sentences there would be an interruption from one of the prisoners: "Oh yes, but Lenin in his speech 'On deceiving the people with slogans of liberty' took a rather different view. . . ."

If the indoctrinator tried to protest, never having heard of the speech in question, the pupil would reply: "You can look it up, it's all in Volume XIV of Lenin's *Collected Works*."

George Blake, with his good knowledge of Russian, would quote genuine passages but after a while he found it more pleasing to play inverted dialectics by making up his own plausible but contradictory Marxist-Leninist-Stalinist dogma.

The French diplomats were less tolerant of the boredom inflicted by the Communist instructors so they resorted to elaborate sarcasm. On one occasion M. Perruche announced, with much detail, that he had an aunt who was a firm believer in Marxist teachings and, being a painter, had renounced "capitalist naturalism" after reading Lenin's *Treatise on Art*. The indoctrinators were very pleased to hear this and asked him to tell the group more about his distinguished aunt.

"She paints while riding a bicycle," explained the French minister blandly. "She belongs to '*L'acromégalisme sénile.*'"*

"And what is that?" inquired the indoctrinator. "Please explain."

"Oh, that is a French school of painting," said M. Perruche airily.

It is inconceivable that sessions like this could have had any profound effect on Blake.

---

* A disturbance of the pituitary gland resulting in the abnormal enlargement of the bones of the head, hands, and feet.

CHAPTER TEN

THE MAN FROM MOSCOW

The death rate was still rising at Hadjang when the Communists decided to move the V.I.P.s to a farmhouse at Moo-Yong-Nee, where they stood a chance of recovering and surviving. On their way through Man-po they were met by someone who, by that time, had taken on the quality of an old friend: Choe, the officer who had arrested the five Britons at the Seoul legation and hauled down the Union Jack. He was now a colonel and told Blake that he had been badly wounded during the second battle of Seoul.

Colonel Choe escorted the prisoners to the farmhouse and stayed with them. The building had four rooms and a kitchen with a hearth and the unbelievable blessing of a warm fire. The Russian-speaking colonel and Blake got on particularly well and Blake was able to win a number of minor favors for the prisoners from him. The guard commander, Lieutenant Pak Yong-se, seeing the colonel's tolerant relationship with all the prisoners, also treated them politely and humanely. He developed, indeed, into a resourceful ally in building what was, by Korean prison standards, an island of gracious living at Moo-Yong-Nee.

Once a month Lieutenant Pak had to go into Man-po to collect the money with which he was supposed to buy the rations locally from the peasants. From one of these trips he returned in triumph bearing a very ancient H.M.V. gramophone and a few very scratchy records. The handle was missing and the spring motor was defunct, so two arias from *Boris Godounov,* sung by Chaliapin, a Tchaikovsky overture, and a rendering of "Auld Lang Syne"—

the latter apparently being booty from the Mess of the Argyll and Sutherland Highlanders—could only be heard when someone had the energy to spin the turntable with his finger.

The sums of money Lieutenant Pak collected in Manpo, although not great, were sufficient to launch him on a series of complicated financial transactions which betrayed a talent for trading that would have made him a rich man in capitalist Hong Kong or Singapore. He and his men were all great smokers and the main object of his business operations was to keep the farmhouse in cigarettes. This was a problem in view of the irregularity of the soldiers' pay. The answer lay in his power of persuasion with the village moneylenders. Lieutenant Pak and the moneylenders spent hours together in negotiations and eventually a line of credit was established on the strength of "the rich, distinguished prisoners'" ability to pay extortionate interests after the war.

With Lieutenant Pak's coup, at the advent of spring, meals became regular, including rice, turnips, cabbage, some meat, and even a marrowbone and a sweet dish when the balance of payments allowed.

Perhaps Pak's greatest achievement for Blake and his companions was his success in borrowing a temperamental old radio set from the village schoolmaster. The electricity supply had been restored in May 1951, after a long interval, and between periods of approved listening to Communist radio stations, the prisoners managed to pick up scraps of news from U.S. Army transmitters. In this way they heard of the repulse of the United Nations troops from the Yalu River and the subsequent offensive by the Chinese "volunteers" army which pushed deep into South Korea. The news of the removal by President Truman of General MacArthur from the supreme command came as a big shock which was only rivaled by an announcement that negotiations for a truce along the 38th parallel had started.

This, then, was the place where the indoctrination of Blake and his coprisoners began in earnest. In fact, they were not the only ones. Their Korean guards also received instruction in the Communist dogma. There was much thumping of textbooks by their officers and hours of dictation from sources such as *The Teachings of Lenin* and *Short History of the Communist Party* (*Bolsheviks*) for the practically illiterate soldiers.

With the prisoners, however, the same methods were not likely to make much progress. Between them, Holt, Owen, Blake, Bishop Cooper, Monsignor Quinlan, Commissioner Lord, and Philip Deane could have held their own in any intellectual company in the world. I am sure Colonel Choe and the other indoctrinators could never have influenced them against their will and, in the relatively civilized circumstances in which Choe conducted his lectures it is far more likely that he and the middle-aged police major who assisted him, were influenced by the prisoners.

About that period of indoctrinations statements were made by several of Blake's fellow prisoners.

Bishop Cecil Cooper said: "They first tried to brainwash us through an interpreter but gave it up as a hopeless job because of the language difficulty. Blake resisted the brainwashing fiercely, arguing with the political officers who were attempting to indoctrinate us."

Commissioner Lord said: "The initial attempts at indoctrination were very amateurish. I think we were the wrong types to work on. . . . Blake was more contemptuous of the propaganda than most of us."

Philip Deane recalled: "The Koreans who indoctrinated us were not effective; we often had to help them with their quotations from Karl Marx and we could always trot out a contradictory quotation, a game we loved to play. . . . The only things the Communist gave us were magazines depicting the triumphant progress of Miss Monica Felton (a prominent member of the British-Soviet Friendship Society in London) and the dean of Canterbury, the late Dr. Hewlett Johnson, through North Korea. We were furious, and Blake was at his angriest and most defiant."

Serious attempts at brainwashing did not begin until the autumn of 1951, when Russian and Chinese specialists ar-

rived to deal with the hitherto impervious British reactionaries.

The mental assault began with a visit by an official of
the North Korean Ministry for Foreign Affairs. On his arrival he let the prisoners know that in the evening he
would make an important announcement. The prisoners
waited in suspense for six hours while he was dining and
resting. At eight o'clock in the evening he reappeared and
said: "Messages have been received from your families.
They are well and are thinking of you."

The prisoners clamored for more news as they crowded
around the visitor. But to all questions he replied that he
was not authorized to say more. However, he would allow
the internees to write short messages home. He also gave
his approval to a request by Captain Holt that he be permitted to send a cable to the Foreign Office informing his
superiors that he and the other members of the British legation were alive and safe.

This and other small favors arranged by the emissary
from the North Korean government were apparently
designed to set the stage for the arrival of the brainwashing experts.

The leader of the team was a Russian, whom the prisoners christened "Blondie." Commissioner Lord recalled:
"After the naïve stuff offered at the indoctrination lectures
by the Koreans, it became soon obvious to all of us that
'Blondie's' techniques were far more advanced. He was a
tall man with aristocratic manners and he was obviously a
university man. He spoke fluent English and he really set
about trying to persuade us that the Communist system
and way of life was the best. George Blake had numerous
sessions with him. Afterwards Blake would return to our
room and tell us he was treating these conversations as a
huge joke. Mind you, Blake never talked a great deal
about what went on when he was alone with 'Blondie.' But
then none of us did. I suppose it is possible Blake was influenced, but if he became a Communist I think he was in-

telligent enough a fellow to go over as a result of his own thinking."

After Blake's trial Commissioner Lord was prepared to accept the conclusion of the attorney general that Blake had become a convert to communism in Korea in 1951, but he was emphatic that he would never have believed it when he was with Blake at the farmhouse.

"None of us guessed that Blake would weaken in these relentless brainwashing sessions by the Communists. I remember his arrogance to the propagandists," Mr. Lord said. All the prisoners at the farmhouse agreed that "Blondie" was the most impressive of the persuaders. I have, therefore, been at some pains to find out who and what he was. My search ended with a real surprise. Although I have been unable to discover his real name, I found out that he was known as Gregory Kuzmitch, or "Kuzma," for short. He was an official of the Political Education Department (*Prosveshtcheny Otdfel*) of the M.G.B., the Ministry of State Security, which controlled all espionage activities abroad. Kuzmitch was one of the highly trained men found serving outside the Soviet Union as cultural attachés, press attachés, correspondents of *T.A.S.S.*, the Soviet news agency, or accompanying trade missions, theatrical and ballet companies on their foreign visits as security officers to prevent defections.

I was able to trace Kuzmitch's diplomatic career prior to his employment as a "brainwasher" in Korea. I discovered that he had served on the staff of Major General Georgi Nikolaievitch Zarubin, who had been Soviet ambassador in Canada until 1947, and afterwards in London, until his appointment at Washington in 1952. Kuzmitch had spent long spells both in Ottawa and London (though in London he used the name of Kuznetzov and the rank of an "attaché"). In 1950 or early in 1951, Kuzmitch was recalled to Moscow and eventually sent to Korea. His task was to turn British and American prisoners around. During his service in the West—he had also spent some months at the Soviet embassy in Sweden—he had acquired a thorough knowledge of the Western way of life; his command of English was almost faultless.

From Moscow's point of view, his acquaintance with Western politics and philosophies proved disastrous. At the end of the war in Korea Gregory Kuzmitch defected to the Americans and was sent to Washington, where he was employed for several years by Mr. Allen Dulles's Central Intelligence Agency. In 1961 he was one of the American agents who evaluated Blake's importance for the C.I.A. After Blake's arrest Mr. Dulles sent three special agents to London to interrogate Blake at Wormwood Scrubs (this was done, of course, with the agreement and assistance of the British government) and to make an assessment of the damage Blake had done to Western agents in Germany and Eastern Europe. One of these American interrogators told a British colleague that Kuzmitch had made a detailed report to the C.I.A. about the impressions he had gained of Blake in Korea, nine years earlier.

Although it was a long time since he had his brainwashing sessions with Blake at Moo-Yong-Nee in 1951, Kuzmitch apparently had been able to provide some interesting information. He made the following points about Blake's reactions to his treatment:

(1) Blake had revealed very little about his work as vice-consul and British Intelligence officer in Seoul.

(2) Neither had Blake given any information about his training or the organization of the British secret service which might have been of use to the communists at that time.

(3) However, Blake had shown a deep disillusionment about Western politics and had been very critical of the American and United Nations intervention in Korea and even more so of Britain's support of this action. While he had not shown signs of being willing to become a convert to communism, Kuzmitch gained the impression that Blake was a "sympathizer" and good material to be "turned round" to the Communist cause.

My information about Kuzmitch can be taken as completely reliable, but not too much should be made of his report about Blake. Kuzmitch was a defector; he had been a senior operative of the Soviet secret service, experienced in subversion. His sincerity toward his new American masters must be taken with a grain of salt. He could have various motives for keeping to himself any special knowledge he might have gained from or about Blake.

Kuzmitch was one of the organizers of the "Red Star Club" for the American, British, and United Nations prisoners of war, at their camp nearby. Membership, which carried valuable privileges such as extra food, cigarettes, warm clothes, and better accommodations, was mainly confined to G.I.s who had been successfully brainwashed or had joined the club out of sheer opportunism. Out of all the "Red Star Clubs" in the P.O.W camps only one Briton and twenty-three Americans chose to stay behind the Iron Curtain when the prisoners of war were freed after the armistice in 1953.

The syllabus for the indoctrination of the G.I.s was of great simplicity. Deane described it thus: "Lessons in American history were given. The annihilation of the Red Indians by the settlers was stressed. Negroes and Filipino boys were challenged about racial discrimination, about segregation and lynching [in America]. Instances of brutality against colored people were stressed. Charles Dickens was quoted as an authority on living conditions in Britain. The conditions described by Dickens, according to the indoctrinator, still prevailed, 'altered somewhat in form but not in essence.' "

Blake did not join the "Red Star Club" and often spoke with contempt of its members, calling them "fools who had sold themselves for a bowl of rice or a few cigarettes."

I am not inclined to agree that Blake was "brainwashed" in the narrow sense of the word, but I would say that many arguments advanced by the Communists have greatly influenced him. Being himself a man always determined to achieve success, he admired the purposeful efforts of the persuaders. He had been shocked, as were all impartial observers, by the deplorable régime of Syngman Rhee. He also knew from personal experience that the be-

havior of many Americans in South Korea was often in-
sensitive and occasionally disgraceful. But, I think, Blake
also realized that, just as hard cases make bad law, the existence of bad government outside the Communist orbit
was not in itself a good reason for adopting communism
as a remedy. Neither does it seem probable that he was
suddenly shaken to the core by the realization that the
West had its shortcomings: he learned that at a tender age
when he watched Rotterdam go up in flames. He may,
however, have been considerably shaken by the racial issue
when one remembers that in 1951 there was not nearly so
much readiness in the West to acknowledge the existence,
let alone the desirability, of a "wind of change."

Taken by itself I do not think that even this could have
sent him running into the Communist paddock but it
might have been a factor in persuading him to shin up the
fence between the two sides, and sit on it.

From this position he could view the mad bulls in both
fields with elevated detachment and score off the equally
immoral contenders with no moral qualms of his own—a
man apart. It was in Berlin that he eventually made his
choice.

The most convincing suggestion to help explain Blake's
final conversion I found in the report which the American
psychiatrist, Dr. Robert J. Lifton, made in 1954 to the U.S.
Department of the Army. With the assistance of the Pentagon he had examined several hundred American ex-
prisoners of war after their return home from Korea. Most
of them had been subjected to indoctrination and brainwashing during their captivity.

Dr. Lifton wrote: "The brainwashing of the prisoners in
Korean camps was essentially an attempt to destroy the in-
dividual's previous personality and remold it in terms of
Communist ideology. It is a process of death and rebirth;
and though few left the prison camps as convinced Communists, none emerged from the ordeal unscathed."

Dr. Lifton placed the subjects of his inquiry into three

basic categories: "the apparent converts," "the obviously confused," and "the apparent resisters."

The "apparent resisters" denounced their captors, as did George Blake, to their fellow prisoners. But Dr. Lifton insists that, while coercion certainly breeds resistance, a proportion of the men who expressed their detestation of the brainwashing "had gained the conviction that reforms of the social and economic system in the West were necessary." The people had been made aware "of shortcomings in the Western democratic and capitalist system, and the method by which they had been given this awareness produced delayed action results after they were released."

If one accepts these conclusions, one could regard Blake as "an apparent resister" who suffered a delayed conversion because he was unable to reestablish his former identity when he regained freedom. Moreover, the double life on which he embarked suited his inclinations to live half of his life in a dreamworld of his own.

CHAPTER ELEVEN

BACK TO FREEDOM

The contrast between conditions at the farmhouse and the death camp of Hadjang, where the bulk of the civilian internees and the prisoners of war had remained, was diminished when "The Tiger" was replaced by a new commandant. Atrocities at Hadjang ceased, although the death rate among the sick and half-starved inmates remained high for some time. The new commandant later moved the camp to Chang-Kang-Djin where better accommodations were provided.

The V.I.P.s at the farm at Moo-Yong-Nee enjoyed many privileges and were allowed to go to Man-po and to take part in the life of the village. Blake and some of the other internees attended a local funeral and visited a school. Then, in October 1951 the missionaries were moved to Man-po. Their new living quarters consisted of dugouts built into the hills. The place was called by the Koreans "The House of Culture." At the farmhouse only the British and French diplomats and journalists remained. Captain Holt told me after his return: "We spent most of the time lying on our beds. It was the boredom which was the worst thing about our imprisonment at that period."

On November 27, 1951, "Blondie" Kuzmitch told the prisoners that a cease-fire agreement had been reached and that the negotiations about a new demarcation line and eventual truce were progressing well. "The war will be over by Christmas," he said with a smile.

One day a fat, jovial Korean general arrived and entertained the British and French diplomats to a luncheon. In the course of the meal he asked Captain Holt and M. Perruche to write letters to Kim Il Sung, the Communist prime minister, expressing their gratitude for the good treatment they had received.

Obviously these letters were to be used during the truce negotiations. After listening politely to the request, Captain Holt replied icily: "I assume, General, you want me to thank His Excellency the prime minister for the humane treatment that led to the deaths of my colleague, Bishop Patrick Burns, the apostolic delegate of the Holy See, of Father Hunt, Father Canavan, Sister Mary Clare, and all the others who died of privations, starvation, and disease? My colleagues and I have been imprisoned and subjected to many inhumanites against all rules of international law and diplomatic convention and practice. Do you wish me to include the details of all this in my letter of thanks to His Excellency?"

The general flinched and said: "Please do not talk like that. You are hurting my feelings. Some mistakes were made but now we are treating you properly, I hope." The general departed without the letters.

When the truce negotiations at Panmunjom broke down,

fighting began again even more savagely than before. North Korean Chinese troops heavily attacked the hill positions on the central front and the Americans withdrew from the embattled "Old Badly" stronghold. The renewed successes of the Communist armies may have had something to do with the fact that conditions at the prison camp remained tolerable.

In the spring of 1953, as the months wore on, restrictions at the farm became even lighter. A Chinese commissar took over control and the diplomats were no longer guarded by armed soldiers. They were allowed to move about quite freely. The brainwashing sessions became more and more infrequent until they ceased altogether.

The end of the strange and often dreadful ordeal for George Blake and his companions came on March 20, 1953, when they were told that they were being taken to Pyongyang. The Britons were first to leave and there was a big farewell party at which M. Perruche, deeply moved, bade them a swift and safe journey home.

The party of seven—Captain Holt, George Blake, Norman Owen, Bishop Cooper, Monsignor Quinlan, Commissioner Lord, and Philip Deane—were driven to the Communist capital in a lorry which had been converted into a caravan with sleeping berth. The journey lasted forty-three hours. Pyongyang had suffered badly from the raids but the big building of the minister of interior, the headquarters of the security police, and other government buildings were still standing.

To their astonishment the Britons were greeted like long-lost brothers when they clambered down from the lorry. Officers saluted and a colonel offered Captain Holt his own room and bed. They were conducted with many bows to the comfortable basement shelters beneath the ministry's offices.

A North Korean brigadier appeared and invited "the guests" to breakfast: a huge bowl of caviar, surrounded by cubes of ice, cooked ham, eggs, spaghetti, real butter, white bread, petit-beurre bisquits and *cowa*.

George Blake, always fastidious about his appearance, asked whether he could wash his shirt, something which he had managed to do even during the worst period at the Hadjang death camp. "We would be honored to have your honorable shirt laundered," replied the colonel with a bow and bore it off for the full Chinese treatment.

The slightly Hollywoodish atmosphere persisted when they were shown into a well-furnished suite of rooms in the underground shelters. The brigadier had summoned a barber and suggested that "the guests" should have their beards removed. Blake staunchly insisted that he wanted to keep his. The barber was followed by a tailor who measured them for suits and overcoats.

Another welcome visitor was a Chinese captain bringing a pile of American newspapers and magazines. These were nearly six months old, but the party read with interest, in *Time* and *Newsweek,* about "the complete destruction of all roads and bridges between the Yalu River and Pyongyang," the latter being described as "a ghost city without a single building remaining."

At the end of the first week the Britons were joined by the French diplomats who, however, received less comfortable quarters and were kept segregated. There were no more attempts at brainwashing but some of the Chinese and Korean officers, all above the rank of major, engaged the Britons in political discussions, designed to pry open the Anglo-American alliance.

"The British are so much more cultured," declared one of the colonels, "so much more mature, so much better behaved. . . . You are certainly more suited for a leading role in world affairs than the Americans. Isn't it unfortunate that the Labour government turned Britain into a satellite of the United States? Imagine all those American soldiers in Britain playing around with your women! And the burden imposed on you by the upkeep of the Yankee aerodromes and all the NATO commitments! It is not possible to believe that a nation with a splendid history like Britain will consent to remain in the humiliating role of an American satellite. . . ."

On April 7 a Chinese major, who spoke fluent English, took the Britons to an office in which some civilians, waiting to meet them, were introduced as correspondents of the Korean *Labour Journal* and other Korean and Chinese newspapers. The journalists said they would like to interview the diplomats.

This was not the first attempt at extracting statements from them. At Man-po they had been visited by two British journalists, Alan Whittington, the corespondent of the London *Daily Worker* and Wilfred Burchett, once an able reporter with the *News Chronicle,* who became a Communist and represented the French Communist organ *L'Humanité* in Korea. The prisoners had learned from the *Daily Worker* of the death of King George VI in February 1952 and the accession to the throne of Princess Elizabeth. Mr. Burchett offered to forward messages to the prisoners' families, which he did, but they all refused to give interviews to their Communist compatriots.

This time the prisoners faced only Chinese and Korean journalists. Captain Holt told them: "As a representative of Her Britannic Majesty and a member of the Foreign Service, I am unable to express any opinions for publication without previous consultations with my government." He then added a few words, to the effect that he hoped there would soon be a fair and just peace.

The reporters turned to Blake: "Could you express any opinion about the murderous bombing by the Americans and the dropping of germ bombs?" Blake replied: "I have nothing to add to what the minister, Captain Holt, has just told you."

Later the Korean radio propagandists broadcast statements ascribed to Captain Holt, Commissioner Lord, and Mr. Deane which they had never made.

The next morning the brigadier read out a message from Comrade Pak Hen-Yen, the minister for foreign affairs of the Korean People's Republic. It stated that "following a request by the British government, transmitted to him by courtesy of the ambassador of the Union of Socialist Soviet Republics, the government of the Korean

People's Republic has ordered the release from internment of His Excellency, the British minister, Vyvyan Holt, Vice-Consul George Blake, legation official Norman Philip Owen, Bishop Alfred Cecil Cooper, Monsignor Thomas Quinlan, Mr. Herbert Lord of the Salvation Army, and Mr. Philip Deane."

The request from the British government was first made to Moscow on July 16, 1950, repeated several times, specifically on August 8, 1951, and in September 1952. It took the Korean Communists thirty-four months to grant it. They gave a rather curious reason for the long imprisonment of the British diplomats, namely that "they were kept under the protection of the North Korean government, until the barbarous American bombing should stop, so that the internees could travel safely to the frontier."

The same night the seven Britons were taken by car to the Manchurian frontier at Antung. The road they took to China runs alongside the main railway and they were able to see the heavy traffic on both. On the road alone they counted nearly a thousand heavily laden lorries heading south, with war supplies and food. Like the roads and railway lines south of Pyongyang these lines of communications to the Yalu and Manchuria had suffered astoundingly little damage from the American air raids so widely publicized in American newspapers and magazines.

At the frontier they were treated like tourists, but they had to give up all written material to the customs officers, though Philip Deane managed to retain his diary, written in Greek, which he kept throughout his imprisonment by concealing it on his body.

At Antung they were taken in American limousines to the best hotel in town. There were scented soap and soft towels in the bathroom and freshly laundered linen on the beds. In the hotel they were greeted by an amiable young Russian, who introduced himself as Pyotr Feodorovitch Vassiliev, second secretary of the Soviet embassy in Peking. He told them their release had been arranged by the Soviet government and that it was his "pleasant duty" to accompany them to Moscow, from where they would be flown to London.

The next stop was Peking, where they had hotel rooms with private bathrooms and a paneled private dining room in which soft-footed waiters served them ten-course meals. Comrade Vassiliev talked of music, ballet, literature, and sport and never introduced a word of politics into the conversation. They traveled from Peking in a brand-new express train and the large and luxuriously upholstered compartments were decorated with Picasso's doves of peace. At the Sino-Soviet frontier they were transferred into a comfortable sleeping car of the Soviet Trans-Siberian express.

It was a long but interesting journey across Siberia and Russia and, as Blake put it, they arrived in Moscow "overfed, rested, and comatose." In Moscow an R.A.F. Hastings, sent from West Berlin, was waiting for them at the airport.

On April 21, 1953, they landed at Gatow R.A.F. airfield near Berlin. A large group of officials, journalists, and photographers had assembled, headed by Major General C.F.C. Coleman, commander in chief British sector of Berlin, his deputy, many British officers, the British consul general, Mr. L. H. Whittal, and a number of German officials. As the Hastings taxied to the waiting group and came to a halt, a British military band struck up. General Coleman entered the aircraft before any of the ex-prisoners became visible. They were informed of the Foreign Office "request" not to talk to reporters or, at any rate, say anything that might have political implication.

After a brief rest in Berlin as guests of General Coleman and the British director of political affairs, Mr. Michael Rose, the seven repatriated men were flown to London. Here security measures were even more stringent than in Berlin, though the reception was no less regal. The aircraft was diverted to the R.A.F. airfield at Abingdon, Berkshire, apparently in the hope of keeping away newspaper reporters. This proved futile. A number of relatives of the returning ex-prisoners had been invited and journalists and photographers talked their way into the enclosure.

The Foreign Secretary, Mr. Anthony Eden (now Lord Avon), recuperating from his first serious operation, had sent Sir Evelyn Shuckburgh to represent him. Sir Evelyn was accompanied by several high Foreign Office officials, including Mr. R. H. Scott, head of the Far Eastern Department. The ambassador of the Republic of Ireland was waiting to greet Monsignor Quinlan, while Bishop Basil Roberts, representing the Archbishop of Canterbury, had come to honor Bishop Cooper. The most colorful group was a contingent of officers of the Salvation Army to welcome Commissioner Lord. They raised their crimson and gold banner and sang "Praise God from whom all blessings flow."

There were cheers and martial music as Captain Holt came down the gangway, followed by his companions, all gripped by deep emotions. They were soon engulfed by an excited crowd of relatives, friends, and reporters.

In the R.A.F. officers' mess refreshments were served and, after some serious conversation between the diplomats and the Foreign Office officials, newspapermen and photographers were allowed in. Scores of questions were fired at the ex-prisoners about their treatment by the Communists, whether they had been brainwashed, tortured, and beaten and whether the statements ascribed to them by Communist radio stations were true.

Captain Holt, Blake, and Owen had already been told in Berlin that Moscow Radio and other Communist stations had broadcast alleged statements including one by Captain Holt, in which he was supposed to have said: "I am deeply grateful to the North Korean government and people for the good, fair, and humane treatment we all enjoyed during our internment. I shall work after my return home to cement friendly relationships between Britain and North Korea. . . ." Commissioner Lord was supposed to have said: "I deprecate in strongest terms the massacre of Korean women and children by American bomber aircraft. . . ." Even stronger words were ascribed to Deane.

After paying tribute to Mr. Eden for his efforts to obtain their release and expressing thanks to the R.A.F.,

Captain Holt told the journalists: "What I said at Pyong-yang was that when I came home I would do my best within the narrow limits of my possibilities to try and help to bring about a fair and just peace. I did say this quite voluntarily. My colleagues, Mr. Blake and Mr. Owen, said nothing at all."

The arrival of the seven Communist ex-prisoners was, of course, reported in the British newspapers, but neither the homecoming nor the various statements designed to correct any impression as to the possible brainwashing results attracted much public attention. During the week the seven men had come home, the British public was far more interested in another event: at Bow Street Magistrate Court John Reginald Christie was revealing the gruesome details of how he had murdered his wife and several other women and hidden the corpses in his house.

The Korean war was still on. The armistice was not signed until July 27. Why the seven men were released months before any of the other United Nations prisoners remained one of the many mysteries of Communist tactics.

Captain Holt was knighted by the queen and after prolonged recuperation was appointed British envoy extraordinary and minister plenipotentiary to the South American republic of El Salvador. He retired from the Foreign Service in 1956 and, his health weakened by his captivity in Korea, he died in 1960, at the age of sixty-four.

At the Foreign Office George Blake was received as one who had upheld the highest traditions of the Foreign Service and, while all the ex-prisoners were questioned, there was never the slightest suspicion that they had failed to withstand the brainwashing techniques employed on them, least of all Blake. There was even some talk of an award, perhaps an O.B.E., but because of Blake's very special position this idea was dropped and, instead, he received a letter from the Foreign Secretary thanking him for his loyal service and expressing sympathy with his sufferings during his imprisonment.

Blake went to his mother at Reigate. To his considerable embarrassment he arrived to find a small crowd of applauding neighbors in front of the house and, as if the destinies presiding over real life were for once seeking to provide a neat and happy ending for the chapter which began with Major Choe's gesture at the Seoul legation, there was a large Union Jack hanging from the window.

Blake was granted sick leave in which to recover from the effects of pneumonia, dysentery, and avitaminosis. He spent most of his time resting, listening to records, and reading French and German books to brush up his command of these languages. The few people he had met in London between his service in Hamburg and his long absence in Korea were out of touch with him and he had hardly any social contacts.

CHAPTER TWELVE

LOVE AND MARRIAGE

When Blake started work again he was given neither rank nor official position. His name disappeared from the Foreign Service List in which he had previously been listed as a vice-consul. He had, of course, received his back payment of all the emoluments due during his years in prison. He was now thirty-one years old and, in the normal course of events, he would have been promoted to a rank equivalent to second secretary in the Foreign Service. But he was now a fullfledged secret agent, a "government official specially employed" of nondescript status.

For a time he lived with his mother in her flat in West London, but she later moved to the country and he took a furnished apartment. He had recovered from the debilitating effects of his imprisonment but he continued to lead a very quiet life. Occasionally he went swimming, and visited his mother and his married sister in Kent. During the following months he made several journeys abroad.

Sixteen years later, in his *Izvestya* interview, Blake stated that at that time he had been appointed deputy head of the "Technical Operations Section" of the Secret Intelligence Service whose agents' assignment was "to eavesdrop on representatives of the U.S.S.R. and other Socialist countries in various parts of the world." In Germany, Blake declared, the "initiator" of these operations was Mr. Peter Lunn, "a senior official of the Secret Intelligence Service," under whom he was later to work.* Such operations—telephone tapping and interception of diplomatic mail—were conducted on a large scale and, Blake sarcastically added, "the S.I.S. squandered on them vast resources."

Sometime later, Blake told in the *Izvestya* article, he became deputy head of the "Y-Section" concerned with obtaining material for the "N-Section," which evaluated information for the prime minister, the Foreign Secretary, and the Chiefs of Staff. In the course of his new duties, Blake alleged, he undertook many operations abroad. One such assignment was "Operation Contrary"—the placing of microphones in the office of the Polish Trade Mission in Brussels, and the wiring of rooms at the Astoria Hotel in Brussels, used by diplomats and trade representatives from Communist countries. "Operation Fantastic" was the placing of hidden microphones at the office of the Soviet commercial attaché in Copenhagen; it was so named, Blake derisively added, because it produced "fantastically useless results." Other operations of his section in which

* Blake apparently refers to Mr. Peter Northcote Lunn, C.M.G., O.B.E., son of Sir Arnold Lunn, the famous alpinist and winter sports pioneer, and himself a well-known ski champion who captained the British Olympic Games ski team in 1936. Mr. Lunn served as a second secretary at the British Control Commission, and later with the British High Commission in Vienna in 1948–50, and in West Germany in 1953–1962. More recently he held a diplomatic post at the British embassy in Beirut. British authorities refuted Blake's allegations.

Blake claims to have been involved included tapping of telephones of the Czechoslovak Export Agency in Cairo and wiring the residence of a second secretary of the Bulgarian embassy in London.

Even if one would accept these stories as true, one must conclude that at this stage of his career Blake had been involved in very minor actions. Indeed, one would expect him to tell taller stories than merely to disclose that the British secret service tapped the telephone of some minor Communist official. It may be that Blake is keeping some more juicy tales for the book he has promised to write.

The fact is that during his initial employment after his return from Korea, Blake was given only minor tasks. His statement that he held the position of a deputy chief of an important section is but one of the familiar overstatements he used to make to exaggerate his own importance.

He had now only a few personal acquaintances among his younger colleagues. He did not frequent bars or nightclubs, he did not like dancing, and he was the very antithesis of a deb's delight.

More surprisingly he seems to have taken care to avoid mixing in consciously "intellectual" company. He enjoyed good talk and he could acquit himself well in any circle, but there may have been the fear that his superiors would look askance at him if he mixed regularly with intellectuals, usually regarded as "left-wing" or "unreliable."

He did not take any deliberate steps, either, to cultivate a social life where he might have met women of his own age or younger. His Korean experiences had given him an authority and poise which at times verged on the solemn; a girl who was merely in search of an amusing boyfriend would probably have taken fright after the first date, although Blake was a handsome man with, I imagine, considerable power to attract women had he cared to exert it. Some of the less charitable people who knew him then were apt to speculate about his apparent disinterest in the opposite sex, but any suspicion that he was a deviate of any kind can be dismissed with complete confidence. Certainly, he seemed shy with women, but no more so than many young Englishmen, and a good deal less so than one might have expected in view of a life which had given him precious little opportunity for female companionship.

Although he did not make real efforts to make friends at his office, he did want to be liked, and it was obvious that he suffered by his self-imposed isolation. He complained that he could not sleep at night and that he missed the rest in the afternoons, having been used to dozing for many hours on a mattress during his last year of captivity in Korea. Although many of his colleagues, and particularly the female staff of secretaries and typists, felt sorry for him, knowing of the terrible hardships he had endured during his imprisonment, he was not a popular member. He had some strange habits, which caused his colleagues to raise their eyebrows. He wore shabby, crumpled clothes and he told them that he liked to walk barefoot in his leisure time, a habit he had acquired in Korea. Even at the office he sometimes took off his shoes and socks and picked his toes, which many found "extremely disgusting" and ascribed it to Blake's foreign origin.

It seems that his behavior at that period was a symptom of yet another bout of frustration. Convinced that he could tackle much more important and complex tasks than those assigned to him, he began to pester his superiors for an assignment abroad, preferably in Germany. But, at first, they were not in a hurry to do so. They decided he required a longer period of training and experience. Obviously, they were aware of his nervous tension, which they ascribed to the hardships of his long imprisonment, and they wanted to give him a chance to settle down. In one sense George Blake was very lucky to be back at work in the department.

As I have mentioned, the Foreign Office twice broke its own rules that employment should be confined "to natural-born British subjects, of parents similarly born," and Blake's return to duty was yet another occasion on which these rules were transgressed.

In retrospect this was all the more remarkable because his return to secret work not only signified the confidence

his superiors must have had in him but it was also in
marked contrast to the action the authorities were taking
elsewhere. While Blake had been in Korean prison camps,
Donald Maclean, head of the American Department of
the Foreign Office, had disappeared and gone over to the
Russians. The defection of Maclean and his friend, Guy
Burgess, to Moscow, the row it caused in the House of
Commons and the British press, not to mention the alarm
it aroused in Washington, all combined to provoke a fierce
"screening" of civil servants. A number of foreign-born officials were removed from their posts as a result.

Sir Winston Churchill announced on October 9, 1954,
that after two thousand civil servants had been interviewed, another seven thousand were to be "investigated
by special security procedure as to their reliability in employment on secret work." His successor, Sir Anthony
Eden (now Lord Avon), appointed on November 23,
1955, a Conference of Privy Councillors to examine "the
security procedures now applied in the public services and
to consider whether any further precautions are called for
and should be taken."

The White Paper, containing the recommendations of
the conference "insofar as it could properly be made public," did not appear until Blake had already taken up his
new and very secret assignment in Berlin, but it is worth
quoting as an indication of Whitehall's attitude at that
time. The privy councillors emphasized the importance of
"the relations between security risk and defects of character and conduct" and the need "for stringent security precautions notably in the Foreign Service and the defense
field." The report stated that "whereas once the main risk
to be guarded against was espionage by foreign powers
carried out by professional agents, today the chief risks are
presented by Communists and by other persons who for
one reason or another are subject to Communist influence." The privy councillors warned that "the Communist
faith overrides a man's normal loyalties to his country and
induces the belief that it is justifiable to hand over secret
information to the Communist party or to a Communist

foreign power. The risk from Communists is not confined to party members, either open or underground, but extends to sympathizers with communism."

They also said that it was "important to impress not only on heads of departments but on supervisory officers generally that it is their duty to know their staff and that they must not fail to report anything which affects security."

Obviously there was nothing adverse to report on George Blake's performance of his duties or his private life, before or after the privy councillors issued their recommendations. Anybody, indeed, with a special interest in his private life would have noted only one significant development, and that with approval.

At his office he had met a beautiful young girl, who had been sent from another section to work for him as a secretary. She was twenty-year-old Gillian Forsyth Allan who, after grammar school, a domestic-science college, and a year at a finishing school in Switzerland, had begun to work at the Foreign Office a few months before George's return from Korea. Her two-years-older sister also worked there. It was only natural that Gillian should be accepted for highly confidential work; her father, Colonel Arthur John William Allan, after distinguished service in the army, was the Foreign Office's Russian linguist.

Gillian was a slender, beautiful girl, very gentle and rather quiet, and she possessed great intelligence and an excellent education. When she began to work for George Blake, she must have found him restless and very tense. Much later she told of his nervous habit of twisting off his sleeve buttons when talking or dictating.

During the summer George had spent a two-week holiday in Spain with his mother and younger sister—his elder sister, Mrs. Elizabeth Wilson, was married to an ex-Royal Navy officer and lived in Kent—and on his return he told his colleagues that he did not particularly enjoy his visit to Spain because he did not like the Franco régime.

Having received his accumulated back pay, George Blake had plenty of spending money. But his habits were frugal. One day in the late summer, he asked his secretary to come with him to a theater. Soon they were going out regularly. Gillian's father, Colonel Allan, had met George at the office and one day invited him to the family home at "The Warren" in Weybridge, Surrey. Blake, the lonely young man, became a frequent visitor. Obviously, his visits were prompted by his desire to see more of the younger daughter of the house. But he was also befriended by the family, and he shared with Colonel Allan the interest in the Russian language and Russian people—though they did not share the opinion of the Soviet system, an opinion which Blake kept very much to himself.

I have been told by Blake's colleagues and relations that Gillian Allan was Blake's first and only love, and I am sure that this was so. However, he did not contemplate asking her to marry him. He certainly found it difficult to settle down. At times he could be jovial and full of good intentions and plans for the future. But this alternated with periods of depression which often lasted for days, when he remained almost silent and seemed to take little notice of Gillian. He told her that he could not see himself as a "respectable householder and family man," that he did not like to accept commitments, acquire possessions, and have domestic responsibilities. This desire of keeping his independence and—as he put it—"not to clutter up my life," was so strong that he did not even want to have a flat, or own furniture, or even a car or a record player.

They did, of course, discuss marriage, but George told Gillian that he had no right to marry. He was going through an intense training and he knew that he would be soon posted abroad, as a secret agent, with all the uncertainties and dangers this sort of job involved. Half in jest—but betraying some inferiority complexes—he pointed to his "peculiar habits," but Gillian laughed it off.

By the late summer of 1954, Blake was told that he would soon be sent to Berlin and attached to the Secret Intelligence Service station at the office of the British military commandant. At the same time Gillian had a chance of being posted as a secretary to a British embassy overseas.

One evening Gillian asked George Blake: "Shall we get married?" As she later told in a newspaper, George was surprised. He tried to put her off, though he told her that he loved her deeply. He said that she would find life with him very difficult, that he hated the idea of making her unhappy. Besides, there were some other factors, which had to be considered very seriously: he was "a foreigner," half-Jewish, who had spent only four years out of his thirty-two in Britain, and had obviously not been able to assimilate the English customs and way of life. Would her parents and family not resent this? Would they approve of Gillian's marriage with a stranger. Then, there was a question of money. Could he provide for a wife, for children, for a household in a manner Gillian had been accustomed to?

Gillian waved his doubts away. They talked it over with her parents, who had grown very fond of George and welcomed him as their future son-in-law, despite the doubts he himself had advanced. In September 1954, George Blake and Gillian Allan announced their engagement. If some of their Foreign Office colleagues were somewhat surprised, George's superiors were well satisfied. A secret agent in Berlin would be in many ways less vulnerable if married and looked after by an English wife.

His assignment was to come through almost immediately and the wedding was arranged in a hurry. George's room was at 5, All Souls Place, Great Portland Street, and the banns were called at the parish church of the district, St. Peter and St. Thomas, Marylebone. The wedding took place on September 23, officiated by the Reverend John Stott. An Anglican ceremony presented no difficulty in view of Blake's religious upbringing in his mother's faith, the Dutch Protestant Reform Church.

When George signed the marriage register, he described himself as a "government official (Foreign Office)," and gave the name of his father ("deceased") as "Albert William Blake." This was, of course, inaccurate. His fa-

ther's name had been Behar. George had adopted the
name of "Blake" only after his arrival in Britain, and so
later did his mother and sisters.

It was a white wedding, George donning a morning coat
for the first time in his life and obviously feeling extremely
uncomfortable. Having no close friend, he asked his
bride's brother to be his best man. While there were many
family members and friends of the Allans present, on the
bridegroom's side there was only his mother, his two sisters, and his brother-in-law, with Uncle Anthony Beijderwellen and his wife, who arrived from Holland. George
had also sent an invitation to Commander D. W. Child,
who was now managing director of a yacht holidays
agency in London. Many officials and secretaries from the
Foreign Office attended the reception and bade farewell to
the young couple who left for their honeymoon in the
South of France.

Blake's post in Berlin did not, after all, come as early as
it was expected and the newlyweds lived for a few months
with George's mother at her flat in Charleville Mansions,
Baron's Court, in West London.

Then, at the end of March and somewhat suddenly,
Blake was told that he would be sent to Berlin within two
weeks.

CHAPTER THIRTEEN

IN THE BERLIN CAULDRON

The exact date on which Blake was enlisted by Soviet
agents in London and agreed to work for the K.G.B. has
never been established. It is significant that after his arrest
on April 4, 1961—in the room of the chief of the Secret
Intelligence Service—the charges read to him at Bow

Street Police Station by Superintendent Louis Gale put the earliest date on which he was alleged to have "communicated information which may be directly or indirectly useful to an enemy," as April 14, 1955, the day after his arrival in West Berlin.

At his trial at the Old Bailey, however, several new points were added to the indictment, and the period relating to one of the charges was substantially advanced to as early a date as September 1, 1953, five months after his return from Korea. The reason for this was that only a day or two after his detention a black notebook found among Blake's belongings was carefully examined. It contained names, some in code, addresses, and telephone numbers. This notebook put officers of the security directorate on the trail of several of Blake's early Soviet contacts, including Ivan Skripov, a second secretary at the Soviet embassy, who arrived in London in 1952 and subsequently became Blake's first "controller." At the initial stage Blake shared Skripov with the Krogers (who had arrived in London in 1954 to prepare the ground for Lonsdale), but later was handed over to Nicolai Borisovich Korovin. This man, who came to London ostensibly as a senior counsellor of the Soviet embassy, was a high official of the K.G.B. For several years he directed not only Blake, but also members of the Portland Naval Spy Ring and, from 1956 on, the admiralty clerk William Vassall.

There is no doubt that it was on Korovin's orders that Blake applied for a position in Germany. Although he had worked for Korovin from the autumn of 1953 until the early spring of 1955 and betrayed operations of the Technical Department of S.I.S. during his initial employment there, his really valuable work for the K.G.B. began only after his arrival in Berlin. Korovin must have been impressed by Blake's skill and eagerness and confident that he could do much more important work in Germany. Blake needed no encouragement; he longed to escape the routine work and impatiently looked forward to an assignment, which meant promotion.

The news of his appointment to the S.I.S. station at

West Berlin's Olympia Stadium Buildings must have made Blake—and Korovin—exultant: it was a move that took him to a position of intense interest to the K.G.B.

The Berlin that George Blake came to know so well was the world's political hot spot. Sometimes it would slip from the headlines, but even in quiet periods the governments of the East and the West were sensitive to every happening in the divided and exposed capital of the Reich they had conquered.

On the surface both halves of Berlin, one prosperous, one shabby, might have seemed just overpopulated, bustling cities; but underneath, the witch's brew of intrigue, espionage, and propaganda was always boiling and bubbling away.

In June 1953 the cauldron was stirred into seething activity when the East German régime demanded increased productivity quotas from its subjects. The workers rebelled and fifty thousand people ran riot in the streets of East Berlin. Moscow, of course, blamed the unrest in its East German colony on "subversive agitation by agents of America and Britain." After Soviet tanks had quelled the uprising, stringent measures were introduced to control the population. They ultimately culminated in the sealing off of East Berlin by the invidious Wall. At first, however, nothing could prevent the sharp increase in the number of refugees crossing the border to West Berlin and freedom. Neither could the Communists stop the activities of a multitude of organizations, determined to continue anti-Communist propaganda and intelligence. The broadcasting stations of Radio Free Europe and R.I.A.S. worked overtime.

The Communists across the border retaliated with political threats and by sending more and more secret agents into West Berlin and by ensnaring West German officials. In scores of clubs, coffeehouses and night dives of every description the buying and selling of "secret information" developed into a way of living for hundreds of free-lance "agents." They were nicknamed the *Hundert Mark Jungen* (hundred-mark boys) who were offering to lay bare the innermost workings of the Kremlin, Whitehall, or the Pentagon for the price of a good dinner.

Neutral observers estimated that, in 1955, there were at least seven thousand spies and informers earning a dishonest living in Berlin. The trade had gone from strength to strength. In the winter of 1961, at the height of the Berlin Wall crisis, a Swedish diplomat thought that over twelve thousand spies of many countries were in full- or part-time employment there.

A favorite meeting place for agents was the large Café Warsaw in East Berlin. When I knew it best in 1955—at the time of George Blake's arrival—it had developed into a sort of stock exchange for secrets, with half the tables taken up by Soviet, Czech, Polish, British, American, French, and East and West German agents. The going rate for a scrap of negotiable information could fall as low as five pounds. A few dollars were enough to make many of the boys change sides between cups of coffee.

Spies of many nations operated—and still do—from re-seemingly genuine public-relations services and economic seemingly genuine public-relations services, and economic consultants are making nice profits out of the business of espionage. Sometimes the operators combine their spying activities for either side with genuine commercial activities on behalf of East-West trade relations.

The drugging and kidnapping in July 1954 of Dr. Otto John, head of the West German Security Office, and his reappearance and trial in 1956, caused a worldwide sensation, but has never been satisfactorily explained. Dr. John worked for both the British and Dr. Adenauer's secret services. In 1956 he was sentenced in Bonn to four years and, after his release he has been fighting to clear himself of treason charges. In a book published in 1969, John stated: "I was kidnapped because the Russians believed I was the key figure who could satisfy them whether or not some of their Western informers—such as Philby and Blake—were genuine Communists or double agents of the British Secret Intelligence Service."

While Dr. John's case was to gain a very special significance, kidnappings and disappearances as such were almost commonplace in Berlin. Many Germans, White Russians, Ukrainians, and other Eastern nationals, who worked against the Communists, and indeed many quite innocent people, were abducted by Soviet and East German agents and most of them disappeared without a trace.

Blake himself was to be involved in some of such kidnappings.

This then was the climate of West Berlin when he and his wife arrived there in April 1955. They were allocated a five-room flat on the fourth floor of a large, modern block of flats at 26, Platanen Allee in Charlottenburg, Berlin's select residential West End. Situated between the park of Grunewald and the seventeenth-century castle housing the mausoleums of the Hohenzollern kings and emperors, it is the most pleasant district of Berlin. The building at Platanen Allee had been taken over by the British authorities for their officers and officials. Only British, or British-sponsored tenants lived there.

The flat, like all the others, had been furnished rather sparsely by the British authorities. Nearly all the other British residents at Platanen Allee had made their married quarters more comfortable by buying some of their own furniture, carpets, curtains, and ornaments. When Gillian suggested that they, too, should make some improvements, George protested, declaring that he did not want to own any property and remarking that, after all, they did not know how long they would stay in Berlin.

Neither did he or his wife take part in the social life of the British colony in West Berlin. They rarely accepted invitations to the numerous cocktail parties and after-dinner coffee gatherings held by British officers and officials, British newspaper correspondents, and visiting businessmen.

A British officer who lived next door to the Blakes for two years told me that he hardly knew them. His acquaintance with his neighbors was limited to passing the time of the day when he met them in the elevator or on the staircase, although he made several attempts to get to know them better because he thought them charming young people.

Luxuries which Blake and his wife did permit themselves were occasional visits to the theater and, more frequently, to concerts. Gillian only knew a little German, while George was fluent in that language and greatly attracted by German *avant-garde* plays. They both shared a love of music. Once or twice a week George took his wife out to dine in one of the smart restaurants. He was particularly fond of French cuisine and developed a taste for wine, although he very rarely drank hard liquor. One of their haunts was the *Maison de France,* in the French sector, which provided excellent French food and where there was dancing at night. George was not a good dancer, but he tried to please his wife, Gillian later recalled that her husband was often absent for days, and would also go out in the evening and return next morning. He explained to her that he had to meet his contacts and, at times, to spend a night away from home in order to make sure that he was not followed when visiting another British agent. Even on Sundays he would sometimes go out alone, saying he liked to "absorb" the place and to get to know Berlin well.

Only much later, after the trial, Gillian Blake must have realized that at least on some of such occasions her husband had been in the Soviet zone, or was meeting his Communist masters at a "safe house." She knew, of course, that he was engaged in secret work, but they agreed never to discuss it. He always referred to the British secret service as "The Firm," and sometimes he told her that "The Firm" was pleased with his work and that he had received a commendation. "In the sort of work he was doing, one is bound to lead more than one life," she stated after his trial. "One has to take on different names and different personalities for different sorts of work, according to whom you are contacting. The whole life is a matter of aliases and shams and deceits. I knew some of his aliases, like 'Max de Vries' (which was the old cover name he had used during his Resistance days in the war). But George didn't go into details, although occasionally he did talk to me about people he met. . . ."

Poor Gillian trusted her husband. She thought that he was devotedly serving her country. She never knew until his arrest that all the time he betrayed secret information to the Russians.

Blake showed his wife every consideration. To compensate her for his frequent absences he sometimes suggested that they should have a night out in the West End. When she remarked that this was rather extravagant, George told her they could afford it and there was no need to be stingy. "I always got plenty of housekeeping money," she recalled, "I'm not very organized about money, and George wasn't either. He was not careless, but he never got down to working out exact budgets." So they went to the Ritz, where they served Oriental dishes, to Kottler's, which was a typical old-German beer house where one got gargantuan helpings, or to Kempinski, where they would sit outside in the pavement café on a mild night.

Blake was not doing much exercise and put on weight. His wife teased him about his middle-aged spread and insisted that he should learn to play tennis and take up riding, but the only sport he was keen on was swimming.

The Blakes did not join the various clubs open to British officers and their families. But he took advantage of the excellent swimming pool at the Olympia Stadium next to his office. He also joined the British Equitation Club and went riding, sometimes together with his wife. His salary, augmented by a special foreign allowance, was sufficient to allow him and his wife a carefree life, particularly as he spent little on clothes or entertaining.

During the late summer of 1955 the Blakes spent a short holiday in Italy at Lake Garda. They went there in the secondhand Ford which Blake had bought, after much prodding by Gillian, from a fellow official who was returning home. In winter they went to Austria, and Gillian introduced him to skiing, which she had learned at finishing school in Switzerland, and they spent two happy weeks at St. Anton on Arlberg.

Blake's official position was that of "a Foreign Office official attached to the Political Department of the G.O.C. British sector Berlin." The commandant was Major General R. C. Cottrell Hill, who had been only recently appointed to this post, after having spent three years in Malaya and two as director of military training at the War Office. It was explained to Blake that he would have nothing to do with the military establishment, but that his superior would be the head of station of the Secret Intelligence Service who, in turn, was subordinated to Mr. Edward Heywood Peck, a Foreign Office counselor and deputy to the commandant as his political adviser.*

In Germany, things had radically changed since Blake had returned from his first assignment in 1948. The German Federal Republic had been established, and since 1954 West Germany had regained full sovereignty. The Allied high commissioners of Great Britain, the United States, and France had become ambassadors to the new German government of Dr. Adenauer in Bonn. At the time of Blake's appointment the British ambassador was Sir Frederick Hoyer-Millar (now Lord Inchyra), who afterwards was permanent under secretary of state at the Foreign Office until 1961.

In the realm of intelligence work, the British secret service was only a junior partner to the mighty organization which the American Central Intelligence Agency (C.I.A.) had established in West Germany in conjunction with General Reinhard Gehlen.

This German officer has proved himself over the past thirty years one of the great spy masters of all times, and has been compared to Cromwell's John Thurloe and Napoleon's Joseph Fouché. Like them, he had changed his allegiance from one political extreme to another, being motivated only by his fanatical hatred of communism.

* Knight in 1966, Sir Edward Peck was from 1961 to 1966 an assistant under secretary at the Foreign Office, later British high commissioner in Kenya, and since 1968 had been a deputy under secretary of state at the Foreign Office.

Serving in the Intelligence Department of the small army of the Weimar Republic since the late 1920s, he gained rapid promotion after the Nazis came to power and rose during the war to become the chief of Hitler's intelligence office at the high command headquarters. Although his department was supposedly restricted to the evaluation of intelligence reports submitted to the führer by the *Abwehr* (Military Ingelligence), he soon superseded all other secret service agencies and conducted all espionage, sabotage, and subversive activities, as well as psychological warfare, against the Soviet Union and throughout Eastern Europe. His activities covered the vast embattled area from the Baltic to Vladivostok and from the Arctic to the Mediterranean. Again and again he outwitted Soviet espionage, succeeded in "turning round" many captured Soviet officers, and sent them back as his agents. Among his almost legendary exploits during the war was the successful infiltration of agents into Stalin's war council in 1942. Other of Gehlen's agents penetrated the headquarters of Marshal Zhukov and the Leningrad command. Many of the initial German victories in Russia were justifiably put to Gehlen's credit; and Hitler showered honors upon him.

In March 1945 Gehlen paid his last respects to the Führer in the underground bunker in Berlin and departed for his headquarters at Zossen. There he had urgent discussions with some of his trusted aides about what should be done before the Red tide engulfed the fatherland.

All of them knew that capture by the Red Army would mean torture and death. All their actions were now based on the premise that the West and the Communists would soon be hostile, even if they did not go for each other's throats as soon as they had shaken hands across the prostrate body of Germany. In this these German officers were more foreseeing than many Western politicians.

Gehlen had accumulated vast archives on the military strength of the Soviet Union, her economic potentials, manpower, raw material resources, and her secret industrial centers established during the war. He had uniquely detailed dossiers on all Soviet leaders and military commanders, and above all on the complex and worldwide espionage machine. He was certain that he and the Western world would need them again. Tens of thousands of microfilm reels were packed into steel canisters, and Gehlen with a group of his officers, disguised as refugees, took them to Bavaria. The archives were buried near a lonely farm on an almost inaccessible mountain peak. There the men watched the advance tank units of the U.S. Seventh Army race through the valley below. When Gehlen and his friends gave themselves up to the Americans, however, they were at first met with total and infuriating indifference, being treated as ordinary prisoners of war.

Gehlen had a difficult time persuading some of the brusque young American officers of his importance but when, at last, he managed to talk himself into the presence of Brigadier General Rush Patterson, chief of U.S. Seventh Army Intelligence, the nature of the treasure he could bestow on the Western Allies was quickly appreciated. He was taken to General Eisenhower, and thereafter flown in great secrecy to Washington where he met men who also had a shrewd idea of the Stalinist danger ahead: General "Wild Bill" Donovan, head of O.S.S., General Bedell Smith, and Allen Welsh Dulles, who were building up the new Central Intelligence Agency. A deal was clinched and, in effect, the Americans gave Gehlen back his organization he had created for Hitler. He returned to Germany to set up the "Bureau Gehlen," financed by the Americans to a tune of $20 million per year, to conduct espionage against the Soviet Union and the emerging Communist satellite countries in the East, as well as to combat Soviet espionage not only in West Germany but throughout Europe.

He reassembled his own skilled staff and recruited many former *Abwehr* and Gestapo officers and members of the S.S. security service—including a number of wanted war criminals, who assumed new identities. Soon they were working at full pressure. At Pullach in Bavaria the "Gehlen Bureau" was housed in a complex of buildings and underground vaults stretching over thirty-six acres and

hidden from the outside world by tall stone walls and elec-
trified wire fences, and guarded by watchtowers, electronic
devices, and patrols of dog handlers. Within less than two
years after the war Gehlen's staff at Pullach, in a dozen
West German cities, and particularly in West Berlin grew
to over four thousand. Hundreds of agents and informers
were infiltrated into the Soviet zone and into the Soviet
Union itself—many were dropped by parachute—and into
Poland, Czechoslovakia, and the Balkans.

Not surprisingly Gehlen soon became the most feared
and hated man on the other side of the Iron Curtain. In
1952 Stalin's espionage boss, Beria, offered a reward of
$100,000 for Gehlen's assassination. Gehlen hardly ever
appeared in public and was known as the "Shadow General" and "The Man of a Thousand Mysteries."

In 1954, after the German Federal Republic became
fully sovereign, the Americans made an agreement with
Dr. Adenauer by which the "Bureau Gehlen" was transferred to the German government and became the
Bundes-Nachrichtendienst—the Federal German Intelligence Service. Adenauer now referred to Gehlen as "my
beloved general." Until his retirement in 1968 Gehlen was
the supreme chief of all German espionage, counterespionage, and Security Department, all the time closely collab-
orating with the American C.I.A., his original sponsors and
financers.

Like Adenauer, Gehlen had little love for the British. In
any case, he was deeply indebted to the Americans and,
although basic information was at times exchanged between his office and the British Military Intelligence H.Q.s
at Wahnerheide and the Secret Intelligence Service station
at the Olympia Stadium Buildings in West Berlin, the
British were usually left out in the cold.

Thus, Blake was given the task to organize a group of
agents and informers through whom information from the
Soviet orbit, and particularly about the activities of the Soviet espionage based in East Germany, could be obtained.
He seemed to apply himself to this task with great devotion and skill. His superiors realized that it was an uphill

task; neither he nor they could ever match Gehlen's mighty machine. But not in their wildest nightmares did Blake's chiefs at Olympia Stadium ever dream that he was already all set to betray every instruction they gave him, every piece of information he gathered, and every document he saw to the Societ espionage he was supposd to be fighting.

One day, in the autumn of 1955, after his return from his holiday in Italy, Blake approached his station chief with a suggestion which, however strange it might have sounded to the uninitiated, was an accepted method of espionage. He told them that—through one of his informers whom he suspected the Russians had "planted" on him, and whom he treated with utmost caution—he probably could establish a direct personal contact with the K.G.B. chiefs at Karlshorst. He would, of course, have to pose as a secret defector, pretending to be prepared to work for the Communists behind the back of his British chiefs. He would have to procure some seemingly valuable material to gain the Russians' trust. There is no doubt that he acted on orders, if not yet from the Soviet H.Q.s at Karlshorst, from his London "controller" Korovin. Such orders could have been conveyed to him through a "cut-out" agent, perhaps during his holiday in Italy, or on one of his brief visits to London he had undertaken on official business.

In 1970, nine years after his trial and four years after his escape, when he reappeared in public in Moscow and unloaded his allegations against the British Secret Ingelligence Service, naming several of his former chiefs, British secret service officials would not dispute in private—although they would not admit it in public—that George Blake became a double agent with the knowledge and connivance of his superiors in West Berlin.

The use of double agents is as old as spying and it is always a sordid and dangerous performance. A double agent is a person who, with the encouragement of his own side, pretends to betray his country to the enemy. He does this by handing over information, some fake, some genuine.

In this way he aims at winning the confidence of the enemy. If he succeeds, he can mislead the adversaries by planting impressive but false information on them and, at the same time, he can extract some of their secrets. The double agent can gradually burrow his way into the enemy's organization until he is accepted as a part of it. From this vantage point he can find out how it is organized, what it is trying to do, and who is working for it.

If a British secret agent, known as such to the Soviet secret service, approaches its chiefs and offers his services as a double agent, pretending either that he has become a Communist convert, or that he is doing it for money, the Soviet spy masters will accept him, but they will treat him with utmost caution.

This is a tremendous snag and makes the planting of a double agent in the opponent's organization extremely difficult. The Soviet spy masters will examine everything he supplies with greatest care and suspicion and, to test him, they will soon begin to press him for more and more secrets. When the enemy is as competent and tough as the Soviet secret service, the pressure will become intense, perhaps unbearable. The Russians never trust mercenary or reluctant traitors. In some cases, genuine converts to communism, who offered to work for Moscow but later became hesitant or repented, were discreetly denounced to the security organization of their own country. I know of at least two British traitors who were unmasked by M.I.5 by the courtesy of the Soviet secret service who dropped and denounced them.

To convince Communist spy masters and to succeed in bringing back to one's own side material of real value, the double agent in the service of the West would have to give away genuine secrets and he would have to pose as a sincere convert.

Examples of double agents becoming triple agents—men who penetrate the enemy organization and are then forced to rat on their original masters—are many in the history of espionage. The battle of wits between Western and

Communist secret services has, by its nature, produced the biggest-ever crop of such triple agents, on both sides.

But all this did not, of course, apply to Blake, as far as the Russians were concerned. He had already sufficiently proved his loyalty to the Communist cause to deserve their trust, even though they would treat him with caution, probing every one of his moves and actions for a long time, before being completely convinced of his genuineness. Had Blake ratted on his Soviet masters, he would have been quietly "liquidated." When his betrayal was discovered by the British, he was sent to prison for forty-two years, which was another kind of liquidation.

Thus it was that George Blake went into what his superiors at Olympia Stadium Buildings regarded as the lion's den at Karlshorst. He had, of course, to observe every precaution and make his first meetings with K.G.B. officers took as clandestine as possible. Had he contacted them without much ceremony as friends, British security officers, whom he expected to watch him, would have immediately discovered the ruse and his game would have been up. He told his British superiors that he would arrange secret "treffs" (meetings) with Soviet emissaries and use "cutout" men. His Soviet masters must have been broadly smiling about Blake's clever scheme.

His meetings with Major Grigory Stolov, Boris Jakovlevich Nalivaiko (who was one of the Soviet "advisers" to the newly established East German Ministry of State Security), Lieutenant Colonel Ivan Malinovski, and eventually with the chief of the K.G.B. Karlshorst H.Q.s, Major General Nicolai Kaverntzev, offered no particular difficulties, neither did the communication and exchange of information during the next four years of Blake's conspiracy. This was, at least, partly due to the peculiar conditions which at that time prevailed in the divided city.

In the mid-fifties food and household articles were in short supply throughout the Communist-ruled "Democratic Republic" of East Germany. But the Communists in East Berlin strove frantically to compete with the increasingly glamorous display of affluence this side of the Brandenburger Tor. West Berlin had by then many large departmental stores and shops, well stocked with goods not only from Western Germany, which was developing a prosperous economy, but also from America, Britain, France, and Italy.

In the Eastern sector of Berlin the rate of exchange was five East marks for one deutsche mark. This meant that the goods available in the Communist sector were very much cheaper for West Berliners. The "Wall" had not yet been erected and people could move fairly freely from the British, American, and French sectors into East Berlin and return home without difficulty. Thousands of West Berliners made daily shopping expeditions across the border, despite appeals to the contrary by West Berlin's city authorities and the Chamber of Commerce, who pointed out that it was wrong to spend good money in Communist stores.

In deference to these appeals, the British military commandant ordered all officers and other ranks and all officials under his jurisdiction to refrain from shopping in East Berlin, except for vegetables and flowers, which came from the farms in Brandenburg in the Communist zone. A few other articles, exempt from the British commandant's shopping ban, were books, newspapers, phonographs, records, and sheet music. This was to prove that the British were no more afraid of Communist culture and propaganda than they were of Communist greengrocery.

Anyway, the regulations concerning all the other goods were honored more in the breach than the observance. Most British wives traveled regularly either by car or on the elevated railway to East Berlin, and returned laden with bargains of every kind. Blake discouraged his wife to do this, but two or three times a month he would go to East Berlin. He could reach the huge store known as "KO," the *Kaufhaus des Ostens*, in a few minutes. This institution was the shop window for Communist prosperity. It had been established by the East German government in an attempt to prove that consumer goods were not the sole prerogative of neon-lit, capitalist West Berlin.

There was no need for Blake to explain his behavior to either of his employers. The British might have been a little worried that if he acted too openly the Russians might smell the rat and suspect him of being a stool pigeon. The Russians knew, of course, that he acted as a double agent on their behalf, and hoped only that the British would not discover it. Therefore, Blake embarked on a prolonged charade, the real purpose of which was to bamboozle the British.

Soviet espionage methods embody elaborate rules, designed to avoid personal contact between agents when information is being passed. Operators use a *yafka*, which is a hideout belonging to a "cutout," a person never engaged himself in espionage; or more simply they arrange for a *dybok*, a hiding place, or "letterbox," where microfilms and documents can be left for collection by a seemingly harmless messenger.

Any assistant in the vast KO emporium could have been a "cutout," and any shopping list which Blake handed over the counter could have contained a brief, coded message. A coat or a book, left in a cloakroom, could easily have contained enough information on microdot films to fill a shelf of files when enlarged. The coat or the book could have been collected hours, even days, later when the cloakroom ticket had been forwarded to a secret address.

In this way it would not have been necessary for Blake to meet any of his Soviet masters. His statement to British security officers after his arrest that he did not know the K.G.B. chiefs could be accepted as true, though it was not. All he needed to know was the correct place to leave the information or to collect such "valuable" material from the Russians as he pretended to obtain from them in exchange. He could tell the British that he got instructions concerning changes in a *yafka* or a *dybok* delivered to him under the impersonal system, which is used by intelligence agents all over the world.

Blake never made any secret of his excursions to East Berlin. He would return with his purchases piled in the back of his car, each parcel wrapped in the red-and-white-striped paper of the store, decorated with little red stars and the initials "KO." Sometimes he showed his bargains to colleagues, commenting: "The Communists are doing some dumping. These things are even cheaper than the stuff we can buy at the NAAFI store. . . ."

At the Olympia Stadium Buildings the duped British officials were rubbing their hands. They were busily producing fake, but impressive-looking, "documents" and fabricated "information," which Blake took to "those stupid Russians." In their innocence they never doubted that, through Blake, they had got the upper hand over the K.G.B. In their eyes Blake had become a highly successful double agent. He brought back to the Olympia Stadium Buildings what his superiors believed to be valuable information. By catching several Communist spies he continued to put up a convincing performance.

That his "catches" were parts of the conspiracy, his British chiefs never discovered. In order to enable him to work undisturbed and unsuspected, General Karverntzev and his assistants were prepared to sacrifice a few of their minor German informers in West Berlin. Thus they protected and enhanced Blake's reputation.

The loss of expendable German agents, most of them mercenaries anyway, was a cheap price for the Russians to pay for the services they were getting from a senior agent of the British secret service placed in such an important position that he could deliver material of first-class value. They were, of course, never mystified by the fake information, which the British officials prepared for them with so much trouble. Blake would have pointed out to them every single one of the fabricated documents, and the papers and microfilms would end in the wastepaper baskets, or rather in the incinerators at Karlshorst, without attracting as much as an amused glance.

CHAPTER FOURTEEN

WORKING FOR BOTH SIDES

Blake's duties with the Secret Intelligence Service included not only active intelligence work, that is the gathering of information, but also watching Communist spies, aimed at defeating the other side's plots and ploys. To begin with he was concerned with finding out if any Germans employed by the British were also working for the Russians. Another double agent, less adept than he, could have turned out extremely dangerous and put his own work, and indeed his future, in jeopardy.

He tried, therefore, to impress on his British superiors that he should be given sole control over all German informers and agents. He succeeded in this to a very large degree. He was in command of a large network of British agents in East Germany and Czechoslovakia. The K.G.B. was regularly informed of their whereabouts and activities. They had to be left at large lest suspicion fall on Blake had they been arrested in too quick a succession. But those who proved themselves too efficient and produced really harmful information were disposed of. Arrests of such British agents were accepted at the Olympia Stadium Buildings as a calculated risk.

I have a long list of agents Blake had betrayed between 1955 and 1959, but in deference to the regulations of the Official Secrets Act, I shall mention only a few, whose names became known through "show trials" in East Germany.

In 1955 Hans Joachim Koch, a then forty-three-year-old radio operator, was arrested when emptying a "dead-letter box" in Pankow Park, which Blake had arranged and of which he gave information to the K.G.B. Koch, a wartime sergeant in the S.S. division Prince Eugen, served the "Bureau Gehlen" and later the British since 1951 and rendered good services during the East Berlin uprising in 1953. He became too efficient for the K.G.B.'s liking and had to be disposed of. He was sentenced to death and executed.

At about the same time Johann Baumgart, an official of the East German railways, who had produced twenty-five remarkable reports about railway transports, was given away by Blake and sentenced to fifteen years' imprisonment. Ewald Jantke, a former Luftwaffe radio operator, and Arno Gugel, son of a Gestapo official, who with a young woman named Ursula Lehmann had formed a successful "cell" in East Germany, were betrayed when Jantke became too cocky and joined the East German People's Police. It is characteristic of Blake's attitude to women that he saved Ursula. While Jantke was sentenced in 1956 to fifteen years and Gugel to ten, Blake arranged for Ursula's escape to West Berlin, either with or without approval of his K.G.B. masters.

Blake was instrumental in "burning" an outpost established in Dresden, which kept in contact with the secret service in West Berlin by exchanging stamps for collectors. Its leader, Helmuth Weisenfeld, posed as a philatelic dealer and sent and received stamp collections to a cover address in West Berlin. An elaborate system had been established by which either single stamps or complete sets of new Soviet and East German postage issues were marked with microdots.

As long as the Russians and the East German Ministry of State Security could intercept the mail and decode the messages, everything went on unmolested. But when the code was changed, and Blake was unable to supply the key, Weisenfeld's fate was sealed.

Among other victims were Arnold Kieser, an engineer in Berlin-Koepenick, who communicated with his married daughter, Hannelore Frühwald in West Berlin. She was unaware that her father's letters contained coded messages when she was instructed to pass them on. In 1958 Kieser was arrested and sentenced to lifelong imprisonment. Once again, Blake protected the woman.

This list could be continued almost interminably. Blake efficiently delivered Western agents to the Russians without ever being suspected of the betrayals. He had, of course, to prove to his British superiors all the time his ability to discover and catch some of the Soviet agents in West Berlin, and he discharged this duty, at times, in an almost farcical manner.

One of such cases was that of an attractive brunette, Fräulein Ursula Schmidt, aged twenty-nine. She worked as a typist at a R.A.F. base and supplemented her earnings with a retainer of 1200 marks (about £105) a month from the Russians. She gave them secret documents about the equipment in British and American fighter-bombers. She and her two German helpers were treated surprisingly leniently. They all got sentences of under five years. On another occasion Blake "discovered" that the top secret list of telephone numbers and extensions of the offices of the British military commandant at the Olympia Stadium Buildings had got into the hands of the Soviet agents. It must have been with a wry smile that Blake noticed that his own "secret" number—Berlin 941–109—was included.

George Blake's life in Berlin was regulated by his long working hours, like that of any conscientious civil servant. He commuted between his flat in Charlottenburg and his office at the Olympia Stadium Buildings in his official Volkswagen car. Usually he went home for lunch, probably to be with his wife, because he often stayed out late at night. To his wife he remained considerate and affectionate. He carefully kept his home life separate from his sordid involvements.

His wife later recalled: "George's office was less than five minutes away by car. But I never went to his office and we never met at the stadium. I myself went quite a lot to the stadium, where there was a laundry for the British families, cleaners, a tailor, and duty-free shops."

Once in 1956, the Blakes gave a big party. This was af-

ter the christening of their first child, a boy born at the
British Military Hospital at Spandau. Gillian insisted that
the child should be baptized in London, and Blake readily
agreed. He drove his wife and child to the Hook of Holland and they sailed to Harwich. The boy was christened in
the fashionable church of St. Michael's, Chester Square.
He was named Anthony after Blake's Uncle Beijderwellen,
who was the godfather. When they returned to Berlin,
Blake and his wife invited some of the British officials and
officers from the stadium.

After Anthony was born, Blake was touchingly concerned about his wife's well-being. He asked his mother to
come to Berlin. She stayed for a few weeks to help her
daughter-in-law, although Gillian had a reliable German
maid to look after the rough domestic work. Neighbors noticed that Blake was helping his wife, washing up in the
kitchen, and doing the shopping.

One day Blake was told by one of his superiors at the
Olympia Stadium Buildings that a most useful informer
was available to work as his chief assistant. The British official seemed to be particularly impressed with this man
because he had previously worked for General Reinhard
Gehlen. But Blake was warned not to disclose his identity
to this man and not to receive him at the office or at his
home at Platanen Allee.

The informer was Horst Eitner, code-named "Micky,"
and he was destined to play the role of Nemesis in Blake's
life. Eitner's name was not mentioned at Blake's trial—at
least not during the public hearing—and the British public
only learned of his existence and his connection with the
Blake case when in December 1961—seven months after
Blake had been sent to prison for three years. He was described in German newspapers as the spy who had worked
with Blake and had been sentenced for betraying secrets to
the Russians.

In fact, Eitner was one of the most important if shadowy
actors in the Blake drama.

When the war ended, Horst Eitner was a lance corporal
in the *Feldpolizei*, the military police. Like millions of

German soldiers Eitner came out of an Allied P.O.W. camp to find himself jobless and homeless. Being bright, energetic, and anxious to eat, he plunged into the black market. Later, after trying his hand on many jobs, he turned to a more uplifting way of life: he got a job as a book canvasser.

He pursued this wearing occupation not one day longer when he heard from a wartime comrade that General Reinhard Gehlen was back in the intelligence business and was taking on operators by the hundred. He was taken on by Gehlen, received a thorough training at one of Gehlen's spy schools at Worishofen, and soon proved himself an efficient operator. One of his first successful spy catches was the case of a former U.S. Intelligence officer Michael R. Rothkrug, of Westport, Connecticut, who had set up as a businessman in Berlin, but was in fact earning his living as a secret agent for the Russians. Rothkrug was arrested, tried, and convicted.

Eitner capped his success by helping to trap a glamorous cabaret dancer, Maria Knuth, and her boyfriend, Police Chief Inspector Hermann Westbold. She was helping him augment his salary by forty-five pounds a week from the Russians with the information she extracted from American officers in her cozy apartment in Cologne.

Eitner's status as a spy rose steadily until he was one of Gehlen's chief operators, with a fair degree of freedom to act in the American zones of Germany and Austria. In Vienna he exposed two former U.S. Army officers, who were working for the Soviet spy center at Baden. Naturally Eitner did not have things all his own way and his stock fell a little when one of his quarries, Walter Laube, apparently an important K.G.B. agent, escaped.

One day he seems to have overstepped even the widely spaced limits laid down by his patient boss and Gehlen fired him.

Eitner was again out of a job and very nearly broke. He could have gone to the Russians who would probably have received him with open arms, but he knew that they were hard and pitiless taskmasters compared with the Americans, which left him with the British. They were not so openhanded, as the Americans, but they did pay reasonably if one provided the goods. So, Eitner decided to pay a visit at the elegant building of the former gambling casino at Bad Oeynhausen not far from Hanover, the H.Q. of British Intelligence in Western Germany.

British secret service chiefs in Germany knew Eitner by reputation. For one thing the American Intelligence had informed them of the details of the Knuth-Westbold case. These details included the fact that copies of secret documents relating to the disposition of B.A.O.R. had been found in the cabaret girl's apartment. Horst Eitner got a job from them but he had to take a big cut in wages; the British basic rate for the job then was only twenty-seven pounds a week.

After initial briefing Eitner was told to go to Berlin, where he would be mainly employed on active intelligence. This was in 1955 and by then the British were more interested in Berlin rather than in trailing minor German spies in West Germany.

The fatal partnership of Blake and Eitner was about to begin. Blake, when he first met him, told him he was a Dutchman, working for the British, and that his name was "Max de Vries." A remarkable friendship grew between the two men who were by temperament and background the exact opposite of each other.

Horst Eitner, of the same age as Blake, was the son of a German artisan, had spent his boyhood in the Hitler Youth, and had a very sketchy education. He was a boisterous hail-fellow-well-met. He relished telling risqué stories and he drank expensive wine and champagne because it was expensive, when he really preferred beer. Blake was fascinated by his vulgarity and, I think, he might have envied Eitner his uncomplicated "philosophy" of life.

Eitner used to have many girl friends and liked to boast about his virile exploits. But, eventually, he fell seriously in love with a pretty, twenty-five-year-old Polish brunette, called Brigitte, who had spent several years in a Russian labor camp before becoming a "displaced person." Eitner married her and became quite a family man, living in a smart flat in Wieland Strasse in Charlottenburg, only a few hundred yards from Blake's home. He was then paid about forty pounds a week by the British. Their first child, a girl, was born soon after Blake's arrival. She had a misformed hip which remained for many months in plaster. Eitner and Brigitte fretted badly about the baby and Blake often brought little presents for Brigitte to cheer her up.

In order that Eitner should remain unaware of the proximity of his new partner's address, Blake rented a furnished room not far from the Eitner's place, under his *nom de guerre* of Max de Vries. He slept there occasionally, particularly when, late at night, he failed to shake Eitner off.

In 1962 when Horst was in prison I went to see his wife in Berlin. She described Max de Vries to me as "a charming man and very good company; he loved to joke and tell stories about his time in the British navy in which, he told us, he had served as an officer during the war. . . ."

She said: "But Max could be moody too, you know. One minute he was gay and laughing and suddenly he would turn very serious and dry up. He told me he was a bachelor and a 'bit of a monk,' not interested in girls. I once suggested that I would introduce him to one of my girl friends, but he refused to make a date with her. I never knew then, of course, that he was married. He had a small room nearby, I believe it was somewhere near the Zoological Garden. Sometimes he would collect my husband and they went to his digs. My husband always complained Max was walking so quickly that he had difficulty in keeping up with him. But, of course, Max was quite an athletic type, he did not smoke and drank very little. Quite unlike my Horst, who loved his drink. . . .

"No, I knew nothing about their business. I had an inkling that it had something to do with politics. . . . I knew Horst had been in the intelligence business before we married, but I did not know whether he was carrying on in this line. He earned good money and he looked after me and the kids, though we had our quarrels. . . . When

Max and he discussed their business I had to leave the room.

"Once, I believe in 1958, it must have been about a year before Max stopped coming, I overheard a row. Max was asking my husband for 'the list,' I think he said, 'the list of all agents,' but Horst did not want to give it to him. But they made it up again. . . ."

I inquired how Brigitte discovered that Max was George Blake.

"Oh, my goodness, that was a pretty shock," she said. "I never knew that Max de Vries was a British official and that his name was Blake and that he was married and had children. And he was a proper toff, too. Would you believe that? Well, it was not until his trial in London. Then I read in the *Berliner Morgenpost* all about him getting forty-two years and there was a picture of Max with a funny beard. It said in the paper it was a photograph taken after he came back from Korea in 1953. But it was Max all right. I recognized him immediately and I was completely stunned. . . . Horst was already in prison. Such a shame . . . Then I too was charged and spent many months in prison, although I never did anything wrong, I swear by the Holy Virgin. . . ."

Brigitte Eitner is not a sophisticated woman and her knowledge of politics and world affairs is limited. But in her feminine way, I think, she sized up George Blake very accurately.

Horst and Max were working in close harmony, but each kept one big secret to himself. Eitner did not suspect that Blake had established contact with the Russians. Blake, as yet, did not realize that Eitner had become a double agent, working for the Russians against the British.

A routine case in which they were involved, for the British, was that of a forty-four-year-old maiden lady, Irmgard Roemer, employed as a secretary in the West German Foreign Office, who spied for the Russians and was a spiritualist in her leisure time. She supplied copies of many documents to a Soviet agent, Carl Helfmann, who paid her small sums of money ranging from twenty pounds to a hundred pounds. Altogether she had received 3200 marks (about £280) for the sheaves of paper she brought home from the office, after laboriously copying all the documents she could find. She spent all the money on financing a spiritualist circle, run by the eighty-year-old "sage," Wilhelm Altmuller.

Irmgard Roemer, who during her trial insisted that "foreign spirits" had commanded her to copy the documents, was sentenced to three years' imprisonment after a psychiatrist had told the court that her sense of responsibility had been diminished by "erotic disturbance": apparently she was still a virgin when Helfmann seduced her at the age of forty-three. Helfman did not escape so lightly. He was sentenced to eight years.

Among the other "expendable" Soviet agents hauled in were Victor and Erika Schneider, both in their early forties. They had been employed by the Russians at least two years when Eitner began to investigate their case and reported to Blake.

It was a case that illuminated the sordid state of affairs in Germany. Schneider was a former S.S. officer who had served in the *Sicherheitsdienst* of the Gestapo. Ironically, his greatest wartime achievement had been to assist in the offensive against the Communist network, the "Red Orchestra" in Berlin in 1942. After the war he became manager in the office of the official newssheet *Informations-Dienst Wirtschaftsbild* of Dr. Adenauer's Christian-Democratic party. The office of the West German government party was used as a *dybok* (letter box) of the Soviet secret service in Berlin.

When the British secret agents finished their inquiries, the embarrassing case was handed over to the German government to deal with itself. The Schneiders were given mild sentences of two years' imprisonment and Schneider told the court that he and his wife would emigrate after their release.

Another sacrificial offering of Soviet agents was made when a roundup of "Hundred-Mark Boys" was carried out after Eitner collected the evidence. It put an end to a disarmingly simple but at times effective espionage technique used by a gang which consisted of Jurgen Ascher, a twenty-three-year-old radio mechanic, his wife Gertrud, Peter Mull, a twenty-eight-year-old electrician, Hans Pflaum, a young carpenter, and Guenther Schultheiss, a salesman. They were systematically stealing documents from British army cars and offices. Young Gertrud also enticed some information from N.C.O.s with the equally direct and traditional methods of a woman spy. Pflaum stole a can of, what he believed, "special oil" used by the R.A.F. in Hunter jet fighters, and a complete stabilizer for British tank cannon.

Exploits like these were mainly Eitner's concern. Blake was after much bigger game.

CHAPTER FIFTEEN

THE BETRAYAL OF THE BERLIN TUNNEL

What information was Blake giving to the Russians during the years he worked at the British secret service H.Q. in Berlin? At his trial the judge said that Blake "had rendered much of Britain's efforts completely useless." Soon after his arrest six British agents in Germany were taken by the Russians, and a few weeks after Blake's trial it transpired that at least forty British agents in Europe and, the Middle East were apprehended by Communist counterespionage, many of them disappearing without trace and never heard of again.

Today we know that George Blake had a terrible record of treachery and many scores of lives, including those of quite innocent people, on his conscience. In his statement to the *Izvestya* he told of how he had betrayed Britain again and again. Sean Bourke maintained that Blake boasted to him that he had "given away one hundred British, American and German agents to the Russians"—indeed, he said, he had lost count of them.

But, besides the human lives destroyed—and he seems entirely unconcerned about the sorrow and misery his crimes have caused to the families of his victims—Blake inflicted untold harm to the political and economic interests not only of the country of his adoption, but to the entire free world.

One exploit of which he appeared to be particularly proud was his betrayal of the Berlin telecommunication tunnel. In the *Izvestya* he stated that he informed the Russians about it already in 1953, before his arrival in West Berlin. He knew, he said, of the planning and preparations for this tunnel when he attended secret conferences of high S.I.S. and C.I.A. officials in London. But this is an outright lie, put forward to gullible Russian readers of the official paper, apparently to show Blake as a man of remarkable foresight and also to ridicule the intelligence services of the West.

The truth is that Blake learned of the existence of the tunnel only several months after his arrival in West Berlin and, indeed, after it had been in good use for some months.

Whatever one might think about the equity of the methods employed, one must not apply normal moral standards to espionage operations. At worst, the secret service organizations of the West were paying the Soviet spy masters in their own coin. For a long time the Americans, the British, and the "Bureau Gehlen" were trying to find a way for tapping Soviet telephone lines, which run under their noses on the border of West and East Berlin. Obviously, if this could be achieved, valuable information could have been obtained by technical means and without endangering the lives of agents. In 1953 General Gehlen approached the American and British secret services with an ingenious plan. It was to establish a tap link, by connecting a cable to the telephone lines laid in shallow channels near the border.

One of Gehlen's top agents, Major Werner Wilhelm Haase, volunteered for the operation. He served during the war in a German engineers' regiment and was an electronics expert. To protect him in case of capture, he was issued fake documents in the name of "Wilhelm Heissler." One watertight cable was to be laid from a dugout in West Berlin's Kiefholtz Strasse across the Heidenkamp Canal, another across the Jungfern Lake north of Potsdam.

During the night of November 13, 1953, Haase stood at the bank of the canal. He had a model boat, driven by a battery, to which the link cable from the dugout was attached. He launched the toy vessel across the water. On the opposite bank was one of his helpers who was supposed to make the connection. Suddenly several men emerged from the dark on both banks. Haase was overwhelmed and dragged into a motorboat, which crossed to the other bank. There his helper had already been seized. Haase's kidnapping took place on West Berlin territory, in the American zone. He was tried by the Supreme Court of East Germany and sentenced to death, the sentence being formally commuted into one of lifelong imprisonment. But he was never heard of again. The other attempt at laying a cable across the lake also failed. The agent who tackled it, Christopher Komarek, was captured and, being regarded as an East German subject, charged with high treason and executed. Both schemes were betrayed by a Soviet agent, Hans Geyer, who, under the alias of "Henry Toll," succeeded in infiltrating the "Bureau Gehlen" and obtained knowledge of the plan.

Some months later the plan to tap Communist telephone lines was taken up once again. This time it was a much more ambitious enterprise than the rather naïve and amateurish undertaking of Major Haase.

A tunnel was built deep beneath the border dividing the city in the southeast. Gehlen provided the men to build it, all of them highly trusted, and the local knowledge. The American C.I.A. provided the finance (it was later estimated that the tunnel and its equipment cost more than $1 million) while the British supplied much of the electronic equipment and some of the operators, most of whom came from the U.S. Army Signal Corps.

The tunnel, starting twenty-four feet beneath street level in a semi-deserted and bomb-scarred corner of the suburb of Rudow near a cemetery, ran for about six hundred yards under the barbed-wire fences of the border into Alt Glienicke in East Berlin. Near its end, along the Schoenfelder Motorroad lay the main telephone lines connecting the East German government offices, the Karlshorst K.G.B. headquarters, and the Soviet army command with direct trunk lines to Warsaw and Moscow.

The tunnel was a solid structure of cast-iron tubes about seven feet in diameter, with several large underground chambers crammed with electronic equipment, transformers, amplifiers, teleprinters, and a complex system of cables ending in a shaft where the connections were made with the East Berlin lines. The tunnel had an air-conditioning unit and was lit and heated by electricity. Two strong steel doors and barbed-wire entanglements secured it from its eastern end against a sudden entry of unwelcome visitors.

The extensive digging and unloading of building material could not be concealed from patrols of the East German police across the boundary. The Americans went, therefore, to the trouble and expense of erecting near the entrance of the tunnel two small buildings, on which roofs radar equipment was installed. The U.S. military commandant notified his Soviet number opposite in East Berlin that the U.S. Air Force was building a new radar station to be used for the air traffic from and to the American airfield at Buckow. The Russians accepted this explanation, having themselves built a large number of radar stations all along the border.

Blake claimed in the *Izvestya* that he had betrayed the existence of the tunnel before it could become operational. This, like many other of his statements, is an empty boast. The Soviet telephone lines under the Schoenfelder Road

were tapped. The control room was manned by highly
trained operators around the clock, the "tap" lasted for
many months, and the British equipment proved excellent.
This was angrily admitted by the Soviet official after the
discovery.

The resulting information obtained was described by
Western Intelligence officers as "incalculable" and of the
utmost value. They are still strictly classified.

All this does not detract from the fact that Blake did
betray the tunnel. He must have done it sometime in April
1956, because the Russians would not have waited long
before pouncing on this highly dangerous establishment.

Khrushchev and Bulganin had just concluded their visit
in London, which coincided with the unfortunate "Frog-
man Crabb incident." On April 15 Soviet K.G.B. officers,
with a posse of heavily armed East German police, burst
into the tunnel having frantically dug an entrance near
the cemetery. But the tunnel had an elaborate alarm system. The steel doors were hurriedly closed by the men inside. After the Russians had smashed them, they found the
tunnel deserted, even though a coffee percolator was still
bubbling in the small recreation room.

How Blake obtained the knowledge of the tunnel must
be left to conjecture. Only oblique reference to this betrayal was made at his trial, and this in secret session. It is
possible that he had found at the Olympia Stadium Buildings some notes when ransacking the desk of one of his
superiors. He often stayed behind after normal office
hours, pretending to complete some urgent work, and he
had, of course, a free run of the offices.

He must have purloined some fairly detailed description,
or even a plan of the tunnel, because he apparently made
a clever drawing of it. This, at least, was claimed to have
come from Blake, when it was published in a Soviet
pamphlet designed to warn Soviet officers and officials of
the activities of Western agents.

A few days after the discovery of the tunnel Colonel
Kotsuba of the K.G.B. called a press conference in East
Berlin and bitterly complained about the "perfidy of the

American and British aggressors." For six weeks fifteen thousand selected East Berliners were conducted on sight-seeing tours through the tunnel to view "the criminal con-spiracy of Gehlen terrorists and capitalist warmongers." Strong protest notes were fired from Moscow to London, Washington, and Bonn. Blake's betrayal caused not only the loss of extremely valuable means of information, but created great embarrassment to the Western governments.

At the Olympia Stadium Buildings, an inquest was con-ducted with similar intensity to the one conducted at the American Intelligence headquarters at Dahlem and at the "Gehlen Bureau" at Pullach. The investigations produced no result beyond the realization that only someone in a senior post at either of the offices could have betrayed the existence of the tunnel to the Russians, who had not unearthed it by chance.

If Blake proved himself a cunning operator by his dis-covery and betrayal of the tunnel, he also showed ruthless-ness and cold-blooded cruelty in some of his other exploits.

As I have mentioned, the block of flats in the Platanen Allee in Charlottenburg, where Blake lived, was exclu-sively reserved for the families of British officers and offi-cials.

There was only one exception. Two floors below Blake's flat lived a German. The other tenants got only an occa-sional and fleeting glimpse of him. None knew that the man, who lived under an assumed name, was Lieutenant General Robert Bialek, former inspector general of the East German People's Police.

He had been in charge of the East Berlin department of the "S.S.D.," the state security service of the East German Communist government, when he defected to the West and was given political asylum in 1953, in the British zone. For a long time he was kept in hiding because of the very real danger of assassination or kidnapping by his old service. Eventually, working for the British secret service, General Bialek was given the accommodation at Platanen Allee.

General Sir William Oliver, then British commandant of

the British zone, ordered his security officers to take special precautions to protect Bialek. Automatic locks were fitted to the doors of his flat, steel shutters to the windows, and a special alarm system was connected to a British security office. Every care was taken to ensure that Bialek's real identity remained unknown even to the British officers and their families living in the block.

Bialek lived in constant fear for his life. He never ventured out without being escorted by a British security officer. As an additional precaution he kept an Alsatian dog, and one evening in February 1956, he took it out for a short walk, without waiting for his escort to arrive.

Two men emerged from the shadow at the corner of Platanen Allee and Leistik Strasse. They hurled themselves on Bialek and forced him into a waiting car.

The British commandant and the British government made sharp and repeated protests, but the Soviet authorities denied all knowledge of Bialek's whereabouts. It was soon established, however, that he had been taken to the H.Q. of the "S.S.D." in East Berlin and put to death after prolonged "interrogations."

Investigations produced evidence that Bialek had been called out from his home by somebody whom he must have trusted. The man was never identified. When Blake was unmasked five years later, the case was reopened. Although there was still only circumstantial evidence, the detectives and security officers now had little doubt that it was Blake who had set the trap for Bialek. He was one of the very few people who knew the defector's identity. He had been Bialek's neighbor and he knew his daily habits. He had a very good motive to deliver him to the Russians.

An even more flagrant conspiracy in which Blake played a part was the kidnapping of a man who worked for the anti-Communist radio station R.I.A.S. in West Berlin.

The K.G.B. and the East German Ministry of State Security were making great efforts to obtain evidence that R.I.A.S. was controlled by Western secret services. To this purpose they wanted to get into their hands one of the journalists or newscasters who prepared the daily broadcasts. Their choice fell on a woman journalist, Lise Stein. A Soviet double agent, Meisel, was infiltrated into the staff of R.I.A.S. and became friendly with her. One day he brought her a box of chocolates treated with a strong sleeping drug. Miss Stein was to be collected from her home by two K.G.B. hatchet men, once she became unconscious. However, she ate only two of the sweets and, when the men entered her flat and tried to drag her out, she managed to shout for help and put them to flight.

The operation code-named "Duck" failed, but the Soviet agents were not discouraged. They now turned to one of Miss Stein's colleagues. Hans Joachim Wiesbach. He suffered from tuberculosis and was hardly able to resist when the kidnappers came, bundled him into a car, and took him across the boundary to East Berlin. During his prolonged solitary confinement Wiesbach was subjected to the usual "psychological treatment" and fed with promises that, if told what his interrogators wanted him to tell, he would go free.

He was told he would be put on trial but this was only a matter of form. He signed the confessions which the interrogators had written and a show trial was staged. Meekly Wiesbach repeated his confessions, telling how British, American, and Gehlen agents went in and out at the R.I.A.S. offices, wrote the scripts, and were in full control. The confessions were used by the Communists for a propaganda campaign designed to discredit R.I.A.S. as well as the Western governments and their secret services. The diabolic sequel was that Wiesbach was sentenced to death—he had been charged with high treason because he had left the Eastern zone some years before and was, therefore, regarded as a subject of the East German "Democratic Republic"—and he was executed.

Only years later was it discovered that the betrayer Meisel was one of Blake's agents, and that Blake himself had assisted in devising both the "Operation Duck" and Wiesbach's kidnapping. There is no doubt that he supplied to the Communist spy masters—Russian, Polish, Czech, and East German—many names of British agents, some of whom were at first left unmolested but carefully watched. Thus, Communist counterespionage was able to gain knowledge of many British secret service operations before it pounced upon these men and women.

Moreover, Blake had access to dossiers and knew the names, or code names, and the whereabouts of British networks and outposts overseas—not only in Germany— when he worked for two years in various sections of the Foreigh Office in London, before and after his stay in Berlin between 1955 and 1959. He revealed the methods used by the Secret Intelligence Service and its agents to acquire information and convey it back to Britain.

Besides the flagrant cases mentioned—and many others—Blake was also involved in the disappearance of members of the N.T.S. organization.

This was—and still is—an anti-Communist organization created many years ago by Russian refugees. Its initials stand in Russian for *Nationalny Trudovoy Soyuz*, freely translated into English as "National Alliance of Russian Solidarists." In Germany it collaborates with the Western secret services, and Gerald Brooke, young London lecturer, was enlisted by N.T.S. leaders to smuggle propaganda material into Russia when he went to Moscow in 1965. He fell into a trap and paid for his abortive mission with five years' imprisonment until he was exchanged for the Krogers.

The K.G.B. pursued N.T.S. members with unremitting hatred. Several of its leading members were kidnapped and liquidated. In 1953 Moscow sent three "executioners" to Frankfurt with orders to assassinate Georgi Okolovitch, the N.T.S. chairman, but the leader of the "Mobile Group"—as traveling executioners are called in K.G.B. jargon—Captain Nicolai Kholkov, changed his mind and surrendered to American counterespionage officers. He handed over an arsenal of strange murder tools, which he had brought from Moscow: a silver case which shot poisoned bullets through the tips of artificial cigarettes, an electrically fired miniature revolver, pistols equipped with silencers which made no more noise than a snap of the fingers, and a selection of poison pills.

. . Blake was then still in London and there is no evidence of his complicity in the Kholkov case. But after his arrival in Berlin he must have been ordered to report anything he could gather about the activities of the N.T.S.

When four N.T.S. agents, Yakuta, Novikov, Chmelnitzky, and Kudratzev, who successfully worked under various aliases and disguises in East Germany, Poland, and the Soviet Union, suddenly disappeared, a shudder ran through the Olympia Stadium Buildings. Their names were known to only a handful of British and American officials. It was clear that the four agents had been betrayed by someone who had firsthand knowledge of their activities. But no one thought the traitor might be inside that office. Again, only years later, Blake's role in this case was established and, as far as I know, he admitted at his trial that he "had helped Soviet counterespionage to apprehend these men."

How terrible Blake's betrayals were, and how much suffering and loss of life they have caused, all this is dwarfed by the far-reaching implications of his handiwork in the politico-diplomatic sphere. The full meaning of the remark by the lord chief justice at his trial that Blake "had rendered much of Britain's efforts completely useless" has never been fully understood by ordinary men and women. There is now little doubt that these words, cautiously expressed, referred to Blake's betrayals of secret policy decisions in the cabinet rooms of London and Washington. Decisions, on which not just the lives of a handful of agents depended, but the peace of the world and the fate of millions of men, women, and children.

CHAPTER SIXTEEN

CABINET SECRETS

In 1970 [first publication of this book], when relations between Britain and the United States on one hand, and the Soviet Union on the other are almost friendly, if only because of the repercussions of the "cultural revolution" in China and Chairman Mao's hostility toward Moscow, it is not easy to envisage the grave situation and the maneuvers and intrigues of the Cold War which bedeviled the world at the period we are concerned with.

Since 1948, when the Iron Curtain firmly descended across Europe, one of the main Communist objectives had been plain to see. That was the entrenchment of Communist régimes in all the areas over which Moscow had gained control since the end of the war. The bloody suppression of the revolts in East Berlin in 1953, in Hungary in 1956, and the invasion of Czechoslovakia in 1968 were some of the later symptoms of Stalinist and neo-Stalinist policy. All the time it was evident that the Communists regarded West Berlin as a finger pointing at its political deficiencies, a source of embarrassment and even a sign of weakness. In the totalitarian Communist ocean West Berlin stood out like a rock of freedom. Again and again, Moscow tried to wipe it out, to starve its inhabitants into submission. In 1948 the Allies saved the city by the famous airlift by which the population, cut off from all supply routes, was sustained for many months, until the Russians had to give in.

When the Berlin blockade ended in September 1949, the Western powers repeatedly suggested that there should be negotiations for a solution of the German problem as a whole and Berlin in particular. Moscow's answer was always *"niet!"* The United Nations set up a special commission, in 1951, to examine the possibility of holding elections throughout Germany and to find out the chances of agreement between Britain, America, France, and Russia on the future of the country. The commission was refused permission to enter the Soviet zone.

Stalin's death and the Korean truce in 1953 raised hopes that a peaceful settlement might be negotiated. The hopes were smashed by the Soviet tanks called in to quell the riots against the Communist régime by the citizens of East Berlin. The number of East Germans "voting for freedom with their feet" by running the gauntlet of barbed wire, watchtowers, and police dogs along the western border grew to a flood.

Protracted diplomatic exchanges led to a fruitless meeting of the "Big Four" foreign ministers in Berlin at the beginning of 1954, but the accession to power of Khrushchev rekindled hopes of a sane settlement.

At the first so-called Summit Conference in Geneva in July 1955, President Eisenhower, the prime ministers of Britain and France, and Khrushchev and Bulganin reached an agreement, directing their foreign ministers to negotiate "a settlement of the German question and the reunification of Germany by means of free elections in conformity with the national interests of the German people and the interests of European security."

George Blake had started work in Berlin a few months before this summit meeting.

Before and after the summit, during the preliminary exchanges and subsequent negotiations of the "settlement," the Foreign Office in London deluged the British secret service headquarters in Berlin with memoranda and questionnaires on every aspect of the Berlin problem.

Blake saw most of these documents and he assisted in the task of answering them.

These secret exchanges concerned the attitude and morale of the Germans, political trends in East and West

Germany, the economic situation, problems of military power of the Communist forces in the Soviet zone, and above all the evaluation of the real intentions of the Russians and their East German satellites.

There were also constant exchanges of opinion between the British ambassador in Bonn, Sir Frederick Hoyer-Millar, and General R. C. Cottrell-Hill, the British commandant in Berlin and his director of political affairs, Mr. E. H. Peck.

The results of all these labors were placed before Mr. Harold Macmillan, then the Foreign Secretary, and his advisers and submitted to the cabinet.

Blake's reports included in these documents must to some unknown extent have influenced decisions at the highest level.

The summit meeting was followed by a conference of the four foreign ministers in Geneva in October 1955. After weeks of useless bickering it was adjourned on the sixteenth of November.

The West, especially Britain, made further attempts in 1956 and 1957 to resume negotiations. When Khrushchev and Bulganin came to London in April 1956, Germany and Berlin were at the top of the agenda.

At the time the Olympia Stadium office was receiving the most precise indications of the doubts and hopes current within the Foreign Office and the cabinet by virtue of the questionnaires that had to be answered. And there can be little doubt that discussions within the office provided a lot more facts to an intelligent listener.

Even from only the brief disclosures during the public hearing at Blake's trial one can deduce that, with documents and reports coming into their hands during that period, the Russians could guess at the innermost thoughts of the British Foreign Secretary. To put it mildly, their negotiating position was strong. Did Mr. Selwyn Lloyd, who had succeeded Mr. Macmillan at the Foreign Office, ponder the uncanny insight of Shepilov and Gromyko?

The Western powers tried to reopen talks in July 1957 and during the following winter. Suddenly, in November

1958, Khrushchev made another onslaught on the freedom of West Berlin, demanding the withdrawal of all troops from Berlin and the creation of a "demilitarized free city."

Originally, the British Foreign Office was not entirely opposed to this idea, provided that real safeguards for Berlin's freedom could be extracted from Moscow. Selwyn Lloyd had cautiously suggested it to the U.S. secretary of state, but it found no favor with Mr. John Foster Dulles, and his refusal earned him the accusation of "brinkmanship." The British proposal, aimed at achieving a *détente* with Moscow, seemed to have died, when suddenly in November 1958 it was brought to life again by Mr. Khrushchev. The tone of his note was aggressive, but his proposal had a startling resemblance to the recently shelved proposals made in utmost secrecy to America and France by Selwyn Lloyd. It seemed that *Khrushchev knew all that was worth knowing about the secret exchanges between the Western powers.*

On January 11, 1959, when Blake was still in Berlin, the Soviet government presented notes in London, Washington, and Paris proposing that a conference be called to draft a German peace treaty. But the main condition was that the Communist "German Democratic Republic" must be admitted to the talks alongside the German Federal Republic. The Russians also said their proposals were subject to a time limit of six months. If the proposals were not accepted they threatened to conclude a separate peace treaty with the "Democratic Republic" of East Germany.

Again the Kremlin was aware of the fact that the Western Allies were in disagreement on some of the basic questions of this proposal. One of its worst features was that it would have jeopardized the freedom of Berlin by removing the responsibility for its fate from the four powers and placing it in the hands of a Communist puppet régime, which could claim it had no obligation to allow freedom of access to the city. It menaced the rights of the Western powers to maintain troops in West Berlin. The threat of a "six months' limit" to further negotiations looked like a very possible detonator for World War III.

Although the Allies refused to negotiate under the menace of an ultimatum, which Khrushchev later withdrew, they subsequently yielded to the Soviet demand that representatives of the East German Communist régime be admitted to the conference on an equal footing with those of the Federal Republic.

Once again Moscow seemed to have *inside information about the British Foreign Offices' efforts* to get Washington's agreement to this compromise. That is precisely what happened. Mr. Dulles bowed very reluctantly to the urgent pleas from London. On February 21, 1959, Mr. Macmillan, the prime minister, and his Foreign Secretary, Mr. Selwyn Lloyd, went to Moscow in an effort to shift the dangerous logjam and prepare the new Big Four meeting. They stayed in the Soviet Union for eleven days, kicking their heels for the first few while Mr. Khrushchev refused to see them after the initial reception. He said he had a toothache, which was as good a way as any to say that he was awaiting up-to-date reports on British foreign policy from his secret service office in Berlin.

After their return from Moscow Mr. Macmillan and Mr. Selwyn Lloyd visited Dr. Adenauer in Bonn and President Eisenhower in Washington. During this period, as can be imagined, there was the utmost interest in any indication of the next Allied moves over Berlin, the sort of information which a senior political agent could supply.

On May 11, 1959, the four foreign ministers met again in Geneva. The Western plan was submitted on May 14. Mr. Gromyko rejected it out of hand, as if he had seen its main contents before and thought he could get more if he tried hard enough. The conference dragged on a while, went into recess on June 20, resumed on July 13, and was adjourned on August 5. Khrushchev had suspended his threat to sign a separate peace treaty with East Germany and went to Washington on President Eisenhower's invitation.

The German question was put into cold storage until the summit meeting which was to have taken place in

Paris in the spring of 1960. All the participants arrived but the meeting never took place.

Moscow had discovered an American "spy conspiracy"—the sending of U.S. aircraft with photographic equipment into Soviet airspace. It was a rather belated "discovery," because the Russians had complained about such flights before. But this time Mr. Khrushchev said he would not talk unless President Eisenhower apologized for the U-2 "spy plane" incident. President Eisenhower and America were not in an apologetic mood. The summit meeting was called off.

George Blake returned from Berlin to London on April 14, 1959, before the Geneva conference had begun. During that conference and the abortive summit meeting in Paris, he was busy at his desk. But his career as the great traitor was rapidly nearing its end. Now he was himself in fatal danger. He did now know it, even though he might have sensed it.

It took almost two years before fate caught up with him. For the time he must have been greatly pleased with his achievement. I do not doubt that he had received suitable commendations from his Soviet masters.

Many years before Moscow officially proclaimed him a "merited agent of the Soviet Union" and bestowed on him high decorations, political leaders and journalists were compelled to pay grudging tributes to his exploits. The extent of his activities was still not known and, therefore, not evaluated. But immediately after his trial—when British newspapers were still gagged by urgent government requests not to publish comments, and while the prime minister still refused to answer questions in the House of Commons—foreign newspapers, particularly in the United States and Germany, began to publish startling revelations about at least some of the terrifying aspects of his treachery.

The *New York Herald-Tribune*, whose publisher was the former U.S. ambassador in London, Mr. John Hay Whitney, bluntly stated: "George Blake learned of every plan, every intended tactical move and of all projects the West worked out on the problems of Berlin and Germany. . . . The United States might in future withhold from the British government its secrets, regarding Britain as a sieve. . . ."

The *New York Times* said: "The Western Allies worked out the plans for negotiations with Moscow in secret conferences with the German government. Western memoranda, plans, strategic ideas and projected moves . . . are believed to have been in the hands of the Soviets before these conferences even began. They were supplied by Blake. . . ."

At the same time German newspapers began to reveal the results of inquiries made in Bonn and Berlin. Several wrote that Blake had supplied the Russians with copies of vital documents the German government had submitted to the British Foreign Office.

The newspaper *Der Tag* wrote: "Numberless secret documents from the archives of the Foreign Ministry were handed over to the Soviets. In many cases Blake had secured photographs of lengthy documents, mainly about the Berlin question. From personnel files and secret dossiers Blake gave the names of British secret agents to his Soviet contacts. . . . The entire British secret service appears to be endangered, because it must be assumed that the Soviets know the identity of British secret agents and they could use this knowledge for conveying faked information to London."

Deutsche Zeitung (Cologne) stated that "only the future might show how much harm was done by Blake" and added that NATO Allies would be careful in the future before imparting secrets to Britain.

The Cologne *Stadt Anzeiger,* Dr. Adenauer's mouthpiece, declared that "Blake betrayed not only British secrets but also those of the Allied Powers. He possessed knowledge of the organization, secret agents, contact places of British and Allied secret service organizations, including the Organization Gehlen and the U.S. Intelligence. Blake will, therefore, be questioned intensively by American and German security officials. He has nothing to lose now and it can be assumed that he will 'unload' his conscience. Only then will it be possible to assess the whole extent of the enormous damage he had caused in Germany."

Die Welt wrote: "Blake did not betray military secrets. But he betrayed vital political secrets when working as a double agent, for both Britain and Russia. . . ."

Many more disclosures were still to come.

The pertinent question is whether Blake would have really been in the position of gaining knowledge of these top secret plans. The answer is—yes.

First, as already mentioned, he saw all the relevant questionnaires and read notes received at the Stadium from the Foreign Office. He made photographic copies of these documents. The investigations after his arrest elicited the fact that he often used to stay alone at the Stadium office. A security officer arranged that all doors should be locked, when all officials were out, but Blake was just locked in, pretending that he had some urgent work to complete. He did then use his camera freely, producing microfilms, knowing that he would remain undisturbed, and that no one would enter the offices.

Secondly, after he returned in April 1959 to London, he had good opportunities for gathering information at the Foreign Office itself, being regarded as fully trustworthy, a senior agent who had proved his mettle in Berlin.

By the spring of 1959 Blake's Soviet masters must have come to the conclusion that Berlin was getting to be too hot a spot for Blake, and that he would be more useful to them in London or elsewhere. They told him to apply for a new posting. Probably in agreement with the K.G.B., Blake suggested a Middle East station of the S.I.S. His father's family still lived in Cairo, and he indicated that he could make contacts there. Blake had good reasons of his own to leave Berlin. His discovery that his right-hand man Eitner was also a Russian double agent, as well as some other events, must have worried him in the extreme.

CHAPTER SEVENTEEN

TRAITOR BETRAYED

In October 1958 a sensational arrest was made at Bremerhaven, the naval base of the German Federal Republic. Horst Heinz Ludwig, a thirty-four-year-old Lieutenant Commander, who had just returned to Germany from the Royal Navy Fleet Air Arm base at Lossiemouth in Scotland, having completed a three-month special training with the Royal Navy arranged for foreign NATO officers, was charged with *Landes Verrat* (high treason). Ludwig was accused of having spied for the Russians since 1955 and having betrayed naval and military secrets of the German Federal Republic and her British and American allies. A few days later several other arrests were made and Chief Petty Officer Fritz Briesemeier, Ludwig's sister, Frau Hanni Jaeger and her husband Werner Jaeger, an insurance broker, were charged with similar offenses.

Only few details of the accusations were made known and the German authorities were in no hurry to put Ludwig and his accomplices on trial. They were kept in custody and appeared in court on January 25, 1960.

George Blake knew the details of the charges and Ludwig's background. This knowledge must have been additional reason for his decision to leave Germany at the earliest possible date.

Lieutenant Commander Ludwig started his military service as a young conscript in Hitler's army shortly before the end of the war. After his release from an Allied P.O.W. camp he went to the Soviet zone, where his parents lived, and in 1947 became an engineering student in Jena University, graduating in 1950. In March 1951 he fled to the West and found employment with an American-controlled labor unit engaged in minesweeping in the port of Bremerhaven. There he met Fritz Briesemeier who served with him in a minesweeper. In 1955 Ludwig volunteered for the new German *Bundeswehr*, was commissioned, and received initial training as an air-force pilot. Many young German officers were sent for advanced training to America and Ludwig went to the U.S. Air Force base at Pensacola, Florida. While attempting to land on an American aircraft carrier he crashed into the sea and suffered serious injuries. He recovered and returned to Germany.

In July 1958 he was sent to the Royal Navy station at Lossiemouth, where he received further training in de Haviland *Sea Vixen* aircraft, also being earmarked for training in the new British all-weather naval fighter, the supermarine *Scimitar*. In October of that year he was suddenly recalled and arrested.

At his trial in January 1960, when Blake was already back in London, Lieutenant Commander Ludwig described how he had been slowly drawn into the net of Soviet espionage by a mixture of threats, blackmail, and bribery.

In 1954, when he was still working in American minesweepers off Bremerhaven, his father visited him and suggested that he should meet some people who had approached him in East Germany. The father told him that he and his wife would be "in trouble" if their son should refuse. In December Ludwig went to East Berlin and met two agents of the Soviet or East German secret service. They warned him that his parents would "not remain free" should he refuse to comply with their orders. One was that he should join the *Bundeswehr* and volunteer for flying duties.

.. This Ludwig did, very reluctantly. Subsequently he had many meetings with a Soviet agent whose code name was "Schütz." It was on this man's order that he requested to be included in the team sent to the U.S. Air Force base in Florida. Schütz told him exactly what to look for during his training in America and how to send his reports to cover addresses.

Later he was introduced in Berlin to a man whom he knew as "Victor." When this contact man learned that Ludwig knew Chief Petty Officer Briesemeier, then serving with the German navy, he ordered him to bring Briesemeier "for a holiday" to Berlin. After several meetings Briesemeier agreed to work with Ludwig for the Russians.

Commander Ludwig made a full confession, saying that during the three years he had worked for the Russians, he had received a total of six thousand marks (about £550). He tried to disentangle himself for a long time, but he was always frightened that the Communists would harm his parents.

Chief Officer Briesemeier cynically stated that he had betrayed secrets solely for money. He said he received a total of 7800 marks.

He also began to make some startling remarks during the public hearing at the trial—most of the proceedings were held in secret—when he was interrupted by the president of the court, but he had time to say that he believed that "Victor" was a double agent who worked for the British and told him that he had served in the Royal Navy.

The name of "Victor" was again mentioned at another spy trial on December 10, 1960, almost a year after Ludwig, Briesemeier, and the Jaegers were convicted.

This time, though "Victor's" identity was not disclosed, it appears that the court and the German authorities knew full well who "Victor" was.

At that trial two messengers at the German Ministry of Interior, Wilhelm Knipp and Joseph Paul, were charged with high treason and made qualified confessions. They admitted to having copied about three thousand documents, but they said they had sold them to an agent who, they believed, worked for the British secret service. This man's name was "Victor." The two accused insisted that they would not have spied for the Russians.

The German prosecutor described the case as one of the worst examples of espionage ever discovered in Germany. He said that most of Bonn's security and defense plans, including some secret NATO instructions, had become known to Soviet and East German spies as a result of it. Members of the ministry staff said on the witness stand that they often wondered why the two messengers always locked the door of their restroom during the lunch hour and refused to be disturbed.

In their defense Knipp and Paul said they had been subjected to great temptation. Security arrangements at the ministry were very slack. They were able to collect files from the desks of high officials during the lunch hour without being disturbed. They photographed the documents with the camera provided by their mysterious friend "Victor." They also opened envelopes given to them for dispatch to the Ministries of Foreign Affairs and Defense. On one occasion a key they had made from a wax impression broke off in the lock of a dispatch case they had to carry to the Ministry of Defense.

"Victor," their mysterious employer, paid them a retainer of five thousand deutsche marks (about forty-five pounds) a month and a "bonus" for each film they delivered, usually once a week, to an accommodation address. Knipp was sentenced to ten years' and Paul to nine years' forced labor.

In order not to keep the reader in suspense I want to add here that at the trial of Horst Eitner in November 1961, it was established that he had used the code name "Victor," when working for the British secret service. The two messengers had good reasons to believe that they were supplying the stolen secrets to a British, or perhaps an American, agent. But "Victor" passed on these secrets to his Russian masters. Eitner had been at that time a double agent for at least three years, and probably longer.

After the arrests of Lieutenant Commander Ludwig and his accomplices in 1958 and the increasing counterespionage activities of the new German secret service under

Major General Reinhard Gehlen, the situation had become
so serious that Blake decided to end his association with
Eitner.

There was yet another and even more weighty reason
why Blake was in a hurry to shake Berlin's dust off his
feet. Through one of his Soviet contacts he had met a
Czech agent, who called himself "Sowa."

It can be assumed that Blake supplied Sowa with information of particular interest to the Czechoslovak secret
service. Sowa reciprocated by introducing Blake to a man
who occupied an exalted position in the German Federal
Republic. This man was fifty-eight-year-old Alfred Frenzel, a member of the German Bundestag (Parliament) in
Bonn, member of its Defense Committee, and a prominent
front-bench speaker for the Social Democratic party, then
in opposition to Dr. Adenauer's government.

Herr Alfred Frenzel, M.P., was decidedly an interesting
man to meet. After the occupation of Czechoslovakia by
the Nazis in March 1939, this German-speaking native of
the Sudetenland and a Socialist since his youth, fled to
Britain and enlisted there, at the outbreak of the war, at
first in the Free Czechoslovak Brigade (formed by the ex-
iled President Benes) and later in the R.A.F. Czech
squadron.

After the end of the war Frenzel went to Germany,
served for a time with the British Control Commission and
later applied for German citizenship, claiming that as a
native of the Sudetenland, he was a German. He became a
trade-union official and quickly climbed the ladder in the
renascent Social Democratic party, then led by Dr. Schu-
macher and Willy Brandt. For several years he was a
member of its executive and chairman of its organization
in southern Bavaria. In 1950 he won a seat in the Ba-
varian Landtag and in 1953 was elected to the Bonn Parliament. As a member of the Defense Committee he was
concerned with Germany's participation in NATO officers
and took part in inspections of NATO installations.

Being fleunt in English, which he acquired during his

service with the Royal Air Force during the war, he made many friends among British and American officers; on several occasions he was a guest at the München-Gladbach H.Q. of the British army of the Rhine and at the U.S. rocket base near Heidelberg.

Herr Frenzel, a big, obese epicure, missed only one thing in his splendid career, which propelled him from a poor glassblower to an influential Bonn politician. This was sufficient funds to indulge his many appetites, which ranged from high-class cuisine and old brandy to pretty women. The Communist secret services were prepared to provide the necessary funds, at a price. It was Blake's mysterious friend, "Sowa," who recruited the German politician for the Czech espionage center in Berlin. From 1956 onwards Frenzel supplied documents which came into his possession as a member of the Defense Committee of the Bonn Parliament, and every scrap of information gathered from his friends at the British and American military headquarters.

Blake met him in 1958 and it appears that Frenzel was under the impression that the young man was a genuine British agent. He probably supplied Blake with information, not being adverse to accept payments from any source. Later, however, probably through "Sowa," Herr Frenzel was enlightened about Blake's double role. With Eitner on his hands, Blake did not cherish Herr Frenzel's friendship, rightly assuming that the venal, fat politician's days were numbered. Frenzel was spending money far beyond his legitimate income as an M.P. and, when in his cups, was careless with his talk.

Unexpectedly, Frenzel prevailed until the end of October 1960. He was arrested after addressing a meeting of former anti-Nazi Resistance members in Bonn. Just before the meeting he had handed secret documents to two Czech agents. Frenzel had been suspected for some time, having been observed meeting Czech agents. The two men who collected the documents on October 28, 1960, were also arrested and admitted to being members of a Czech espionage organization in Germany.

By a strange fate the dates of Frenzel's and Blake's trials coincided: Frenzel stood in the dock on April 26, 1961, and his trial lasted for a week, ending with a sentence of fifteen years' imprisonment. Blake was sentenced on May 3. Again, Frenzel gained his freedom only a few weeks after Blake's escape from prison, serving—like Blake—only five and a half years. But the ex-parliamentarian did not escape. He was exchanged on December 28, 1966, for a German journalist, Fräulein Martina Kischke, arrested by the Russians in August 1966 in Alma Ata, capital of Kazakhstan, and accused of espionage.

At the time of Frenzel's arrest and the events which finally led to the unmasking of Horst Eitner, Blake was already in Beirut as a student at the British Middle East College for Arabic Studies. The arrests and trials in Germany must have caused him constant worry because of the danger that at least one of his former accomplices in Berlin would talk and give him away.

The Blakes left Berlin on April 13, 1959. Mrs. Blake was expecting her second child, which was born in a London hospital soon after their arrival. It was another boy and he was christened James. Blake once again became a "civil servant," commuting between his pleasant semidetached house at Bickley in Kent and Whitehall. His wife later described his apparently humdrum life: dressed in a dark suit, soft collar, and sober tie, carrying a rolled umbrella, he would take the 9:14 A.M. train to Victoria, to arrive shortly before ten at his office. His wife bought him a bowler hat, but he did not like to wear it, and he was constantly losing his umbrellas. He seemed to admire the new fashion adopted by young people in England and yet unknown to him: Edwardian-styled clothes, drainpipe trousers, long hairstyle. He would have loved to emulate it, but he had to dress respectably.

Usually he returned home by 7:00 P.M. There was nothing about his habits that would betray his double life. Only after his trial was it said that Superintendent George Smith of the Special Branch had a hunch that Blake was meeting spy contacts during those evening journeys home. It seems that instead of taking the 6:24 P.M. train from Victoria to Bickley, he would catch an earlier one, leaving Victoria at 6:18 P.M. for Bromley South and meeting a contact for the few minutes at Bromley, before changing there for the later train to take him to the next station, Bickley. This fleeting encounter, perhaps once or twice a week, would have been sufficient to enable Blake to hand over microfilm, hidden in a folded newspaper, to a man on the crowded platform during the rush hour.

When spending evenings at home, after the two boys were put to bed, he used to read a lot, often Russian books and many newspapers and political magazines. He was also still interested in philosophy and theology, a strange throwback to his youth when he had played with the idea of studying for Holy Orders.

The family spent their summer holiday in 1959 at the fine villa of his uncle Mijnheer Anthony Beijderwellen at Zandvoort near Amsterdam. Blake expected to be sent in the autumn to the college at Beirut and his main occupation was to prepare himself for his Middle East assignment.

He was not ignorant of the affairs of that politically so unruly area. The three years he had spent in Cairo as a boy counted little, but during his stay in Berlin he had met a number of Arab politicians and emissaries. Soon after Colonel Nasser came to power in Egypt, the first of many trade, technical, and military missions from Cairo arrived in Berlin and went on to Poland, Czechoslovakia, and Moscow. Nasser engaged a number of pilots from East Germany and Russia to replace Britons and Frenchmen. The Suez crisis brought about close political and economic cooperation between Nasser and the Soviet Union and opened the Middle East to Communist influence.

One of the prominent Arab leaders who was a frequent visitor to Berlin, Warsaw, and Moscow was Colonel Abdel Hamid Serraj, in 1956 chief of the Syrian security police and head of the secret service. Later he became vicepresident of the United Arab Republic. Blake met Colonel

Serraj and other of Nasser's notabilities in Berlin. They gave rise to suggestions at his trial that he was involved in the exposure of the alleged British espionage cell in Cairo in 1956 and the imprisonment of Mr. James Swinburn and Mr. James Zarb by the Egyptians. It was established that Blake, having access to secret files, gave their names and those of other Britons in Cairo to the Russians. Swinburn was charged with being the head of a British espionage cell, said to have been operating for four years prior to 1956.

When George Blake arrived in Beirut in September 1960, he did so as a student. The Foreign Office had entered him at *M.E.C.A.S.*, a college with a strange past, a curious present, and an uncertain future. *M.E.C.A.S.*, the Middle East College for Arabic Studies was founded under the aegis of the Foreign Office many years ago. During the British mandate in Palestine it was situated in Jerusalem.

In the last war it became the center for the training of British officers of the Arab Legion under General Glubb and of special agents of the S.O.E., which had its southeastern headquarters at Cairo. Officers of the Jewish units, which fought beside the British forces in Africa, were trained there, and one of the chief instructors was Major Abba Eban, later foreign minister of Israel.

When Britain relinquished the Palestine mandate, the Foreign Office moved *M.E.C.A.S.* from Jerusalem to Lebanon, where the government was headed by the pro-Western President El Khoury. The college was housed in a former monastery of the Christian Maronites at the village of Shemlan, about twenty miles from Beirut.

Communist propaganda was blowing strongly through the Middle East. Arab nationalities denounced the British college as a center of British imperialism and espionage.

It is true that *M.E.C.A.S.* has always been financed and run by the Foreign Office, that its tutors have, mainly, been drawn from Foreign Service staff, and that a good proportion of its students have been destined for the foreign, consular, and colonial services as well as for work with the secret service and Military Intelligence departments. On the other hand, there was a fair proportion of nongovernmental students, sent to *M.E.C.A.S.* by oil companies, banks, and industrial and commercial companies with interests in the Middle East.

When George Blake arrived there in the autumn of 1960, there were about forty students in residence on British government grants, a number of privately sponsored students, and a few from Canada, Ghana, Nigeria, East Africa, and the United States. *M.E.C.A.S.* had the world's most intensive course, lasting for eighteen months, at the end of which the candidates could take the Civil Service Commission's Higher and Interpretership examinations.

The realization that Britain required many more Arabic linguists if she was to maintain even the greatly diminished influence in areas such as Jordan, Aden, Kuwait, Bahivain, and so on, the Foreign Office wanted to expand the college and move it to one of the British protectorates on the Red Sea. Despite the unrelenting hostility of Cairo to the "British spy college" the Lebanese government showed itself anxious to continue hospitality to the institution. A landowner, Mr. George Hatti, offered to build new premises and let them to the Foreign Office for a nominal rent. His offer was accepted and some impressive buildings were erected. They included classrooms, assembly, dining and recreation halls, a gymnasium, and a comfortably appointed residential wing.

Blake did not, however, become a residential student. In addition to his grant—the usual fee for *M.E.C.A.S.* students was a hundred pounds a month—paid by the Foreign Office, he continued to draw his salary. He rented a pleasant stone-built house on the edge of the village so that his wife and his two boys, Anthony and baby James, could join him.

As one would expect from his record, Blake was an assiduous student. The principal of *M.E.C.A.S.*, Mr. John Wilton, himself a Foreign Office man who had served in the British embassy in Bulgaria and shared Blake's interest in Eastern European politics, was full of praise for Blake's hard work and the speed with which he learned the elements of Arabic. His superiors decreed that he need only stay at M.E.C.A.S. for nine or ten months instead of taking the full course. It seems that London wanted him for an assignment as quickly as possible.

Shemlan is only a few miles from Beirut, which is one of the world's most enticing places. Set in picturesque surroundings on a lovely bay, it has beautiful weather, beautiful women, luxurious hotels and restaurants, and the world's largest gambling casino. The smart and idle rich of the international set make it their expensive playground, leaving Monte Carlo, Cannes, and Nice more and more to the holiday tourists. Beirut, as can be expected by its location, also attracts politicians, conspirators, plotters, and secret agents from all over the Middle East and North Africa.

The Blakes rarely went near the place. They would occasionally leave the village of Shemlan on a sight-seeing excursion to one of the many archaeological sites in Lebanon but they spent most of the time in their villa in the foothills of the mountains.

Since September 1956, Beirut had had another remarkable British resident. He was Kim Philby who, after his dismissal from the Secret Intelligence Service following the affair of the "Missing Diplomats," Donald Maclean and Guy Burgess, had arrived there as the correspondent of a British Sunday newspaper. In 1955 he was fully exonerated from any complicity with the two traitors by the British prime minister and other cabinet members.

After Philby's unmasking as the supreme Soviet double agent and his flight to Russia in 1963, intensive investigations were carried out by British security officers to find out whether Philby and Blake maintained contact during their stay in Beirut. Their findings were never officially disclosed. But several people came forward to say that they actually did see Philby and Blake together. Mr. Eric Downton, then a special correspondent of the *Daily Telegraph* in Beirut, who knew Philby as a colleague, stated that Philby told him of his visits to Shemlan, although he did not mention Blake. Mr. Downton added that he gained the impression that Philby had contact with Blake.

George Blake had little contact with the British community outside the college. He was still a regular churchgoer and attended services with his family in the Maronite church on Sunday. He was not unfriendly to his fellow students but he seemed absorbed in his work.

All in all life for George Blake at Shemlan seems to have been as good and carefree as at any time since he was a boy. The intrigues of Berlin seemed to have been forgotten, and wartime Holland, Hamburg, and the Korean death camp must all have seemed but remote memories.

But the secret past had started to catch up with George Blake almost as soon as he reached Beirut.

Horst Eitner was still busily operating in Berlin. One day in September 1960, security officers of the German Federal secret service received an anonymous letter denouncing him as a "Russian spy." They shadowed him for several weeks and checked up on the possibility that he was the much-wanted "Victor." In fact, Eitner was denounced by his own wife, who had become jealous of another woman. When I asked, in 1966, the otherwise very communicative Brigitte, she refused to discuss it, but it was all mentioned at her and her husband's trial. In October 1960, about a month after Blake reached Lebanon, Eitner was arrested in Berlin and charged with "intelligence with a potential enemy."

As one would expect of such a man, Eitner was now quite prepared to talk. He stated that late in 1957 or early in 1958, he had been recognized as a British agent on one of his visits to East Berlin. He said he was "kidnapped" by East German security policemen and taken before Colonel Willi Seegebrecht, chief of Section 19 of the East German secret service. During his interrogations he was dismayed to find how very well informed Seegebrecht was about the British secret service activities and its headquarters at the Olympia Stadium Buildings. The Communist spy master seemed to know most of the British agents' identities and their whereabouts.

Whether Seegebrecht mentioned "Max de Vries" to Eitner, or whether he even disclosed that he knew "Max" was George Blake, Eitner did not say. But he said that Seegebrecht offered him an alternative: either he would go back to West Berlin and work as a double agent, or he would be liquidated.

Eitner did not hesitate. The Communists offered him the same pay he was receiving from the British. "We shall pay you sixty pounds a week, but of course, you can keep the money the British pay you," Seegebrecht told him with a grin. "So you will be a prosperous man. . . ."

This is the story Eitner told his interrogators and repeated during his trial, which was held in secret session. For the time he kept the secret of his collaboration with George Blake to himself. As I have mentioned, sometime during the summer of 1958, they confided in each other. They decided to continue working together on the same lines as they had been doing.

In prison Eitner thought of the harsh fate that had overtaken him. Confronted with the possibility of a sentence to life imprisonment, he must have pondered about the contrast between his condition and that of his friend George Blake who, he knew, was safe and comfortable with his family in sunny Lebanon. He decided to write to Blake and ask his senior partner in so many perilous ventures, which had landed him in this desperate plight, for help.

There was no reply and by February 1961, bitter and disillusioned, Horst Eitner asked to be brought before the interrogating judge and unburdened his mind to the German official. He insisted that if he had become a traitor, it was because he had become a double agent at the instigation of the British. And he described the identity of the British agent who, he said, had been a double agent himself.

At first the judge refused to believe Eitner's story. But the methodical procedures of German bureaucracy have their uses. The transcript of Eitner's "fantastic depositions" was sent to the president of the court and the state prosecutor, then hurriedly passed on to the Ministry of Justice at Bonn. There the growing dossier, enlarged by deposition of Eitner's wife Brigitte, who told of the "handsome Englishman" who used to work with her husband and often visited East Berlin, finally landed with a nasty thud on the desk of Herr Dr. Heinrich von Brentano, Adenauer's minister for foreign affairs. It took many weeks between Eitner's first deposition and the day the German authorities passed Eitner's allegation on to the British government.

At first the allegations were disbelieved in London. There was no other evidence against Blake than the confusing "confessions" of a man who could not be trusted and who might have acted out of spite, or to save his own skin, or even by order of the Soviet espionage aiming at compromising the British secret service. There were many conferences between high Foreign Office officials, the head of the Secret Intelligence Service, Sir Dick Goldsmith White, and the director general of security (the so-called M.I.5), Sir Roger Hollis. Blake's past life and activities were carefully scrutinized; instructions went out to S.I.S. stations in Germany and Beirut for immediate reports.

Then came the bombshell.

A Communist defector had come in from the cold, crossing into West Berlin on Christmas day 1960. He was forty-one-year-old Colonel Michael Goleniewski* of the

* This is probably an asumed name. His real name was never established. He became an American citizen in 1963 and worked for the C.I.A., but later quarreled with his new bosses and accused several C.I.A. officials of being double agents of the K.G.B. He was dismissed but later the C.I.A. paid him a "pension" of £170 a month. Later Goleniewski allied himself with critics of the C.I.A. in Congress and continued a bitter campaign, which became subject of a congressional committee inquiry. Although a senior C.I.A. official, Mr. John Norpel, told the committee that Goleniewski's information proved to be one hundred percent accurate, he expressed the opinion that the man later became mentally deranged. There was, probably, some truth in this. By 1967 Goleniewski stated that he was the son of Nicholas II, czar of Russia, that he had escaped the massacre of the czarist family by the Bolsheviks in 1918, and was brought up by a Polish family.

Polish Intelligence Service, third in command of the Polish "Second Bureau" and for two years head of its office in East Berlin. His arrival at the United States headquarters at Berlin-Dahlem was not quite unexpected. When he was still in charge of the Polish Intelligence office at Danzig in 1957, he had approached American consular officials, declaring his disenchantment with the Communist régime, and offered to supply secret information. Treated at first with utmost caution, his *bona fides* were soon established. Since 1958 he had furnished the C.I.A. with invaluable information, which led to the discovery of Communist spy rings in the United States and to the arrest of the American diplomat Irwin Chambers Skarbeck who had become a Soviet agent when the K.G.B. got a sex-blackmail hold on him. Later, in Berlin, Goleniewski worked closely with K.G.B. chiefs at Karlshorst.

Goleniewski was flown to Washington and began to unpack his newest secret to the C.I.A. Almost casually he mentioned that one of the chief British agents in West Berlin, George Blake, had been for years a Soviet spy. It was not until February 21 that a transcript of Goleniewski's information concerning Blake—and others, including members of the Portland Naval Spy Ring, was forwarded by the State Department to London.

The depositions were so detailed that, with the corroboration of hitherto disbelieved evidence from Eitner, Blake's fate was now sealed. On the urgent request from the British authorities Goleniewski was flown with C.I.A. men to London and interrogated by the chiefs of the British secret services. He gave them chapter and verse to his previous depositions. Reports were submitted to the prime minister, Mr. Harold Macmillan, and the Foreign Secretary, Mr. Selwyn Lloyd. Commander Evan Jones, head of the Special Branch, was instructed to investigate and arrange for the surveillance of all contacts Blake had had in London. More Special Branch detectives and security agents were hurriedly dispatched to Berlin, where they once more interviewed Eitner, officials at the Stadium, and agents who had worked with Blake. Their report conveyed to London, left little doubt of the far-reaching implications of Blake's treasonable activities.

The prime minister ordered that Blake should be brought to London from Beirut.

The possibility that Blake might bolt was very real. The Syrian border was only a few miles from Shemlan and in Damascus, at that time there were several Soviet "missions" who would, presumably, be ready to assist him. The Foreign Office sent a message to Blake asking him to come to London "for important consultations." Purposely, the message did not stress particular urgency.

Blake showed no concern when he received the telegram. He discussed it with his wife and remarked that "The Firm" might want him in London for a new assignment. He told several of their acquaintances and the tutors at *M.E.C.A.S.* that he was going to Britain immediately after Easter. The only explanation for his unconcern—apart from possessing iron nerves—might be that he accepted the summons to London with relief: this was the end of the road.

He had replied to the Foreign Office without delay, saying he would leave for London on Easter Monday. He wanted to stay with Gillian, who was expecting her third child within a few weeks, and arrange for her care during his absence. On Easter Sunday they had a few friends—members of the British Council, a tutor and some students from *M.E.C.A.S.*—for drinks in the afternoon. George Blake appeared cheerful and said he would be back in Beirut on the following Satuday for the birthday party of his elder boy. Anthony, who was six. His guests drank to their host's future, teasing George that he would get a high promotion in London.

Blake arrived from Beirut aboard a B.O.A.C. *Comet* aircraft at London Airport on Easter Monday, April 3, 1961. He had been told to report at the Foreign Office on Tuesday morning. Every precaution was taken not to arouse his suspicion and, perhaps, prompt him to take a desperate step. From the air terminal at Victoria he went to his mother's place at Reigate and spent the night there. The only luggage he brought with him was a bulky attaché case and a raincoat.

On Tuesday morning he went to Whitehall. Perhaps he did not expect that as soon as he had entered the office of his department he would be taken to the inner sanctum, the office of Sir Dick Goldsmith White, head of the secret service.

With the chief were two men Blake did not know and, at first, they were not introduced. When Sir Dick told Blake that British authorities had evidence that he had committed offenses under the Official Secrets act and that he would be investigated, Blake did not flinch or deny it. He asked to be allowed to make a full report which, he said, "would explain everything." His chief told him curtly that he would have the opportunity to do so.

Then the older of the two strangers, a tall dark-haired man, introduced himself as Detective Superintendent Louis Gale of the Special Branch. "I am a police officer, Mr. Blake, and this is my colleague, Detective Chief Inspector Ferguson Smith," he said with a wave of his hand toward his companion, a fair-haired man with a fair mustache and blue eyes. Blake did not know that Chief Inspector Smith and two other officers had watched him during the last twenty-four hours, ever since he had stepped off the aircraft from Beirut.

The superintendent asked Blake to come with them and added: "Please do not say anything now. I shall take you to a police station, where you will be cautioned and charged. If you wish you can then make a statement."

Blake remained silent. He left the room with the detectives after a short bow toward the desk at which his chief sat. With Superintendent Gale and Chief Inspector Ferguson Smith he was driven to Bow Street Police Station, where he was formally charged.

The niceties of British law were duly observed. Blake was put before the chief metropolitan magistrate, Sir Robert Blundell, who ordered a special sitting in the late afternoon, at an hour when the Bow Street Police Court does not sit. The usually so diligent court reporters knew nothing of the special court, at which only the magistrate, his clerk, the accused, and police officers were present.

Blake was remanded to custody until April 22. On that day, one month after the end of the trial of the Portland Spy Ring, the chief magistrate issued a brief official notice to newspapers, stating that a former government official had been sent for trial charged with three offenses under the Official Secrets Act.

The statement rated a paragraph near the bottom of the page in most newspapers. It was couched in a manner that seemed safe to assume that it must be a case of a junior civil servant blotting his copybook with a minor indiscretion. The name of the culprit was given as "George Blake, a government official, of no fixed address."

Fleet Street did not think the story looked very promising. Certainly it bore no sign of being a patch on the splendid naval spy case of the mysterious Lonsdale, the Krogers, Harry Houghton and his lover, Missy "Bunty" Gee. That court drama enacted at the Old Bailey during March for a whole week had been as good as a spy thriller. In comparison, this seemed a nonevent.

Gillian Blake, at Shemlan, received a note from her husband, informing her that he had to stay in London, but would write soon, and telling her not to worry. After a few days she received a message from the British ambassador in Beirut, Sir Ponsonby Moore Crosthwaite, saying that her husband had been delayed in London. On Saturday, April 8, Anthony's birthday party took place without his daddy, in a subdued mood. There was no news from London, not even a greetings telegram for the boy from his father.

On Monday, April 10, a woman official from the Foreign Office arrived by air in Beirut and went to Blake's villa at Shemlan. As gently as she could she told Gillian Blake that her husband had been taken into custody and charged with very serious offenses. Mrs. Blake put up a brave face. She later said she realized that her life was shattered, but she had no time to weep. The visitor told her that she must pack some belongings and accompany her with the children to London. She had already booked passage for the following day.

Mrs. Blake went to the general store and paid the grocery bill, telephoned a few friends to tell them that she and the children had to go to England because of a family matter. Then she packed a few suitcases. On April 11, with the two boys and the Foreign Office official she flew to London. She was expecting her confinement within six weeks. After her arrival she was advised not to stay in London, in order to avoid newspaper reporters. She went with the children to the home of friends in Sussex.

A few days later she was allowed to visit her husband at Brixton prison. It was a pathetic reunion, with a Security officer hovering in the background. She was told that George's trial was due to take place at the Central Criminal Court at Old Bailey within three weeks and that the authorities were anxious to have as little publicity as possible.

The story, if not the mystery, of George Blake was drawing to an end—or so it seemed.

CHAPTER EIGHTEEN

THE TRIAL

When at nine minutes past ten in the morning of May 3, 1961, Lord Parker of Waddington, the lord chief justice of England entered Court No. 1 at the Central Criminal Court in the Old Bailey, only a few members of the public were in the gallery but the three rows of benches reserved for press reporters were well filled.

Sir Theobald Mathew, director of public prosecutions, was sitting in front of counsel's bench, occupied by Sir Reginald Manningham-Buller, the attorney general, and Blake's counsel for the defense, Mr. Jeremy Hutchinson, Q.C.

In the well of the courtroom sat three gentlemen, whom only very few people would have recognized as the chiefs of the secret services.

Blake was called into the dock. He was looking younger than his years, clean-shaven, without the beard which has been shown in photographs published after his trial and taken in 1953 after his arrival from Korea. He wore a dark gray suit, sober checked shirt with a blue tie with red spots. He seemed impassive, looking steadily at the lord chief justice, though there was an occasional twitch on his deeply dimpled, sunburned face. His long dark hair was parted low on one side.

The clerk of the court read the indictment, enumerating the five charges under the Official Secrets Act, namely that "for a purpose prejudicial to the safety of the interests of the state, he communicated to another person information which might have been useful to an enemy."

To the question whether he pleaded "guilty" or "not guilty" to these charges, Blake replied, hardly audibly: "Guilty, sir."

Lord Parker then invited the attorney general to present the case for the prosecution. Sir Reginald Manningham-Buller (now Viscount Dilhorne), a tall, massive man, a barrister for thirty-four years, had been a Conservative member of Parliament for nineteen. A product of Eton and Magdalene, Oxford, grandson of the earl of Leicester, married to a daughter of the earl of Crawford, he was a pillar of the Establishment which the prisoner in the dock had let down so invidiously.

The attorney general began in solemn tones: "The charges to which the accused pleaded guilty are of a very serious character. I shall tell the court a little about them in open court, and about his history. Until these matters came to light it was right to say that Blake enjoyed the reputation of a good character. In October 1943 the defendant, who was a British subject, volunteered for service in the Royal Navy and served until 1948. From that date until his arrest he had been employed in the government service both in this country and overseas."

Pointing to the great pile of papers in front of him, the attorney general continued: "As Your Lordship knows from the depositions, he has made a detailed confession. Its contents, except for the short passages to which I propose to refer, must remain secret, and if there is any question of referring to the confession, apart from those parts I shall mention, I shall have to ask you to close the court and sit *in camera.*

"In that statement Blake says that more than ten years ago his philosophical and political views underwent a change and . . . he held the strong conviction that the Communist system was the better one and deserved to triumph. To quote his own words, he resolved to join the Communist side in establishing what he believed to be a balanced and more just society.

"Having reached this conclusion he did not take the course of resigning from the government service. What he did was to approach the Russians and volunteer to work for them.

"His offer was accepted, and I use his own words, he agreed to make available to the Soviet Intelligence Service such information as came his way in the course of his duties in order to promote the cause of communism.

"It appears from his statement that for the past nine and a half years, while employed in the government service and drawing his salary from the state, he had been working as an agent for the Russians, as a spy for them, and communicating a mass of information to them. In short, for the past nine and a half years he had been engaged in betraying his country.

"I cannot publicly reveal the nature of the information he has communicated," Sir Reginald said, "but in his statement he says this, and again I quote his own words: 'I must freely admit that there was not an official document of any importance to which I had access which was not passed to my Soviet contacts.'

"And he had access to information of very great importance," Sir Reginald added gravely.

Referring to the trial of the "naval spies"—Lonsdale, the Krogers, Harry Houghton, and Miss Gee—the attorney-general continued: "Recently Your Lordship tried in this court another serious case where the charge was conspiracy to commit breaches of the Official Secrets Act. That was a grave case but it is right that I should say that the facts of this case bear no resemblance or connection to the facts of that case, but that this is an even graver case is clearly shown by the confession made by the accused. It is not necessary for me to say anything more at this stage on behalf of the prosecution."

The lord chief justice asked whether the attorney general now wanted the court to be closed. Sir Reginald replied that he understood that "counsel for the defense would be better able to put forward his plea of mitigation if the court was cleared.

"I accordingly apply to Your Lordship that the court be closed on the grounds that matters may be referred to which would be prejudicial to the national safety."

The lord chief justice: "I have a strong dislike of hearing anything *in camera* but I gather you are both satisfied that it would be better?"

Lord Parker now turned to counsel for the defense, Mr. Jeremy Hutchinson, Q.C., and asked him whether that was so.

Mr. Hutchinson: "I have indicated, my lord, some of those matters which I wish to urge in mitigation and which are most vital to this man. I am told that much of what I wish to say should not be said in public and, therefore, my choice must be whether the full facts should be put before you, or whether I should leave out much that should be said, but at least some mitigation should be known to the world in general. In those circumstances my client wishes, in spite of the disadvantages in many ways, to him, that I should have complete freedom to address Your Lordship on all matters."

Nothing was said in open court about the nature of the mitigation put by counsel *in camera*. But the shrewd guess of those who had studied the Blake case is that it referred to the fact that Blake's superiors acquiesced and even encouraged him to become a double agent.

The lord chief justice then ordered that the court should be cleared. The newspaper reporters stood up and left the courtroom while ushers asked the few people in the public gallery to leave.

Wooden shutters were then placed on the glass-paneled swing doors and on all windows, and police constables took up positions in the corridors outside Court No. 1. Everybody, including barristers and solicitors not connected with the trial, was barred from entering it.

After fifty-three minutes, during which Mr. Hutchinson addressed the court on behalf of Blake, ushers removed the shutters, opened the locked doors, and told the group of press reporters they might now enter the courtroom again.

When the court was reopened, the clerk of the court rose and said to Blake: "You stand convicted of felony. Is there anything you wish to say why sentence should not be passed upon you according to law?"

George Blake shook his head, his lips moved as if he would say "No," but no sound came from him that would be audible at the press bench.

He stood upright, at first with his fingers holding the ledge of the dock, then folding his arms. He glanced upward to the public gallery as if looking for a friend or relative; then he looked down from the dock to the benches of the newspapermen on the other side of him.

As the lord chief justice began to address him, Blake looked at him directly with his head slightly inclined to one side, betraying no emotion, but moistening his lips a few times.

Lord Parker said: "Your full written confession reveals that for some years you have been working continuously as an agent and spy for a foreign power. Moreover, the information communicated, though not of a scientific nature, was clearly of the utmost importance to that power and has rendered much of this country's efforts completely useless.

"Indeed, you yourself have said in your confession that there was not an official document of any importance to which you had access which was not passed to your Soviet contact.

"When one realizes that you are a British subject, albeit not by birth, and that throughout this period you were employed by this country—your country—in responsible positions of trust, it is clear that your case is akin to treason. Indeed, it is one of the worst that can be envisaged other than in time of war.

"It would clearly be contrary to the public interest for me to refer in sentencing you to the full contents of your confession. I can, however, say, without hesitation, that no one who has read it could possibly fail to take that view.

"I have listened to all that has been so ably said on your behalf and *I fully recognize that it is unfortunate for you that many matters urged in mitigation cannot be divulged*, but I can say this, that I am perfectly prepared to accept that it was not for money that you did this, but because of your conversion to a genuine belief in the Communist system. Everyone is entitled to their own views, but the gravamen of the case against you is that you never resigned, that you retained your employment in positions of trust in order to betray your country.

"You are not yet thirty-nine years of age. You must know and appreciate the gravity of the offenses to which you have pleaded guilty. Your conduct in many other countries would undoubtedly carry the death penalty. In our law, however, I have no option but to sentence you to imprisonment and for your traitorous conduct extending over so many years there must be a very heavy sentence.

"For a single offense of this kind the highest penalty laid down is fourteen years' imprisonment and the court cannot, therefore, even if so minded, give you a sentence of life imprisonment.

"There are, however, five counts to which you have pleaded guilty, each dealing with separate periods in your life during which you were betraying this country.

"The court will impose upon you a sentence of fourteen years' imprisonment on each of the five counts. Those in respect of counts one, two, and three will be consecutive, and those in respect of counts four and five will be conccurrent, making a total of forty-two years' imprisonment."

All throughout the judge's pronouncement Blake appeared to remain quite impassive, looking straight at the lord chief justice. Only when he heard the words "forty-two years' imprisonment" did he move. He leaned forward slightly. That was all. Motioned by the guard, he turned slowly and descended the steps from the dock to the cells below.

The sequel of the trial in Parliament and press was to be much more dramatic than the trial itself.

The newspaper reporters rushed to the telephones and the evening editions carried banner headlines announcing "the longest prison sentence ever imposed in modern British history. . . ."

Soon the news became the subject of lively discussions when people made their way home from work that evening. In the House of Commons the chamber rapidly emptied when the Rating and Valuation Bill was being debated and M.P.s congregated in the smoking room and bars, discussing the Blake trial. The next morning *The Times* parliamentary correspondence reported that "both sides at Westminster have been shaken by the statements made in court . . . and many M.P.s have been framing questions to put to the prime minister, who has the responsiblity for security."

The newspapers, "gagged" by official requests not to report anything beyond the bare facts of the trial, inevitably printed vague stories about George Blake's life, his appointment as vice-consul at Seoul, and his imprisonment by the Korean Communists. But several M.P.s embarked immediately on their own inquiries about Blake's real position in the government service and discovered that he was a senior man of M.I.6.

When late in the evening the prime minister was told that several questions had been submitted, he decided to forestall an embarrassing situation.

Next afternoon Mr. Macmillan rose after Question Time, during which none of the prepared questions on the Order Paper which concerned Blake had been reached. The prime minister was thus spared replying to embarrassing "supplementary" questions and could hope to have an easy out. He said that he thought it right to make a statement about the grave case of George Blake. "I naturally wish to give the House as much information as I can, consistently with the national interest and without prejudicing any appeal. Blake, who is a British subject by birth,* served with credit through the war with the R.N.V.R. In 1948 he was temporarily employed as vice-consul in Seoul, where he was interned by the Chinese and held for nearly three years in captivity. Although he no doubt underwent a certain amount of ill-treatment in common with others who were interned, he was subject to none of the brainwashing which military prisoners suffered. After his release, and after having been subjected to a very thorough security vetting, Blake was employed for a period with the British military government in Berlin and subsequently attached for a time to the Foreign Office in London. In September 1960 he was sent to learn Arabic in the Lebanon. Blake was never an established member of the Foreign Service. There is no reason to doubt that until 1951 he gave loyal service to this country. . . . It would appear that he voluntarily became a convert to what most members of this House would regard as an evil faith. However regrettable we may regard such a conversion, it does not of course, constitute criminal conduct. But to this he

_____
* Here the prime minister was at variance with the lord chief justice, who correctly said at the trial that Blake was "a British subject albeit not by birth."

added treachery to the state. He agreed, in his own words, to make available to the Soviet Intelligence such information as came his way in the course of his duties. It was for doing this that he was tried and sentenced."

After some interruptions and renewed questions whether it was proper for the prime minister to make such a statement in view of the possibility of an appeal, Mr. Macmillan continued: "Blake's action was not the result of brainwashing or intimidation while a prisoner. Nor did he fall to any of the other kinds of pressure which are sometimes employed in these circumstances. He received no money for his services. He was never at any time a member of the Commnist party or any of its affiliated organizations. What he did was done, in the words of the lord chief justice, as the result of conversion to a genuine belief in the Communist system. In these circumstances suspicion would not easily be aroused in relation to a man who had served his country well for some eight years, who gave every appearance of leading a normal and respectable life, but who had decided to betray his country for ideological reasons. Indeed, having agreed to work for the Russians, he was careful not to arouse suspicion and to conceal his conversion to communism. Eventually, however, his activities were uncovered and the result was his trial at the Old Bailey. He had access to information of importance and he passed it on. As the attorney general said in open court, he has done serious damage to the interests of this country. As to that it would not be right, nor would it be in the public interest, for me to say more than was said in open court yesterday."

Pausing for a moment, the prime minister continued with emphasis: "But I can assure the House that Blake's disclosures will not have done irreparable damage. In particular, he had no access to secret information on defense, nuclear, or atomic matters.

"Such cases as this are, I hope, extremely rare. But by reason of their very nature they are very difficult to detect or prevent by security procedures. No such procedures can guarantee to catch a man who changes his allegiance and skillfully conceals his conversion. *I do not, therefore, think that any inquiry such as that now being conducted in relation to another case* with which Blake's case has no connection and affords no parallel, would serve any useful purpose.* But I can assure the House that I am reviewing all the circumstances with very great care to see whether there are any possible further measures which could be taken to protect this country from treachery of this kind."

Anticipating an attack from the Opposition and demands for full inquiry, the prime minister concluded: "While I recognize to the full the responsibility that rests on H.M. government, I should be very willing to discuss with the leader of the Opposition the circumstances of this case and the matters that arise from it."

The leader of the Opposition, the late Mr. Hugh Gaitskell welcomed the statement because "there was widespread disquiet that this kind of thing could have been allowed to happen and a man could for nine and a half years supply information to the Soviet Union. In these circumstances I consider it right to accept the prime minister's invitation for talks, but some kind of inquiry was necessary to assure the public the right things were being done to prevent this sort of thing happening again."

Mr. Richard Marsh, Labour M.P. for Greenwich (later a member in Mr. Wilson's cabinet), said that "although Blake might not have been an established civil servant he was, in fact, employed by Foreign Office Intelligence."

To this the prime minister replied: "It would not be right for me to add anything said in the court *in camera.*"

It should be remembered that when these matters were discussed in the House of Commons, the British press was still prevented from publishing any relevant information because of the requests conveyed through the so-called D-notices. A remark by Mr. John Hynd, Labour M.P. for Attercliffe, caused some consternation, but remained unanswered by the prime minister. Mr. Hynd said: "The foreign press has already been able to present very full

---

* The committee headed by Lord Romer, inquiring into naval security procedures.

reports of the evidence given *in camera* in this case." German newspapers on the morning after the trial disclosed that Blake had been a senior agent of the British secret service, working for four years in its Berlin headquarters at the Olympia Stadium Buildings.

The British public and, for that matter, members of Parliament did not know anything about this, with the exception, perhaps, of the few people who had seen these German reports.

The next few days went by with newspapers merely reporting that the prime minister had seen Mr. Gaitskell and three Opposition privy councillors.

Then a number of M.P.s on both sides of the House tabled a series of questions about the character of Blake's employment, about the date when Blake's name last appeared on the Foreign Office List, and how long afterwards he had been employed by the Foreign Office. By and by M.P.s had begun to discover that the prime minister's statement had indicated Blake's real position only very vaguely.

The Labour party Opposition "Shadow Cabinet" met and decided to press the prime minister for instituting a full inquiry and to demand a full statement.

Several newspapers now decided to disregard the D-notices. The *Daily Telegraph* and the *Daily Mail* began on the Monday after the trial to publish some details about Blake's life and position. The *Daily Mirror* described the statements made by the prime minister as "feeble, evasive and utterly unsatisfactory," and the *Sunday Pictorial* asked: "Why keep the public in the dark?"

Faced with this onslaught in Parliament and press, not only from the Labour side, but by Conservative newspapers and several Tory M.P.s, the prime minister decided to give some explanation for the decision to impose the "gag" and suppress publication of stories about Blake, particularly after Mr. Gaitskell asked: "Did this procedure not attract so much publicity that it did almost as much damage as the Blake case did itself? Can you give us a rather fuller answer?"

The prime minister stood up and the two party leaders, who had held their private discussions the day before, eyed one another for a few moments. Mr. Macmillan hesitated and then said: "I would rather not add anything publicly. There was some advantage in the time lag of publication."

He was further pressed for a fuller reply. After sitting for a while with his arms folded, Mr. Macmillan finally replied: "I was quite satisfied, for a number of reasons, which I will not reveal, that I was right in what I did. . . . Information can leak or be planted. I do not wish to take this further, except to say that I hope the House trusts my personal word that I believe what I did was right and had some advantage. It is true that the advantage was not sustained for as long a period as I had hoped."

This was an intriguing statement. Several papers commented upon it by saying that "a new mystery over the Blake case was raised in the House of Commons—by the prime minister himself."

Political and parliamentary journalists got busy interpreting the meaning of the prime minister's remarks.

Some claimed to have information from "a high government source" according to which the suppression of news in the British press had served "to save lives of other British agents who might have been betrayed by Blake." These agents, behind the Iron Curtain, were to be quickly withdrawn by the British secret service. But if Blake had betrayed them, he must have done so a long time before his arrest in April and, at the time of his trial in May, the Russians must have been fully aware of the identity and location of these agents. Moreover, the secret service had, of course, sufficient time to withdraw these agents without waiting for the trial and the gag on the British newspapers, after Blake's trial.

The only real explanation for Mr. Macmillan's vacillation was that he tried to protect the secret service chiefs and Blake's immediate superiors—though he was not particularly successful.

The uproar in Parliament and press was followed by an announcement by the prime minister that he had appointed Lord Radcliffe, a lord of appeal, to preside over a committee to inquire into Britain's security services. This announcement was made on May 15, 1961. The terms of reference of the committee were: "In the light of recent convictions for offenses under the Official Secrets Act, to review the security procedures and practices currently followed in the public service and to consider what, if any, changes are required." They were drawn up so cautiously by the prime minister that they precluded the committee from being able to answer the questions uppermost in the minds of ordinary citizens: "What is wrong with the British secret service? How could a double agent work undetected for many years, have access to most guarded secrets of the state, and with apparent ease, betray them to a potential enemy?"

The committee sat for eight months. The report was published in April 1962. Some parts of it were never published at all, because Lord Radcliffe and the four other members decided that their publication "was incompatible with the requirements of national security." While paying respectful tributes to Lord Radcliffe's wisdom, many members of Parliament and political writers in newspapers did not disguise their disappointment. Some described the report as "an attempt at whitewashing the secret service." Indeed, the committee rather surprisingly declared that there was nothing basically wrong with the secret service and proclaimed the self-evident truth that "the sources from which the main threat to national security comes are the intelligence services of foreign powers, and subversive organizations in this country to which the most formidable is the Communist party and its sympathizers." Unexpectedly, the committee came down heavily on the civil service unions and expressed the anxiety at the number of Communists and Communist sympathizers who were holding positions in these unions and who had achieved a higher degree of penetration than in almost any other sector of the trade-union movement. Although the committee stated that none of these officials had been detected in any form of espionage, "the deliberate massing of Communist effort in the civil service unions must be regarded as most dangerous to security."

The main recommendations to improve security were as disappointing as the main text of the report, in which no reference to the Blake case was made. They were:

An all around tightening up of personal checks and investigations of civil servants, particularly those in sensitive posts. No one who has been a captive in Communist hands should be employed in a security-risk job—the only distinct reference to Blake.

British embassies, particularly in Communist countries, should exercise meticulous care.

The security risk of diplomats and officials marrying foreign wives should be borne in mind.

Many recommendations dealt with purely administrative measures in government offices to strengthen day-to-day security, to keep important documents safely, and so on. The only improvement in any of the government departments which the committee regarded as necessary concerned security arrangements in the admiralty—a reference to the treachery of the two civil servants involved in the Naval Spy Ring.

The cabinet had received the report four and a half months before its publication and Mr. Macmillan assured the House of Commons that in the meantime a thorough "vetting" of all civil servants with access to secrets had been carried out most intensively. The report was an anticlimax to the Blake trial and the sensational disclosures which followed it.

Even after a tightening of the security regulations the officials concerned failed to detect in time the admiralty clerk John Vassall, and it must have escaped them that Frank Clifford Bossard, employed on secret scientific and telecommunications work for the Ministry of Defense in Germany and later as an officer of the Intelligence Service in London, had been a Nazi sympathizer and Mosley follower before the war, had been sent (in 1934) to prison for fraud, and in more recent years had been a heavy drinker. At his trial he admitted to having received five thousand pounds from the Russians.

If one wonders how Blake could remain undetected for so many years, one derives little solace from the knowledge that Vassall had been betraying secrets for seven years, and Bossard for at least five years. In a case still before the courts in 1970 the accused has been charged with offenses alleged to have been committed over eight years.

What the nation expected from the Radcliffe Committee and from several others, which followed between 1962 and 1966, was that they would deal with the following main problems: First, examine the competence of the man in command of the departments of the British secret service and Intelligence and the quality of the secret agents employed; second, examine the cooperation between the existing departments, who often vie with each other and overlap in their tasks; third, inquire into the present-day practice of recruitment of recent agents and security officers, which leaves a lot to be desired; fourth, review the organization and finance of the secret service, which many experts consider greatly out of date; finally, examine the practice of handling of secret documents and information which, as the Blake case—and others—had shown, must have been extremely perfunctory.

In fairness to British counterespionage it must be conceded that Britain's liberal laws often prevent the authorities from using methods which are at the disposal of their colleagues elsewhere, particularly in the United States. British public opinion is strongly opposed to methods such as searching a home without a search warrant, the interception of mail, the tapping of telephone conversations, the interrogation of the employers, neighbors, and friends of a suspect, or the detention of a man as a "material witness," without being charged and brought before a magistrate. Lately some of these methods have been applied in Britain, but whenever they become known they cause a public outcry. However, the lesson of the spy cases is that, though it may be unpalatable, the hand of counterespionage authorities must be strengthened. What public opinion, the House of Commons, and the press must jealousy watch is that such methods should be used with great restraint.

After Blake's trial the British people were shocked into attention and the main cause of alarm was the fact that Blake had been a traitor for so many years while holding a position of trust.

Then came the summer, people went on holiday, and Blake's name disappeared from the headlines and was soon forgotten. Another economic crisis was upon us, with a "financial squeeze," a wave of strikes and industrial disputes, and a sadly deflated stock exchange.

One or two brief news items reminded the public of the traitor who had been given the longest prison sentence in Britain's legal history. One was that, three weeks after the trial, Mrs. Gillian Blake had given birth to her third child, a boy, who was christened George Patrick. Some people expressed sympathy for his father, who might not see him until the boy grew up. There was a story in a popular morning paper that Blake had suffered a nervous breakdown after the trial and had been removed to the prison hospital.

Eventually, hardly anybody in Britain talked about the mysterious case of George Blake, until the British people and, indeed, all the world were confronted by the much more sensational case of Captain Ivanov, who shared a mistress with the British secretary of state for war. By 1963, when the "Profumo affair" hit the headlines, most people could hardly recall Blake's name. Their memory certainly received a jolt when in October 1966 the news of his startling escape from Wormwood Scrubs was splashed across the front page.

CHAPTER NINETEEN

THE MODEL PRISONER PONDERS ESCAPE

Blake had certainly not expected to receive such a terrible punishment. Both his defense counsel and his solicitor Mr. A. E. Cox, had warned him that he might be sentenced to fourteen years, a term given to Klaus Fuchs for the betrayal of the West's most closely guarded atomic secrets.

But the lord chief justice made the sentence for three out of five counts of the indictment run consecutively and not concurrently as in all previous spy trials. This was later regarded by eminent lawyers as a questionable decision.

It was never disclosed at the trial that, a few days before it began, the attorney general had a conference with counsel for the defense. It is an unusual practice, but permissible in this case, for it took place in order to prevent national security being harmed by possible statements in open court. I have reason to believe that the attorney general and Blake's counsel also agreed that the plea relating to mitigating circumstances—the acquiescence of Blake's superior to his operating as a double agent—would be put to the court in secret session.

A more puzzling fact was that certain documents, including Blake's diaries, seized at his villa in Shemlan, had been shown to his counsel only at 5:00 P.M. in the afternoon on the day before the trial. Blake's uncle, Anthony Beijderwellen, told me that Blake had been advised to plead "guilty" on all five counts of the indictment under the Official Secrets Act. Beijderwellen insisted that Blake received this advice and accepted it, because he hoped that if he pleaded guilty to all counts and did not contest any of the submissions of the prosecution, he would "get off more lightly."

Blake was unprepared for the severity of the sentence meted out to him. Two days after the trial his solicitor told a newspaper reporter that his client had collapsed in his cell, suffering from shock, and had been admitted to the prison hospital at Wormwood Scrubs. Afterwards the solicitor announced that it had been decided to lodge an appeal against the sentence.

The appeal was heard at the Court of Criminal Appeal on June 19, 1961. Sitting with Mr. Justice Hilbery, the senior queen's bench judge, were Mr. Justice Ashworth and Mr. Justice Paul. Blake, still ill, was not brought from prison for the hearing. Three-quarters of an hour of the hearing was *in camera*, with the public and newspaper reporters excluded. At the beginning of the open session, Mr. Justice Hilbery said that the only ground of appeal was that the sentence was too severe, and he added that the court had read all the submissions made by the defense in mitigation at the Old Bailey.

Mr. Jeremy Hutchinson, Q.C., who again appeared for Blake, said: "The effect of that sentence was to cover the rest of the applicant's natural life. That sentence raises a matter of principle of fundamental importance, not only to the applicant but to the administration of British justice. The sentence is inordinate, unprecedented, and manifestly excessive. To pass consecutive sentences of fourteen years' imprisonment is wrong in principle."

The barrister complained that substantial mitigating circumstances surrounding Blake's conduct—which he was forbidden to mention in open session—had been given no weight by the lord chief justice in passing sentence. He then asked to be allowed to refer to a number of these mitigating factors in open court.

But Mr. Justice Hilbery refused. "We are solely concerned to administer the law. We are not here to scotch some rumor. We are here to consider whether this sentence was wrong in principle or manifestly excessive. What difference does it make to the applicant whether certain submissions were made in public or in private?"

Mr. Hutchinson argued that the sentence had the factual meaning of life imprisonment. But while in modern times life imprisonment meant a maximum of twenty years before remission and, indeed, more recently the norm served in terms of life imprisonment was about ten years, the sentence imposed upon Blake deprived him of the normal chance of remission for good conduct, and also deprived him of the protection of review by the home secretary, from which he would have benefited if sentenced to life imprisonment.

When defense counsel said that during the long months at the prison camp in Korea, Blake was allowed only to read the works of Marx, Engels, Lenin, and Stalin, Mr. Justice Hilbery remarked: "He has not been condemned for having a particular political ideology. He has been condemned for remaining in the service of his country and, in a way which is particularly odious, surreptitiously attempting to do this country as much harm as it was in his power."

Mr. Justice Hilbery announced that the appeal was dismissed and that the Court of Criminal Appeal had upheld the forty-two-year sentence passed at the Old Bailey. He added that the court's reasons would be given later. Four days later a short statement was made public: The Court of Criminal Appeal had found that the lord chief justice's words that "Blake's case was one of the worst that can be envisaged in times of peace" accurately represented the view of the appeal judges who added: "This sentence had a threefold purpose. It was intended to be punitive. It was designed and calculated to deter others. It was meant to be a safeguard to this country."

The legal process had run its course.

At Wormwood Scrubs Blake had settled down to normal prison routine. Indeed, it seemed that he had recovered rather quickly from his nervous collapse and had accepted his fate. It was only after his escape, when the report of Earl Mountbatten's Inquiry was published in

December 1966, that it became known that Blake had been placed on the escape list and was allocated a special security cell. A prisoner on the escape list at Wormwood Scrubs is never kept in a cell with a ventilating shaft under the floor, lest he might try to use it for a getaway; there is light in his cell throughout the night; and all his clothes, except for a shirt and slippers, must be placed outside the cell at night. Such a prisoner wears large patches of cloth, in contrasting colors—orange, red, yellow—on each item of his outer clothing. Regular searches of his cell are frequently made and he is barred from many communal activities.

For a time Blake was subjected to these harrowing experiences but at the beginning of October 1961, the governor of Wormwood Scrubs, after consultation with the prison commissioners, decided to remove Blake from the escape list. By September 20 the director general of security service had informed the prison authorities that the intensive interrogations of Blake, conducted by senior secret service officers, would soon have to come to an end. Thus, the prison commissioners could consider moving Blake from Wormwood Scrubs to another prison, where he would be able to come into contact with other spies. At that time Lonsdale, the chief actor in the Portland Naval Spy Case, was also held at Wormwood Scrubs.

The security service asked the prison commissioners to transfer Blake to Winston Green Prison in Birmingham. But the commissioners replied that it would be a considerable hardship to Blake's wife and mother if he were moved so far from London. In the course of the next two years there were several exchanges between the director general of the security service and the prison commissioners. In December 1963 it was suggested Blake should be sent to Wakefield Prison. But for reasons not explained in the report of the Mountbatten Inquiry Blake stayed at Wormwood Scrubs. He became a model prisoner.

In the autumn of 1961 he asked for permission to take a correspondence course in Arabic. He was not yet allowed—as were many other prisoners—to attend educational classes. One reason for this was that Blake was held in "D" block, which is a security block at Wormwood Scrubs. Teachers conduct their classes in different parts of the prison and are not allowed inside "D" block; prisoners who leave "D" block must always be accompanied by guards. Because of the shortage of guards it would have been difficult to let Blake, and other "D" block prisoners, take part in educational classes held in other blocks.

Hence, Blake was allowed to take a correspondence course with a reputable college. At first the security service received all the original scripts for examination before they were given to Blake and also examined all the essays and material he sent back to the college. Because this caused long delays, it was later arranged for photostat copies to be made of all this matter and the copies were examined by security. The purpose was, of course, to prevent Blake receiving or sending secret communications.

He had regular visits from his wife and mother. Prison rules require that visitors must be within the sight and hearing of a prison officer. In February 1962 there were consultations between the prison authorities and the security service about the desirability of having a security officer present at Blake's visits. But the security service decided against it. Both Mrs. Blake senior and Mrs. Gillian Blake were regarded as fully trustworthy; there was no suspicion that they would exchange any surreptitious messages with the prisoner, or pass any articles forbidden by prison rules.

While Blake thus had a very limited and, from the point of view of the security and prison authorities, safe contact with the outer world, he was able to associate freely with many other prisoners in "D" block. At the end of 1961, Gordon Lonsdale was at Wormwood Scrubs and was surprisingly allocated a cell in the same hall as Blake's. On a number of occasions Lonsdale and Blake met and had long conversations, without a prison officer being present. It was later suggested that these strange meetings between two convicted spies during daily exercises and at film shows and recreational hours were encouraged by the security service in the hope that Lonsdale might be induced to reveal information to Blake. Lonsdale had persistently refused to reveal his real identity and insisted that he was a Canadian.

It was said that hidden microphones were installed and that security officers had monitored the conversations between the two men. This is extremely improbable because a whispered conversation during a walk in the yard could hardly have been monitored by microphones. Bourke does not recall having ever noticed such devices.

When a former prisoner, Mr. Norman Andrews, who had been a "trusted blue band" at Wormwood Scrubs, told the *Sunday Times* in May 1964 about the meetings between Blake and Lonsdale and his story was published, Mr. Henry Brooke (now Lord Brooke), then the home secretary, was questioned in the House of Commons. Miss Alice Bacon, Labour M.P. for Leeds Southeast (afterwards herself a minister of state at the Home Office) asked what instructions were given at Wormwood Scrubs about the association of the two prisoners George Blake and Gordon Lonsdale.

Mr. Brooke firmly denied that any meetings between Blake and Lonsdale had ever taken place in prison. He upheld his denial even after the editor of the *Sunday Times* produced a sworn affidavit by Mr. Norman Andrews that he had seen Blake and Lonsdale talking on several occasions to each other, and twice being together at a film show. On June 4, 1964, Mr. Brooke was again challenged in the House of Commons. This was only a few months before the general election which his party lost. He again rejected the depositions by Mr. Andrews and also another sworn statement by a second prisoner, who said that he had been told by Lonsdale about his meetings with Blake. Mr. Brooke told the House that Mr. Andrews "was a prisoner of doubtful mental state who had been sent to Wormwood Scrubs for psychiatric investigation." Many prisoners undergo psychiatric investigation; indeed this is part of their rehabilitation treatment. Mr. Andrews is today a successful businessman, running two shops and incidentally, not a political adversary of Lord Brooke, but a respected member of his local Conservative club.

When the then home secretary affirmed his denial, Mr. Jo Grimond, M.P., the former leader of the Liberal party, challenged him and the attorney general, Sir John Hobson, to initiate proceedings for perjury against Mr. Andrews and the other prisoner, as they had made sworn statements which the home secretary declared untrue. But the attorney general replied that "there was not sufficient evidence to put either man on a charge," a somewhat strange statement as the written affadavits were in the possession of the *Sunday Times*.

But this was election year and the incident was soon forgotten—until Blake's escape in 1966, when it was once again discussed in the House of Commons and widely commented on in the press. Significantly, the controversy began in May 1964, a week or two after Gordon Lonsdale had left the inhospitable shores of Britain: on April 20, 1964, he was exchanged in Berlin for the British agent Greville Wynne.

In his *Izvestya* interview, six years later, Blake confirmed that he had had regular meetings with Lonsdale, whom he "badly missed after he left prison."

It is, of course, idle to speculate what information Blake could have supplied to Lonsdale when they met in prison. But in view of Blake's escape it might be possible that Lonsdale, after his return to Russia in 1964, had been in some way instrumental in arranging assistance for Blake.

Blake was not prevented from having friendly chats with yet another convicted Soviet spy—William Vassall. In a sworn statement (afterwards published in the *Sunday Times* on November 13, 1966, a few weeks after Blake's escape), another prisoner, Mr. John McGrath, made some startling disclosures about these meetings.

McGrath was in Wormwood Scrubs from 1962 until September 1965. He had been given special remission for his brave assistance to guards, when fighting a fire in the prison. He was a "blue-band leader," that is a trusted prisoner, and allowed to move fairly freely around and do various chores without guards being present. One of his duties was to make tea for prisoners' visitors. McGrath stated that one of the first friends he made was George Blake, because they shared an interest in the Middle East and Arabic. McGrath spent a considerable period there. He recalled that during most of Blake's visits from his family, he arranged tea for them. Blake's visitors were his wife, his mother, his sister and her husband, and his father-in-law.

When Vassall arrived at Wormwood Scrubs, McGrath also became friendly with him. At first Vassall was subject to the usual "escape restrictions." When these were removed he was given a cell opposite Blake's. "The two became close friends and went together to evening classes," Mr. McGrath stated. "In the evening they would spend a great deal of time together and exchange books, sweets, or fruit."

There is no reason whatsoever to doubt Mr. McGrath's sworn statement. He became Vassall's godfather at a baptizing ceremony, when Vassall—the son of an Anglican vicar—became a convert to Roman Catholicism. The ceremony was officiated by Archbishop (now Cardinal) Heenan, who on several occasions visited the prison. In 1965 Vassall was moved to Maidstone Prison, and Blake lost another close companion and ex-fellow spy.

Soon after the Lonsdale-Wynne exchange, at the beginning of May 1964, the governor of Wormwood Scrubs, Mr. T.W.H. Hayes, submitted to the Prison Department at the Home Office a detailed report of information given to him by two prisoners about an alleged plot to get Blake out of prison. The governor was told that a plan had been made to enable Blake to escape to East Germany and then to the Soviet Union.

Although the story sounded like a script from a television thriller, it was carefully examined by the security service. The escape plan was, briefly, as follows:

An ex-prisoner who knew the layout of the prison well would enter the prison, climbing the wall from outside, wearing prison clothes and the blue armband worn by "trustee" prisoners who are allowed to move freely within the prison. This "pimpernel," disguised as a prisoner, would go to the mail shop, where Blake was working, and take him out under some pretext into the corridor.

At that moment a helicopter was to land in the yard behind. Blake and his rescuer would run into the yard and get aboard the helicopter. They would then be taken to East Germany, if the helicopter had a sufficient range, or part of the way and change into another helicopter, if necessary.

The prisoner who told this story to the governor declared that he himself was to be one of the pilots of the helicopter and was to escape together with Blake. The crew of the helicopter were to wear British police uniforms, and the helicopter was to be painted blue, with the word PO-LICE painted in white on the side. It was suggested that prison officers would not know whether there were such things as police helicopters, and they would hesitate when this official-looking party landed in the prison yard to prevent them from taking Blake and his friends with them.

This story might have deserved just a hearty laugh, were it not for the man who told it to the governor. He was, in fact, a qualified pilot who, in 1950 had landed a hired sports aircraft equipped with floats on the sea off the New Jersey coast of the United States, alongside the Polish motor ship *Batory,* which was on a voyage from New York to Southampton. The *Batory* is a well-known luxury liner for holiday cruises and she calls frequently at British ports. The man was picked up by the ship's crew together with his small airplane. When the *Batory* called at Southampton a few days later, the man was arrested by British immigration officers because he had no passport. He spent some time at Winchester Prison and later left Britain. That was fourteen years ago. Eventually he came back to Britain, later committed an offense, and was sentenced to a long term in prison. That was how he finally appeared at Wormwood Scrubs as a fellow prisoner and would-be rescuer of George Blake.

The man was, of course, interrogated by the security

service. He had a history of mental instability and his interrogators came to the conclusion that he had invented the whole fantastic tale. But there was still the other man to investigate, the pimpernel who was to enter the prison and alert Blake. This ex-prisoner was duly found by the police. He was the son of a titled personage, had been educated at Eton, from which he had been expelled, and at Oxford University, from which he had also been expelled. Although the black sheep of his distinguished family, he had many excellent connections which he used for unprincipled sponging. It was not at all unlikely that for a large sum of money he would have been prepared to embark on some daring enterprise, such as the escape of George Blake.

There were protracted investigations inside and outside the prison which kept the security service and the Special Branch of Scotland Yard busy for weeks. Another prisoner was located, who was shortly due to be released, and who told yet another story of a plan for Blake's rescue. After his release he was to obtain employment as a solicitor's clerk. This would have enabled him to come to Wormwood Scrubs and talk to prisoners and prison staff. He was to change his appearance, by plastic surgery, to avoid being recognized by "screws" (prison officers) who had known him. Shortly before the date on which Blake was to be taken over the wall, the "solicitor's clerk" was to put an advertisement in *The Times* (which Blake was permitted to read every day) as a signal for Blake, giving him the date of the operation in a simple code. This man was also mixed up in the helicopter plan, but he claimed that he might have taken part in an alternative escape operation, whereby Blake was to be helped over the wall and collected by yet another conspirator outside the prison.

While the investigations were still going on, another prisoner was released from Wormwood Scrubs on May 13, 1964. Two days later he went to Scotland Yard and said that he knew of a plan to free George Blake. He was seen by Chief Inspector Ferguson Smith of the Special Branch. The man said that he spoke Dutch, having lived in South Africa during the war. One day at Wormwood Scrubs he spoke to a black South African prisoner in Afrikaans, and Blake overheard him. As a result he and Blake became friendly and used to converse in Dutch and French.

The ex-prisoner told the chief inspector that three days before his release, on about May 10, Blake asked him whether he would act as a contact for him to some friends he had "outside." The man replied that he was willing to help because he felt that Blake's sentence had been too harsh. Blake then asked him to give him a telephone number through which he could be contacted. Blake did not give him any names or addresses and did not ask him to see any of his friends, but said that they would approach the ex-prisoner by phone in due course. But he never heard from anybody, although on instructions from the police he made all arrangements to be reached through the telephone number he had given Blake.

On October 29, 1964, a prisoner told the governor of Wormwood Scrubs that an attempt would be made to get Blake out of "D" Hall on Christmas Day. I myself have investigated this case and I can reveal the name of this man because, after his release, he had told his story to a reporter of the *People,* without objecting to the publication of his name.

He is Mr. Peter Holmes, aged thirty-four, who had been in business in Willesden in North London when he got into trouble by selling television sets which he had obtained on credit. He was serving a sentence of twelve months at Wormwood Scrubs when he became very friendly with Blake. One day, according to Mr. Holmes, Blake suggested to him that he could make an easy thousand pounds after his release. Blake said that he wanted to escape and some friends would help him. Another prisoner would escape a month earlier and take a party, including two foreigners *who would be immune from arrest* to the vicinity of the prison. Mr. Holmes was to play a part in arranging the contacts and take Blake, after his escape, in a car to an address in Kensington. Blake did not mention the address, but it appeared that he had the Soviet embassy in mind. This would also explain his alleged reference to the foreigners "immune from arrest" and apparently enjoying diplomatic privileges.

All precautions were taken inside and outside the prison but nothing happened at Christmas 1964, and Earl Mountbatten says in his report that he had been unable to find any evidence to suggest that such an attempt was ever planned or intended.

Obviously, with all these stories of plans for Blake's rescue, the security service and the prison authorities took special precautions to watch Blake's behavior. He was questioned about some of the stories, though never told what the authorities had learned from the prisoners and ex-prisoners who gave them the often fantastic-sounding information. Blake just laughed off any suggestion that he wanted to escape. He repeatedly told the governor Mr. Hayes and senior guards that he had settled down in prison and had accepted his fate.

Indeed, he never caused any trouble. The prison officers reciprocated by allowing him various small privileges. At first he worked in the mailbag shop and for a time in the prison laundry but later was given more pleasant work in the bookbinding shop, where he seemed to be happy.

Like all long-term prisoners he was allowed little luxuries in his cell. His wife had brought him a Bokhara rug for the stone floor, his mother made curtains for the barred window, and he had a shelf full of books. In 1965 Blake was moved to another cell, for which he had asked because the view from the window was better. Here he could look down on the bowling green and the aviary.

A fellow prisoner who was a decorator painted the cell for him a bright pink and primrose. On the walls Blake stuck a few prints, including his favorite picture, showing St. Paul studying. Every Sunday morning, after roll call, prisoners are allowed to visit each other within their block, or "hall," and Blake was having a stream of visitors. Each one brought his mug with him and Blake treated them to coffee. Being a nonsmoker and earning eight shillings a week for his prison work, he had enough money to be able to afford these coffee parties. His Sunday visitors were nicknamed "the intellectual élite" by other prisoners, and they often listened with Blake to B.B.C. critics discussing new books, plays, films, and art exhibitions.

Although Blake was in good health throughout his imprisonment, he was a bit of a hypochondriac and a regular attender of medical checks by the prison doctors. As one of his former fellow prisioners said, "A sore throat, a finger cut at work, a piece of grit in his eye, an ingrown toenail—Blake always took the opportunity to consult the doctors or be taken to the hospital." He made friends with guards and nurses; indeed he must have charmed some of them because every time he visited the hospital he was invited to have a cup of tea and biscuits, and sometimes even got a good lunch at the nurses' canteen.

Not long before his escape Blake complained that his sight was impaired and asked to be examined by an ophthalmologist. Blake told him that he was reading a lot and that the lighting in his cell was not too good. He also remarked that, being forty-two, his eyesight might be changing. The doctor found little wrong with Blake's eyes, but prescribed a pair of glasses. Blake was fitted with a No. 524 National Health frame and minus 2 lenses. He took the glasses with him when he escaped and might have used them as part of his disguise because none of the existing photographs of him shows him wearing spectacles.

Blake had made many friends among prisoners from every walk of life, men of good education and background, who had slipped out and served terms for commercial fraud, false pretenses, or some offense which was not directed against society, as well as professional criminals. Everybody liked George because he was always courteous and helpful. Often he assisted fellow prisoners, who had trouble composing a letter, with letters to their families, or advised them on how to tackle a business matter, instruct a solicitor, or make an application for a job while waiting for release.

He also gave lessons, teaching several prisoners French and German, and one or two even Arabic, and he gave lectures on history and travel in the recreation hall which were well attended. He was certainly a model prisoner and popular with the "screws" because he never caused trouble.

A fellow prisoner "Zeno," a wartime officer in the First Airborne Division, parachuted at Arnhem and decorated for gallantry, who was serving a life sentence for murder in a *crime passionnel* became a close friend of Blake. After his release in 1968 on license—having served more than ten years—he published a book* about prison life in which he devoted to Blake a chapter of almost lyrical eulogy: "George Blake's love for mankind takes a more practical form than the intellectual commitment which I feel when I am alone, and therefore at peace with my fellows," he wrote. "I cannot, as George does, ignore the shortcomings, the crudities, and—above all—the lies, and look as he does only at the tolerable qualities of those with whom we spend our days. His tolerance of prison authority is also greater than mine.

"If I had his knowledge of languages and his patience as a teacher, I still could not give up hours a day of my time to teach any man who asked me to. George does just that. He has a class of young cockneys to whom he teaches French, and he has brought them to a standard whereby one at least will shortly be sitting G.C.E. 'A' level, and the others their 'O' levels. For years George devoted an hour a day to teaching a West Indian to speak German. This was particularly remarkable when I remember that I had the greatest difficulty in understanding the man's English. And yet, steadily and despite the hours he spends on his protégés, he is studying for an honors degree in classical Arabic.

"Sometimes when I go to his cell I am greeted by cockney voices holding an animated conversation in French, or reading to each other from French newspapers or periodicals, and if this is the case I withdraw and return at another time. I may find him alone, standing as he

* "Zeno," *Life* (Macmillan, London, 1968).

sometimes does, and reading the Koran, which rests on a lectern made for him by one of his pupils. Or he may be seated at his table making notes, or again he may be lying on his low bed, reading a tale in Arabic from *The Thousand and One Nights*. Whatever he may be doing, if he is alone I am greeted with a charming smile of welcome, an offer to seat myself, and if the time is right an invitation to take a mug of tea."

Blake certainly succeeded in keeping his sanity in prison. He appeared to have resigned himself to staying there for many long years. At least this was the impression "Zeno" had. He asked, and heard the other prisoners asking, Blake whether he thought of escape. There had been several escapes at that time and only few men were recaptured. Blake just shrugged and said, "What's the point?" But when they pressed him, he explained that if he did escape, he could never see his family again. Where could he go? How could he get out of the country? When some prisoners suggested his Russian friends would help him he brushed it off, saying: "I'm no longer of any use to them, I would be an embarrassment. If I got to their embassy, they'd take me, but they wouldn't be happy about it." When more questions were asked about this subject, Blake would suddenly dry up and walk away.

In fact he never stopped thinking of escape, but he knew that he had to bide his time and wait for the signal from his Soviet friends. When the time came he looked for a man who would be of assistance because he had the knowledge of the "inside." However skilled his Russian rescuers were to carry out the operation, its success depended on the knowledge of the prison's layout.

One man with whom Blake struck up a friendship was Sean Bourke, who was serving a sentence of seven years, and with remission for good conduct was to be released in the summer of 1966.

Sean Alphonsus Bourke was then thirty-two years old. He was born in Limerick and he has all the likable traits of a true Irishman as well as the foibles. He had had an adventurous youth and, as he hismelf told me, was a "rolling stone," often changing his jobs and sometimes living rough. In 1961 he worked in a factory at Crawley in Sussex and, as he put it, "had some differences with the local police," and particularly with Detective Constable Michael Sheldon. One day in the summer of 1961, the police officer received a parcel and opened it in the presence of his wife Elsie. The parcel contained a homemade bomb, the load consisting of a handful of screws, bolts, and nuts. The explosion was not particularly violent. Sheldon's wife escaped with a minor burn, her husband was unscathed, but the ceiling and some furniture were badly damaged. Suspicion fell on Bourke, who allegedly had uttered threats against the policeman.

Bourke was arrested and when his room was searched a box with screws and bolts was found, which an expert described as similar to those in the explosive parcel sent to P. C. Sheldon.

Bourke denied being the culprit, but he was sent for trial. The jury found him guilty and he was given a stiff sentence. Thus he found himself one day at Wormwood Scrubs as George Blake's fellow prisoner.

They were not particularly close. Bourke says that Blake had "intellectual" friends. "Because of his background he tended to be surrounded by a small group which included a City financier—serving a term for fraud—an army officer ("Zeno"), a journalist, and another spy."

Sean Bourke, whom I personally met in January 1970 in Dublin, having previously exchanged many letters with him, told me that he has written a book about "the springing of George Blake." I certainly wish him success for his literary effort and have no desire to anticipate it. Bourke told his version of the escape—and, indeed, several very different versions—to reporters, on television and radio, and to judges in Dublin courts who considered the application of his extradition. He also told me a version, which I could not accept. I shall not, therefore, follow it here, but I feel that I should mention Bourke's account of how he first discussed the escape plan with Blake.

Bourke, never lost for a good yarn, put it like this:

"One day I have just finished writing an article for the prison magazine [he was then the editor of Wormwood Scrubs' *New Horizon*] about the bad food we were getting, when Blake approached me. He was not smiling as usual, but frowning. He said, 'Good morning, Sean. May I speak to you for a moment? I have now been here five years and thus far I have been hoping for an exchange of some sort with the Russians but it is not to happen. If I am to leave here at all before I die I must, as it were, do it under my own steam. . . .'

"So he says simply," Bourke recounted, " 'Look, Sean, would you please consider springing me from jail?' "

"I said yes, of course, George. Just like that," Bourke told me. This was about a month before Bourke was released on July 4, 1966.

Bourke recalls that Blake said, "Thank you, I knew you would do it. I wouldn't have asked anyone else. I know I can trust you. Even if you would have refused, I know you wouldn't tell anyone about my asking you. . . ."

From then on they often discussed the details of the planned escape. Bourke maintains that all the arrangements were to be made by him alone and that Blake never asked him to get in touch with Russians or anybody else. A problem was to find the money. A car was needed, a temporary hiding place had to be found, and the fares to be paid. Rather naïvely, Bourke tried to make me believe that he saved every penny he earned after his release, working in a factory in Acton, and that after Blake's mother, whom he visited, refused to give him money, he found a friend from whom he borrowed either seven-hundred or a thousand pounds—there are again several versions of this—to pay the expenses of the escape.

Blake, meanwhile, carried on as usual. Like to all who knew him at various past phases of his life his mind remained impenetrable to his fellow prisoners. His friend "Zeno" recalls that when in June 1967 Blake's wife asked him for a divorce, he immediately agreed and took it extremely calmly. His fellow prisoners always thought that he was greatly devoted to her and that his reason for staying on in prison was, as he said, his desire to be reunited with his wife and children as a free man and not as a fugitive. Yet, in fact, Blake was preparing himself for the escape for a very long time. There is no doubt that he was in touch with his friends outside, patiently waiting for the signal. To keep himself fit—he knew he would have to make a difficult climb, use a rope ladder, and attempt a long jump, and he never had any athletic prowess—he did Yoga exercises and borrowed a chest expander from another prisoner for his daily workouts.

When the signal came—and it came by means he had been accustomed to use in the past—George Blake was ready.

CHAPTER TWENTY

ESCAPE AND PURSUIT

On the evening of Saturday, October 22, 1966, a slight shower began to fall soon after dusk in London. It was a mild but hazy autumn day. In the West End of the "swinging metropolis," crowds out to enjoy themselves, strolled past well-lit shop windows and gaily illuminated cinemas, restaurants, and cafés, hardly noticing the drizzle.

But the mean streets between Wormwood Scrubs Prison, Kensal Green Cemetery, and the deserted White City Stadium, unpleasant even on a bright summer day, were empty but for an occasional car speeding by.

Inside "D" Hall at Wormwood Scrubs there was a period of "free association." This is part of the syllabus of rehabilitation of the prisoners—particularly those serving long sentences—devised to encourage them in communal activities. The "free period" starts on Saturdays at 5:00

P.M. and ends two hours later, when all prisoners are being locked in their cells for the night. "D" Hall is a large, grim Victorian building. On each of its two longer sides there are cells on four floors; at the two shorter sides are workshops, storerooms, offices of the prison staff, and recreation halls. The "D" block houses usually between three hundred and four hundred prisoners, all serving long sentences and each having a cell to himself. At the two shorter sides of the rectangular building there are large barred windows, looking out into the yards. On one side the distance from the windows to the outer wall is only about eighty feet.

During the "free period," prisoners are allowed to leave their cells, stroll through the corridors, and those who wish to do so gather on the ground floor in the recreation rooms to watch television, play table tennis or chess, or musical instruments. Usually scores of prisoners walk up and down the stairs of the four-story building, leaving and entering their cells, talking in groups on the landings, while some who do not join in these social activities are allowed to stay in their cells, of which the doors remain open during the two hours. There is a general hubbub and a great deal of noise, amplified by the height of the hall's iron staircases, which causes all sounds to reverberate.

On that evening two hundred and ten prisoners from "D" block were allowed to attend a film show, held in a neighboring hall. They were accompanied by two prison officers, and at "D" block there were only two other "screws" left to supervise a hundred and seven prisoners. Blake among them. Shortage of officers is such that no better supervision can be afforded, particularly on a Saturday or Sunday, when a larger number of prison officers are off duty.

At 5:30 P.M. George Blake was watching a television program on I.T.V., featuring an all-in-wrestling show. There was a good deal of excitement, the prisoners shouting funny remarks, and the noise even greater than usual during the "free periods." Blake watched the program for a while and then, passing the two officers, remarked that he thought all professional wrestling bouts were faked and just clowning. He exchanged a few words with the "screws" and said he was going to his cell to read.

That was the last time Blake was seen in the prison by members of the staff. In his report, Earl Mountbatten stated that in his opinion 6:00 P.M. was the latest possible time at which Blake was still inside "D" hall. The way in which he got out can easily be described and was no doubt as easily accomplished, the report adds. During the general hubbub he went up to the landing on the second floor and along the large window above the entrance to the hall. This window was thought by the prison staff to be secure, because it has narrow cast-iron bars, forming some twelve separate window frames. But after Blake's escape it was found that one of the bars was broken, and this left a space large enough for a man to get through. How, when, and by whom this cast-iron bar was broken is a matter of speculation, but the report says that Blake must have found it surprisingly easy to force. The day after his escape, when an examination of all the windows on that landing was carried out, a prison officer broke a similar bar just by kicking it. The officer was wearing a pair of heavy boots, similar to those issued to prisoners, and he only gave a single blow with the heel of his boot. In another experiment a small hammer was used; a bar was hit with one light blow—with a piece of wood placed between the hammer and bar to deafen the noise of clanging metal—and the bar broke. The dull noise, and even the breaking of the glass, could hardly be heard a few yards away. What happened afterwards is, at least in parts, a matter of conjecture. I have some accounts of it from Sean Bourke, but this is hearsay. He can only repeat what Blake told him. And Bourke is a splendid raconteur who never leaves a story unembroidered.

It is unlikely that Blake left the breaking of the bar until the time of his escape. Around the broken bar was found a strip of adhesive tape which had been blackened with shoe polish. It must be, therefore, assumed that Blake had broken the bar at a convenient time, then stuck the black tape around it and left it in position until the moment of the escape, when he had only to push it off with two fingers.

Once out of the window Blake faced a drop of twenty-two feet to the ground. But he had selected the right window: beneath it was the roof of a covered way and he could lower himself on to it. This reduced the drop from the second floor by about half. The second part of the drop was even easier because a large bin with a stout wooden lid was standing on the ground and by lowering himself from the small roof he had to jump only four or five feet to reach the ground.

Running in the shadow of the covered way, he could reach the wall within a few seconds. By 6:00 P.M. the drizzle turned to heavy rain and visibility was poor. The wall was patrolled by only one prison officer, who had to walk all along its perimeter, which takes eight minutes. Another officer was in a small shed connected by telephone with the office of the orderly office. Blake could rightly assume that, if he chose the right moment, neither of them would notice his escape.

From both Bourke's account and the clues discovered by the police, we can follow Blake's progress with some accuracy. On the inside of the wall a rope ladder was found, and Bourke tells how this came about: "I got out of the car and got the rope ladder out of the boot. I looked up at the wall but it was too high. I stood on the roof of the car and threw the ladder and waited for Blake to ascend."

The rope ladder was made of nylon thread, was apparently homemade and each rung was reinforced by a steel knitting needle. This device held the rungs taut and made the climb easy.

From my own wartime experience I know that this sort of reinforced rope ladder was used by Resistance men when escaping from internment camps of the Vichy régime in France. Blake, who had used the famous "Spanish escape route" of S.O.E.'s escape organization in 1942, must have known about it, and he probably advised

Bourke on how to construct it when they were still together in prison. Bourke says he made the ladder himself.

Standing outside, Bourke was waiting for George to emerge. From time to time he glanced toward the main road where buses passed by and a few people plodded through the rain. But the narrow alley remained deserted. It was only a minute or two, but it seemed like hours before Blake appeared on the wall. Now he had to jump, onto the car roof.

"But he jumped badly," Bourke says, and he has once again two versions of what happened then. Interviewed on the "World in Action" television program, he stated that Blake knocked himself unconscious and badly hurt his head when falling from the twenty-foot-high boundary wall. In his evidence to the Dublin High Court some months later, Bourke said: "A minute later Blake was astride the wall. When he jumped he fell on his arm and badly twisted his wrist at an awkward angle." Bourke had to drag the fugitive to the car and took him to the lodgings near the prison.

"Blake was unable to sleep for the pain during his first night of freedom," Bourke recalls. "The next morning I called a doctor, whom I knew for his left-wing sympathies. I gather, I said to Blake, that you are allergic to hospitals and it is, therefore, my duty to treat you at home. Next morning the doctor came and he set to work without questions. At one stage the doctor wanted newspapers to spread out on the table to prepare an embrocation. I handed him a pile of the morning papers I had collected. On all the front pages was a picture of Blake, but the doctor continued his work without saying a word."

The two stayed for some weeks in the flat, of which I shall tell more later.

Inside the prison, the "free period" ended at 7:00 P.M. and prisoners were ordered to return to their cells. The four officers—the two in "D" Hall, and the two who brought back the party from the film show—needed about ten minutes until the usual nightly roll call could be held. It was then that one of them found that Blake was not in his cell. But he did not become suspicious since it takes a little time for all three hundred and seventeen prisoners to return to their cells, and the officer went to Blake's cell again at 7:20 P.M. It was still empty and he notified the orderly officer at the main gate by the house telephone that Blake was missing.

At about the same time another officer, patrolling the wall, discovered the rope ladder hanging on the inside and gave the alarm. He ran outside the prison into the narrow lane called Artillery Road. Almost exactly opposite the spot where the ladder was hanging on the inside wall, he found a pot of pink chrysanthemums, wrapped in crepe paper, propped against the wall. Within three or four minutes Shepherd's Bush Police Station was told by telephone that a prisoner had escaped. The police sergeant on duty was told in another telephone message that the escaped prisoner was George Blake, the spy.

Shepherd's Bush Police Station immediately informed Scotland Yard and within minutes several police cars arrived at the prison, both from Shepherd's Bush and from Scotland Yard, the later carrying several senior officers, including a chief inspector of the Special Branch.

By then it was exactly two hours since George Blake had been last seen in "D" Hall, when he talked to the two prison officers and expressed his disgust about the wrestling match on television. Even taking account of the time he needed to reach the window, push away the broken bar, make his descent, reach and climb the wall, and be driven away by a waiting car, Blake was by at least one and a half hours ahead of any pursuit which could be organized.

By 8:00 P.M. the Information Room at Scotland Yard relayed the message of Blake's escape to all radio cars within Greater London. Five cars including one with plainclothesmen and a van with dogs and their handlers were directed to Wormwood Scrubs and a general search was staged in the vicinity of the prison. Dogs were given the scent of some of Blake's belongings hurriedly brought from his cell. But, as one would expect, the search around the prison remained quite fruitless. Blake must have been miles away by then; indeed he could have reached London Airport and boarded an aircraft to several destinations on the Continent, as well as flights to British cities and Ireland.

"We were sitting already in our little flat in front of a television set, drinking whiskey and laughing about all that hoop-hah. On television they showed a twelve-year-old picture of George, with the beard he had brought from Korea. His own mother wouldn't have recognized him. . . ." Bourke said.

Scotland Yard officers were by then desperately searching for a more recent photograph of Blake. It was discovered that there was no photo of him at the Criminal Records Office, but the chief officer at Wormwood Scrubs found one which was taken in the prison on June 2, 1965, showing him clean-shaven—in contrast to the many pictures published in newspapers at the time of his trial, which were old photographs taken after his arrival from Korea in 1953 when he had donned a fine, dark beard. The question of a photograph was of utmost and urgent importance because prints had to be rapidly distributed to policemen and immigration officers at London Airport and all seaports, not to speak of supplying them to police stations and detectives all over the country, and to Sunday newspapers.

The photograph taken in prison was the only one in existence since Blake's conviction in 1961, and it has never been sent to the Criminal Records Office at Scotland Yard. Police photographers had to work overnight to produce from this only existent picture, showing Blake as he looked in recent years, as many prints as they could. Incidentally, Earl Mountbatten's report states that Scotland Yard had no photographs of the convicted spies Vassall, Bossard, the Krogers, and Ethel Gee, nor one of the train robber Ronald Biggs, who in July 1965 had escaped from Wandsworth Prison.

A request was made to the *News of the World* to publish Blake's description and photograph; at 10:15 P.M. the editor of this large-circulation Sunday newspaper stopped the printing of an edition so as to include them. Several other Sunday newspapers also published the photograph in their last editions.

Later in the evening Blake's description was broadcast over the entire police radio network and particularly to all Special Branch officers at airports, the cross-Channel ferry boat-train to France (which was leaving Victoria Station at 10:00 P.M.), and all seaports. Special attention was given to certain ships in the London docks and to all airfields and flying clubs, where light aircraft might land and take off. Detectives surveyed the neighborhood of Eastern European embassies and legations in London, particularly in Kensington, and questioned passersby and residents in the districts whether they had seen anything that would provide a clue to Blake's arrival. The watch included looking out for any large packing case or crate being taken in or out of Communist embassies, consulates, or offices of trade missions during the night and on the following days. Eight Communist freight vessels berthed in British ports, including three in the Surrey Docks of the Port of London, were under constant watch. Scotland Yard was aware that Blake could also have been taken to one of many lonely spots on the Kent or Essex coast, gone aboard a small fishing vessel or a motorboat, and smuggled across the Channel or the North Sea to the Continent before daybreak. All coastguardsmen were alerted and R.A.F. aircraft sent off on patrols. It was the largest and most costly manhunt staged for many years.

Watch was put on the home of Blake's seventy-year-old mother at Radlett in Hertfordshire, and his sister's house in a town in Kent, as well as several of his former friends whom Blake might have wanted to visit. One of the first persons to be questioned was an official of the British Communist party. His home at Burntwood Lane, Tooting, in southwest London was searched. The man later told reporters: "The police knew that I was a close friend of George Blake and that he worked with me in the party,

before his activities were discovered. I met him again in
'D' wing at Wormwood Scrubs. It is quite likely that he
might try to get in touch with me, but I very much hope
that he is well away and abroad. . . ."

It was less likely that Blake would try to see his wife
and children. While Gillian Blake had stood by him for
several years after his conviction, though she certainly did
not approve of his treasonable activities, by the spring of
1966 their relations had come to an end. On June 18,
1966, it was announced that Blake was filing a petition for
divorce. It appears that he wanted to make it possible for
his wife to be free and, if she wished, to remarry.

The ladder itself provided little hope, but the police
concentrated on the twenty knitting needles, size No. 13,
used to reinforce each of the ladder's rungs. They traced
the markers, but Mr. H. D. King, sales director of Needle
Industries Limited at Redditch, Worcestershire, gave little
hope that the police would be able to trace the person who
bought the needles. "We make millions of such needles a
year and they can be bought in any department store,
Woolworth's branch, or in thousands of haberdashery
shops all over Britain." Bourke was laughing his head off
when he read this. He had bought the needles in Ireland.

The clue of the pink chrysanthemums proved more
promising. The pot was found still wrapped in the florist's
paper but it was a firm which has almost a hundred retail
shops, several within a mile or two of Wormwood Prison.
Without a description of the person who had bought the
flowers in any of these shops, it was hopeless to pursue the
inquiry in this direction. The flowers could have been
bought by a man, a woman, or even a child, and brought
to the man or men, who arranged Blake's rescue, and used
the pot as a "marker" for the spot where the escape car
was to draw up at the wall. In fact it was not a "marker"
at all.

There was yet another clue, which proved extremely important and, indeed, put Scotland Yard upon the trail of
Bourke, who became a suspect almost immediately after

the investigations started. This clue was the tire marks of a car in Artillery Road, near the spot where the flowerpot was found. Scratch marks on the wall indicate that the vehicle had been backed up to it. It was thought that Blake, after he had reached the top of the wall, using the rope ladder, then jumped onto the parked car or van, and that his fall was broken by his rescuers, one of them possibly standing on the vehicle's roof.

Special Branch officers had an early suspicion that one man might have played a leading part in the escape— Blake's former fellow prisoner and close friend, Sean Bourke, the man who had served a long sentence at Wormwood Scrubs for sending the bomb to Detective Sergeant Michael Sheldon at Crawley.

Every prisoner who had served with Blake and had been released from Wormwood Scrubs before his escape was traced and interrogated. All could give a reasonable account of their movements since and particularly on the evening of the escape. Anyway, only one or two could come under initial suspicion. But the police could not find Bourke and, by elimination, and because of his past, he became the main suspect from the very outset.

When the police concentrated on finding Sean Bourke, they learned that he had registered a car soon after his release from prison. It was a secondhand, two-tone Humber Hawk, a 1955 model, and it had the registration number 117 GMX. Every policeman and traffic warden was ordered to look out for it. Five days after Blake's escape the car was found abandoned in Harvist Road, Kilburn, in northwest London. It was subjected to meticulous tests at Scotland Yard laboratories. Almost with certainty it was established that its tires corresponded to the marks left on the wet road outside Wormwood Scrubs on the evening of Blake's escape. Scotland Yard could announce on October 29 that "Blake's escape car had been found in London." Fingerprint experts found in the car many prints of Sean Bourke's, but none of Blake's. This did not exclude the likelihood that Blake was collected in the Humber Hawk;

he could have been wearing gloves, or—being an experienced secret agent—taken great care not to touch anything and not to leave fingerprints behind.

Scotland Yard also investigated another important connection between Blake and Bourke when they were fellow prisoners. As already mentioned, Blake, like all long-term prisoners, was allowed to have a radio set in his cell. Bourke was an amateur radio mechanic and often did repairs at the prison. When I met Bourke in Dublin recently he told me the story of his radio contact with Blake. He had constructed a miniature transmitter—whether alone or with the help of others he wouldn't say—and kept up a regular communication with Blake. On October 22 he took the transmitter, hidden in the chrysanthemum pot, to the spot outside the prison and sent the final signal for the escape. Once Blake arrived, Bourke left the pot behind, a piece of evidence that was to greatly mystify the police and security men.

The transistor set which Blake used did not include the 27–28 megacycle band on which walkie-talkie transmissions are normally made. Nevertheless, as stated in Earl Mountbatten's report, because of the low order of selectivity common in receivers of the type which Blake used, signals could have been received when transmitted on 28 megacycles if the transmission was sufficiently strong at a point on the receiver's tuning dial showing an apparent reception frequency of about 14 megacycles. No special knowledge would be needed to pick up signals in this way. All that was necessary was to tune the receiver until the signal was heard. The point on the dial where this is achieved can be noted for subsequent occasions. But the report points out that the distance from Blake's cell "D-8" to the nearest point outside the prison wall was over a hundred feet, and the combined effect of this distance and the shielding of the building and metal in it "would make it unlikely that a walkie-talkie signal could be picked up on Blake's radio set."

Earl Mountbatten and his technical advisers' conclusion in their inquiry into Blake's escape was, therefore, that it was unlikely that Blake could receive messages from outside on his radio set. Unlikely, but as it was proved, not impossible. Indeed, this was what actually had happened.

In my book *Shadow of a Spy*, which dealt with the Blake case and was published early in 1967, at a time when there was still no trace of Blake and Bourke and it was not even known that both were in Moscow, I wrote the following lines:

I have consulted an eminent radio and electronics expert and, with great respect to Earl Mountbatten and his experts, I disagree. A skilled radio mechanic—such as Sean Bourke—could have slightly modified a transistor set, such as Blake's, and made it possible to receive, however faintly, signals emanating from a powerful transmitter, placed outside the prison wall.

Blake's cell "D-8," for which he had specially asked because he wanted to have "a nicer view of the green and the aviary," was almost at the end of the corridor, on the ground floor, and the distance to the wall, across the yard, was much less than a hundred feet. If, for the sake of argument, one assumes that Blake had help from friends connected with a Communist secret service organization, one can go one step further and say that such secret agents would operate very powerful transmitting apparatus, probably from a car which could at any time of the day, or preferably at night, pass the wall and stop for a few moments to send signals. The question of timing does not arise. Blake could have quite easily been given a message, by word of mouth or in writing, at what hour he should listen. This would apply only to the very first signal. On that occasion his friends would tell him when to listen again.

Blake was an experienced secret agent. During the war, secret agents parachuted by S.O.E. (Special Operations Executive) into Nazi-occupied Europe and equipped with small radio transmitters, were told to listen to signals at "scheduled times," the so-called "skeds." I described this procedure and the system of clandestine radio communications in two of my former books.* The same procedure could be easily adopted by Blake and his foreign secret service friends—if he had any. Bourke, who had been free for many months prior to Blake's escape, could have easily made the necessary contacts, quite apart from his help with the radio set.

Alas, I could now say, I told you so.

Earl Mountbatten stated in his report that Blake did not need to rely at all on such complex communications. He had other ways in which he could have established contact with helpers outside, ways which Lord Mountbatten said were open to less risk of being discovered.

Within Wormwood Scrubs there is a hostel from which usually some fifty prisoners, expecting to be released shortly, go out to work outside the prison. These are the "parole prisoners" and they leave the prison, in plain clothes and unaccompanied every morning, to work in factories, shops, offices, and for local councils. In the evening they return to the prison hostel for the night. This system is an important part of a prisoner's rehabilitation and it makes his transition from prison life to ordinary life easier. The system works well and it is rare that a parole prisoner does not return to the hostel. In any case, he expects to be released within a few weeks and he would risk his good conduct remission and be put back into a cell if he absconded.

The parole prisoners are kept apart from ordinary prisoners, and at Wormwood Scrubs they would normally have no contact with prisoners in "D" Hall, where Blake was held. However, "blue-band trusted prisoners" go about the prison quite freely, are often enlisted to run errands to the hostel warden or do some repairs or cleaning jobs there. There were several of the "trustees" in "D" block with Blake. Any one of them could have carried oral, and even written, messages to and fro, and found a parole prisoner to convey them to somebody outside, for instance by tele-

* *Inside SOE* (Barker, London, 1966) and *They Came from the Sky* (Heinemann, London, 1965).

phone, while working in town during the day. Earl Mountbatten drew special attention to this in his report and
suggested certain changes in the system of parole prisoners and hostels. He also remarked that the trust placed in
parole prisoners had sometimes been badly abused, that
articles were brought into the hostel from outside without
authorization, and that even stolen property had been
found there.

As I later found out, one of the prisoners who used the
hostel was, in fact, approached by Colonel Nicolai Ivanovich Mekhonoshin, who despite his high military rank was
a mere "assistant military attaché" at the Soviet embassy,
being in reality a high K.G.B. official. This man was meeting the colonel at the Waldorf Hotel Bar and at the Cecil
Bar at Shell Mex House in the Strand.

The security authorities were informed about these
meetings and the necessary steps were taken to investigate
the ex-prisoner's role. I was told that he was able to prove
his innocence. He was one of Blake's many pupils, and after his release he was buttonholed by Colonel Mekhonoshin in a bar. The colonel did not tell him how he knew
that he had been in prison with Blake, but he seemed well
informed. The Russian did not make any suggestions relating to Blake. He invited the ex-prisoner to lunch and
asked him about conditions at Wormwood Scrubs, how
Blake spent his day, in which part of the prison he
worked, and so on. When they parted the colonel asked
his guest for his telephone number and said that they must
meet again. But he never telephoned nor did he try to get
in touch with the ex-prisoner again. It does not require
much guessing to deduce that the Russian was looking for
a "contact" and, having found a better one in the meantime, dropped his passing acquaintance.

The hue and cry continued for both George Blake and
Sean Bourke, the latter being politely described by the police as "a man wanted to help us with inquiries." Not the
slightest trace of Blake's whereabouts was found until the
end of January, but Bourke left a long trail behind him,
which led from London to Ireland and back.

Chief Inspector Stephen Cunningham and another officer of the Special Branch went "on information received" to Limerick City, hoping to find Bourke. They were told by his seventy-one-year-old mother that he had visited her during the week of October 10 to 15, 1966, and when he left told her that he was going to Dublin and London on some important business. That was the week before Blake's escape. Bourke arrived in London from Dublin on the sixteenth and took a furnished two-room flatlet at 28, Highlever Road, North Kensington, at a house belonging to sixty-year-old German-born Mrs. Lottie Heveringham. He told the landlady that he got her address from an estate agency in Paddington and that he lived in Croydon, giving his last address as 5, Bank Road, Croydon. The police later found that there is no such place.

The new tenant gave his name as "Mr. Sigworth" and said he would stay for two months, but might go abroad on business at an earlier date. "He was a handsome man, in his early thirties, about five feet ten inches tall, well built, with dark brown hair, and a fine beard and mustache, looking like an artist." Mrs. Heveringham told me a few months later, when the police had discovered the identity of her tenant, "I asked him for a month's rent in advance and he immediately agreed. He pulled from his pocket a big bundle of notes, all 'fivers'; he must have had several hundred pounds on him. He paid nineteen pounds, the weekly rent I asked was four pounds fifteen and I gave him the keys." The landlady showed me the flat, by then inhabited by a new tenant. It was simply but comfortably furnished. Mr. Sigworth told Mrs. Heveringham he would bring his own television set. She did not see much of him. In fact Bourke did not move in until the day before the "springing." He was staying at the International Language Club in Park Hill Road in East Croydon, using another alias. He kept his room at the club during October, when he had already taken the flat in Highlever Road.

The intriguing though not surprising fact about the flat which Bourke had chosen was that Highlever Road is within a short walking distance from Wormwood Scrubs.

It leads to Little Wormwood Scrubs Green, opposite the prison, and is separated from it only by the Metropolitan Underground line.

The landlady saw very little of her tenant; she lived at the back of the house. Moreover, she was ill for several days and later was visiting a friend in the country. But she saw him a few times, once when he moved in and arrived in a two-tone Humber, with a large television set, a typewriter, and two suitcases. About ten days after he moved in—which was after Blake's escape—Mrs. Heveringham saw him again, but he had no beard and was clean-shaven. She remarked to a neighbor that she did not recognize her tenant, he looked quite different, and she was sorry that he had taken off his fine beard.

I must shamefacedly admit that Sean Bourke endeared himself to me by the jolly cops-and-robber game he played in this deadly serious conspiracy. He would not tell me whether the "clean-shaven tenant" was he, or whether Mrs. Heveringham, in fact, saw Blake and, on the dimly lit staircase on a foggy November evening, mistook him for her real tenant. "It could have been either of us," he said. "But Blake never left the flat, so it must have been me. . . ."

The mystery of the luxuriant growth was eventually satisfactorily solved. After Blake and Bourke left—the landlady never discovered that both used the flat—Mrs. Heveringham went to clean it in anticipation of new tenants. She found in one of the rooms a few books. One was *The Great Train Robbery* by Peta Fordham. From the other fell out a small parcel wrapped in tissue paper. When she unwrapped it she got a shock: it contained a false beard and a false mustache, looking exactly like the whiskers which had adorned, a few weeks before, the handsome face of her friendly tenant. The landlady, perhaps because she saw the book, decided that she must have harbored one of the fugitive train robbers. She immediately telephoned the local police station, and within minutes the house was full of detectives.

Special Branch Superintendent William Marchant and his men took bottles, glasses, crockery, and kitchen utensils to Scotland Yard, while fingerprint experts busily examined every piece of furniture. Several fingerprints were identified as those of both Blake's and Bourke's.

But by then the two wanted men were many hundred miles away.

Bourke mentioned several times that he and Blake used false passports for their journeys to the Continent. He repeated this in evidence before the Dublin court when his extradition case was heard in November 1968 and January 1969. But he did not give any details, or say from whom and when they obtained the forged documents.

Had Scotland Yard known about certain happenings in West Berlin in the autumn of 1966, Blake and Bourke might have been caught on their journeys after the jail-break. In October 1966 a young woman, twenty-four-year-old Elvira Baumgarten was arrested in West Berlin on a charge of having illegally obtained passports and identity cards and passed them to suspected Communist agents.

Frau Baumgarten was an assistant in an elegant beauty salon in Tiergarten Strasse. She was married to a college lecturer and scholar of Celtic history and language. But the couple had separated in 1963. Early in 1964 Dr. Baumgarten—who is in no way involved in his ex-wife's alleged activities—was in Dublin, attending a postgraduate course at Trinity College. His wife visited him there, either to attempt a reconciliation or to discuss divorce proceedings. It appears that on that occasion she obtained at least one Irish passport issued for a man aged about thirty-seven.

After her arrest in West Berlin in October 1966, Frau Baumgarten admitted to the investigating judge, Dr. Hans Dobbert, that she had given this and another passport and two identity cards, to a "Major Alexander," a Russian whom she had met some months earlier. She had obtained duplicates of her own passport and identity card, having reported to the police that she had lost them. She also gave these documents to "Major Alexander." She explained that she had several friends in East Germany who wanted to escape to the West. She had met "Major Alexander" at a party at the home of two Arabs, Yubrail Khoury, a thirty-six-year-old Lebanese, and Yamal al-Fahdi Handam, a twenty-four-year-old Jordanian, who lived in a luxurious apartment in Tauentzien Strasse in West Berlin. "Major Alexander" had promised to pass the passports to her friends in East Germany, who would thus be able to travel legally to West Berlin.

Investigations by the West Berlin police resulted in the arrests of the two men, who had been for some time under surveillance as suspected Communist agents. The Lebanese had been living in West Berlin for some years, ostensibly as the representative of a Beirut commercial company; the Jordanian had arrived a year before and had registered with the West Berlin police as a student. After their arrest, the two men denied having had any truck with Communist agents and said that they had met "Major Alexander" by chance and did not know his identity.

It will be remembered that "Lonsdale" served part of his sentence at Wormwood Scrubs, together with Blake. Their other fellow prisoner was Bourke. It is not at all a farfetched assumption that "Major Alexander" was Lonsdale; and if he was not, he was one of Lonsdale's K.G.B. colleagues. In the course of the protracted investigations into the background of Blake's escape, several clues emerged, pointing to Lonsdale's participation in the enterprise.

At first, the West Berlin authorities did not connect the woman and the two men with Blake's escape. But further investigations brought to light that Frau Baumgarten had met "Gordon Lonsdale" soon after he arrived in East Berlin, following his exchange for the British agent Wynne. Frau Baumgarten, accompanied by Yubrail Khoury, had visited East Berlin in 1964, shortly before her journey to Dublin.

There are many threads in the tangled web of the Blake story and many indications that the K.G.B. prepared the ground for the "springing" of George Blake in terms of a long-term operation. Quite apart from Blake's usefulness—and that it prevails is proved by the important position he now holds—his escape certainly enhanced the prestige of the K.G.B. It also reassured its agents that their chiefs kept faith with those in trouble and that the K.G.B. has the power and the means to rescue them. After all, the K.G.B. has a special department—the *Transpornty Otdeyl* which, besides maintaining communications with networks and spies abroad, has a "special transportation section," which deals with escapes. Scores of successful operations of this kind, particularly in the United States, were and are being carried out by this section. The meticulous preparations for, and the execution of, the "disappearances" of Donald Maclean and Guy Burgess, and later of Mrs. Melinda Maclean, spring to mind.

When the Soviet government succeeded in clinching the excellent bargain with the British by which they got Lonsdale back for Mr. Wynne, Moscow hoped for a similar barter in the case of Blake. Once the K.G.B. realized that it would not come off—and Blake himself explicitly told Sean Bourke that it was off*—plans for his springing" were begun. Sean Bourke firmly maintains that he had not been "hired" by the Russians, and had not been in direct contact with the Soviet embassy or overt Soviet agents. This is difficult to believe, but I accept Bourke's word for it. The K.G.B. does not work so crudely. There were certainly no members of the Soviet embassy lurking around Wormwood Scrubs on that rainy October night. The K.G.B. does not carelessly expose its agents to a possible arrest. Not even pseudo-diplomats are sent to hold a rope ladder for a convict to jump over a prison wall. The risks of an international incident, which would only expose clumsiness, are carefully avoided. The K.G.B. employs more subtle and usually safer means to achieve results.

* See page 216.

As we have seen, a number of Blake's former fellow prisoners had been approached by mysterious characters with strange propositions over a period which began two years before Bourke volunteered to help Blake. Some of these approaches had probably only the purpose to obtain information about the prison's layout. Even the bizarre plan of the helicopter abduction appears less fantastic when viewed with hindsight.

Turning back to the passport affair of Mrs. Baumgarten and the two Arabs, the German counterespionage office (*Bundesamt für Verfassungsschutz*) firmly believed that the passports had been manufactured for Blake. Special Branch Officers journeyed to West Berlin and were given facilities to interrogate the woman and the two men at Moabit Central Prison. They got little out of them, simply because the prisoners did not know to what use the passports were eventually put by "Major Alexander."

The three suppliers were jailed in West Berlin on September 28, 1967, having spent nearly a year in custody while investigations continued in several countries. They were sentenced only for passport offenses; Mrs. Baumgarten was jailed for fifteen months, Khoury was sent to prison for two and a half years, and Handam for ten months. At the trial the judge asked each of them several times: "Do you know whether the forged passports were used for the escape of the British spy Blake?" and every time the accused replied that they did not. One would hardly expect them to admit it, even if they did know, which is unlikely.

The passports could have been very useful. With his somewhat Oriental looks, and his fluent mastery of Arabic, Blake could easily have posed as a Lebanese or Jordanian and traveled on a passport the Russians had obtained from Khoury. The Irish passport would have fitted Sean Bourke, who could not possibly conceal his lilting brogue.

Bourke gave several versions of how he financed his operation. He said he asked Blake's mother, Mrs. Catherine Gertrud Beijderwellen Blake, for £ 750. At that time the old lady worked as a housekeeper for a family in Hertfordshire. Bourke said that she refused and that "she was very frightened" and did not want to talk to him. On different occasions, Bourke later gave different versions of how he got the money to finance the escape. On one, he said that he borrowed seven hundred pounds from a friend; on others he stated that, after Mrs. Blake's refusal he approached three friends in London, "unconnected with Blake," who provided eight hundred pounds, and that he used two hundred pounds from his own savings. When his abandoned Humber car, which he says he used for the "springing" operation was subsequently examined by the police, a number of paper bands were found, of the kind bank cashiers use to wrap around bundles of bank notes. The bands have printed inscriptions of the value of the bundle. In the car such wrappers for a total of fourteen hundred pounds were found. After his return from Moscow to Dublin Bourke gave two explanations of this. According to one of his versions, the wrappers must have belonged to a bookmaker who previously owned the car; according to his other version the car was the property of a butcher's wife and she probably left these wrappers behind. The previous owners of the car were traced by the police. None of them knew anything about the wrappers, none had ever cashed such large sums at the bank. The friends from whom Bourke claimed to have borrowed the money were never traced.

If, as I believe, the operation was financed by the K.G.B., money was, of course, no object. Soviet spy masters can be very generous indeed. When one of their chief agents in the United States, Gerhard Eisler, was unwisely released pending his trial, he jumped his bail of $23,500 his employers had put up and escaped, disguised as a seaman aboard the Polish ship *Batory*, to emerge soon after in East Germany. In December 1964 Ivor Alexandrovich Ivanov, a senior agent of the K.G.B. was tried before the federal court at Newark, New Jersey, for espionage. Holding the rank of a colonel, he had arrived in America two years earlier to take up the modest job of chauffeur for Amtorg, the Soviet trade agency in New York. With another spy he was soon engaged in ferreting out secrets of the computerized communication system of the U.S. Strategic Air Command. When they were eventually caught, copies of top secret documents and blueprints of launch silos, propellent terminals, and missile fuel tanks, purloined from the headquarters of 821st Combat Group, and drawings of the secret Titan missile base at the 451st Stratetic Missile Unit were found in Ivanov's possession. He was sentenced to thirty years' imprisonment, his accomplice Butenko to twenty years. Ivanov appealed and the appeals court at Philadelphia freed him on bail of $100,000, paid into court by the Soviet embassy in Washington. Behind the unusual move was a pledge given by the Soviet government to the U.S. Department of State that Ivanov would not try to escape. It was this pledge that carried more weight than the $100,000 bail.

Compared with these amounts, the expenses of Blake's "springing" were mere chicken feed to the K.G.B.

About Blake's and his own movements after the escape, Sean Bourke gave many versions. Before dealing with his various statements after his return from Moscow, it seems necessary to give a brief account how this came about. After his visit to the British embassy in Moscow on September 4, 1967, when he asked for a passport or a travel document which would enable him to go home, his request was passed by the British Foreign Office to the Irish government in Dublin. Ireland had no diplomatic relations with the Soviet Union and no representation in Moscow. Mr. Frank Aitken, the Irish minister of external affairs dealt personally with this matter. Bourke was issued a document, was given a Soviet exit visa, and arrived on October 23, 1968, in Ireland. He flew to Shannon from Düsseldorf, apparently having traveled from Moscow to Prague and Vienna two or three weeks earlier. Earlier that month, his brother Kevin received from him a letter bearing an Austrian stamp and postmark.

The British authorities were not unaware of his departure from Moscow and his pending arrival in Ireland. The Foreign Office sent a note to the Irish government, requesting Bourke's arrest and making an application for his extradition on a warrant on two charges, one being of "helping a prisoner to escape" and a second, under the Offenses Against the Person Act, of "causing to be sent to Michael John Sheldon, a police officer, a letter threatening to kill him." The second charge related to Bourke's old quarrel with the Crawley police detective to whom he was alleged to have sent a bomb in 1961 and for which he received a sentence of seven years' imprisonment. Now it was alleged that some months after his release from Wormwood Scrubs Bourke sent a letter to Sheldon—apparently dated January 1, 1966, which must have been just when he was off to Moscow after Blake's "springing"—in which he told Sheldon that he would settle his old account with him and kill him. Incidentally, Bourke firmly denies it. Two Special Branch detectives went to Dublin to await Bourke's arrival there, expecting that the extradition would be granted.

During a stop at Schipold Airport (Amsterdam), a team from the Granada Television program "World in Action" boarded the aircraft and accompanied Bourke to Dublin. They interviewed and filmed him during the flight and on his arrival at Shannon Airport. He posed willingly for newspaper photographers at the airport. Later a spokesman of Granada Television Company said that the meeting at Amsterdam was "by arrangement with Mr. Bourke, who agreed to being interviewed and filmed."

Irish police officers were present, but he was not arrested. The Eire Extradition Act, 1965, and treaties with Britain make a British warrant valid in the Irish Republic, but the wanted person has the right to oppose it in court within fourteen days. Bourke was driven to Gresham Hotel, a luxury hotel in Dublin's O'Connell Street, where there was a sort of a party at which he made many statements.

Ten days after his arrival he was arrested at his hotel room by Guardai (police) Inspector John O'Driscoll, was allowed to telephone his solicitor, Mr. John Gore-Grimes, and was taken to the Dublin District Court. There the magistrate told him that his arrest was made on a British extradition warrant on an alleged offense under Section 29 of the Prison Act, 152, namely "aiding and abetting the escape of a convicted prisoner," an offense which carries a two-year jail sentence, and asked him whether he understood the provisions of the Extradition Act, to which Bourke replied: "Yes, I do, Your Worship." The magistrate then ordered his extradition and told him he could appeal against the order within fourteen days. The police opposed bail and Bourke was remanded to custody. The magistrate remarked that Bourke had no passport.

Within hours Bourke's solicitor arranged for writs opposing the magistrate's decision to be served on the commissioner of police and the attorney general, and a few days later he lodged an appeal with the High Court. Bourke spent only a few days in custody. On November 4, he was released on bail of two thousand pounds, of which one thousand was deposited by himself, while two other people provided sureties of five hundred each. Bourke then moved back to Gresham Hotel, where the charges for room and breakfast are five pounds a night. He gave many more interviews and appeared on television.

The appeal was heard in January 1969 and lasted for three days.

It was stated with all the trimmings of a *cause célèbre*. The judge was Mr. Justice O'Keefe, president of the Irish High Court; the state was represented by the attorney general; for Bourke appeared Mr. Declan Costello, a leading Dublin barrister, who holds the title of a state counsel, equivalent to that of a British Q.C. He was assisted by junior counsel. Much of the proceedings was taken up by long depositions by Bourke himself. The president of the High Court asked him why he helped Blake to escape. Bourke's reply was: "I considered that his savage sentence had been the result of a trick by a very angry English Establishment. I looked upon him as a political prisoner who had been sacrificed a great deal for what he believed in." Bourke certainly knew how to play up to the gallery; nothing goes down better in Ireland than a bit of baiting the English.

He had to convince the court that in aiding Blake his motives were political not humanitarian. Only thus could he escape extradition, because the legal provisions of the act only protect political offenders but not "criminals," whatever their humanitarian motives might be. Mr. Nial McCarthy, who appeared with the attorney general, tried to prove that Bourke did not, in fact, act from any political motives. He asked and was permitted to replay a record of the verbose statements Bourke had made on Radio Eireann. Bourke's voice boomed through the courtroom: "I have never been a Communist. . . . I don't care for politics. . . . I sprang Blake, the Russian spy, from a slow lingering death. . . ." This presented Bourke as a charitable man, but not a political offender. Bourke had quickly to rethink his position, and he did this very well. He now told the court: "As a result of many conversations with Blake, I had come to the conclusion that his ideas of a just society coincided with my own. This is, briefly, my reason for having helped him."

In a reserved judgment, President O'Keefe gave the High Court decision on February 3, 1969. The appeal was allowed and the extradition order was set aside. He awarded the cost to the plaintiff.

In a long summary he gave the reasons for the judgment in favor of Bourke. They were almost entirely legal arguments. The judge stated the difficulty in making the decision was whether Bourke's part in helping Blake to escape was "an offense connected with a political offense." Without doubt, the forty-two-year sentence given to Blake was for political offenses, the betraying of British secrets to the Russians, he said. "But no one has yet defined the precise terms of an offense connected with a political offense, neither did the Extradition Act define it." In the circumstances the judge decided to direct that the plaintiff be released.

The judge made a significant remark about the escape as Bourke had described it in court: "For the purpose of this case I must accept that Bourke did help in the escape of Blake, although I have reservations in my mind that the escape was carried out in the way Bourke said in evidence before this court."

Whatever was in the judge's mind, Bourke was a free man. Within minutes after the judgment was read out, Bourke, surrounded by journalists, said he would be sending a "victory telegram to Blake." It would simply say: "George, Victory. Letter following. Best Wishes Sean."

He told reporters who asked him about the many contradictory stories he had told: "Oh, forget it. I am happy. The first thing I am going to do is to have a couple of celebration pints of Guinness. Then I am going home to rewrite a chapter of my book. . . ."

The most striking thing about Sean Bourke's stories is the amazing number of versions of every incident. In television interviews he gave a detailed description of how he "dispatched Blake from London Airport, via Paris and Berlin to Moscow." They passed policemen and security officers unmolested. "The British were supposed to be looking for him and he wasn't even disguised. It was terribly simple."

But soon afterwards, in newspaper and radio interviews, he abandoned the story of the air journey. He was now telling a thrilling tale of how he bought a van, built a false floor compartment, and "squeezed Blake into it." He drove the van, with Blake inside, to the Dover ferry and, after crossing the Channel, through France and West Germany to the East. Most of the time Blake was sitting next to him, or even driving himself. Every time they approached a frontier, Blake crept into the hidden compartment. Eventually they reached East Germany and took leave from each other. Why? Because Bourke decided to return to Britain and, according to this version, he actually did. But after a while he changed his mind and made off again, all the way across Western Europe to East Germany and then to Moscow. This would surely be adventure enough. But, no, there were yet more versions to come.

In court this story was told: "Blake was taken out of Britain in December 1966, was driven to Dover and then by ferry to Ostend in Belgium. Then he reached East Germany." Bourke was not with him, said Bourke's counsel, Mr. Costello, who submitted this version to the court on his client's instruction. He did not say how and by whom "Blake was taken out of Britain."

This is the only version which deserves to be accepted, because it is nearest the truth. Blake was taken out of Britain by others than Bourke—and it does not need a particularly shrewd guess to imagine who they were.

According to the submission of Bourke's counsel, Bourke remained for a short time in Britain after "Blake had been taken out" and made a railway journey to West Berlin. There he crossed though "Checkpoint Charlie" to East Berlin, where he was met by a Russian colonel and put on an aircraft for Moscow. This, apparently was early in January, and the date coincides with Bourke giving up his flat in Highlever Road. Blake had preceded him by at least three weeks.

About his life with George Blake in Moscow, Bourke has told many stories. Their friendship did not endure for long. Bourke remained in Blake's flat for six months but, as Bourke put it, "once Blake had reached his sanctuary he reverted to type and treated me with contempt." It seems Blake wasn't anymore the kind and helpful mate Bourke knew at Wormwood Scrubs. "Blake stalked about in a long red dressing gown and took to calling me 'Robert,' the name the Russians put in my false passport. One day I overheard him saying to one of the K.G.B. men who came and went: 'Of course, he is only an Irish peasant. . . .' " He began to order Bourke about: "He told me, 'With effect from today, all noise must cease within this flat at 11:00 P.M. I wish to sleep from eleven o'clock onwards.' One day I heard Blake saying to the K.G.B. officer, Stanislav, 'The Irishman must remain in the Soviet Union, against his will if necessary . . . or . . .' " Blake did not finish the sentence, but the meaning was clear, says Bourke, and from then on he lived in fear of his life.

"When I heard myself betrayed by Blake to the K.G.B., I went to the British embassy for help, but they asked me to leave. I was desperate and ran to a forest outside Moscow and hid there, but finally I went back and gave myself up. I realized it was just a matter of choosing the form of my death—stay in the forest and freeze or starve to death, or go back to the flat and get it over quickly with a bullet."

But he wasn't shot. Although Blake hardly spoke to him anymore and when he did, called him coldly "Mr. Bourke," the K.G.B. was very kind: they sent him on a sight-seeing holiday to Leningrad and other places, and after he returned to Moscow, they gave him a flat on his own and an allowance of £120 a month. He says from then on he had a very good time, met a nice girl, Nerissa, and got engaged to her. Indeed, he hopes to go to Moscow, collect her, and marry her.

When he eventually decided to return to Ireland, the K.G.B. officials tried to discourage him, but were not too difficult. "They did not want me to go to Britain, however, and they suggested I should go to South America, where they would pay me a pension for life. Even as I boarded the plane they tried to change my mind. But I really wanted to get back to my own people. I had had enough there and I didn't fit in, and wanted to get back to the West. And, of course, I wanted to write a book about all this. . . ."

Such are some of the stories galore which Sean Bourke has been telling since he returned from Moscow. He is a born entertainer and he deserves the great popularity he enjoys in Dublin's pubs. He must have forgiven Blake for suggesting his "liquidation," because he sent him the victory telegram and occasionally writes to him.

He told me his book will be published in Britain and many other countries, and he hopes that a film will be made about his adventures. When I last saw him in Dublin in January 1970, he looked forward to a bright future, having been paid more than ten thousand pounds in advance of the very substantial fees and royalties he expected from the sales of his book and the serialization of his story in many journals.

I wish him well. But I cannot help thinking it was a bizarre twist of fate that a man like Blake should, at least to some degree, owe his rescue from prison to a man such as Bourke. Perhaps it is poetic justice.

Although I have accumulated much information from reliable sources about George Blake's life in Moscow during the past four years, I decided not to compete with Sean Bourke on this account. I am convinced that he will produce a much more amusing story than I could, or would care, to write.

I expect that like his colleague Kim Philby, George Blake will himself make a fitting contribution to the spate of Communist propaganda literature. Traitors' memoirs are in great demand. We haven't heard the last of the most recent bearer of the Order of Lenin and the Order of the Red Banner.

About the Author

E. H. Cookridge wrote from firsthand experience. Himself a wartime secret agent (he was imprisoned in Dachau and Buchenwald by the Nazis), he met George Blake during the war and worked with him both then and after the end of military hostilities. Also a political journalist and a House of Commons lobby correspondent of many years' standing, he had access to unpublished files and a mass of top-secret information.

An authority on espionage activities, Cookridge wrote many books on the subject that have been published in various editions throughout the world, such as *Gehlen: Spy of the Century* and *History of the British Secret Service.*

FOR YOUR EYES ONLY!

True stories of international espionage that read like the best espionage thrillers....

The Ballantine Espionage/Intelligence Library

11